Marianne Pade (Ed.) – On Renaissance Commentaries

Noctes Neolatinae
Neo-Latin Texts and Studies

Herausgegeben von
Marc Laureys und Karl August Neuhausen

Band 4

On Renaissance Commentaries
edited by Marianne Pade

Georg Olms Verlag
Hildesheim · Zürich · New York
2005

On Renaissance Commentaries

edited by Marianne Pade

Georg Olms Verlag
Hildesheim · Zürich · New York
2005

Gedruckt mit freundlicher Unterstützung der
Stiftung Pegasus Limited for the Promotion of Neo-Latin Studies.

*

Das Werk ist urheberrechtlich geschützt. Jede Verwertung außerhalb der
engen Grenzen des Urheberrechtsgesetzes ist ohne Zustimmung des Verlages
unzulässig und strafbar. Das gilt insbesondere für Vervielfältigungen,
Übersetzungen, Mikroverfilmungen und die Einspeicherung
und Verarbeitung in elektronischen Systemen.

Die Deutsche Bibliothek verzeichnet diese Publikation
in der Deutschen Nationalbibliografie; detaillierte bibliografische Daten
sind im Internet über *http://dnb.d-nb.de* abrufbar.

ISO 9706
Gedruckt auf säurefreiem und alterungsbeständigem Papier
Herstellung: dp-Service, 56626 Andernach
Alle Rechte vorbehalten
Printed in Germany
© Georg Olms Verlag AG, Hildesheim 2005
www.olms.de
ISBN 3-487-12955-8

Preface

The six essays collected in this volume were presented during a special session on "Renaissance Commentary," organized and chaired by Marianne Pade, at the Twelfth International Congress for Neo-Latin Studies at the University of Bonn, August 3–9, 2003. Three of the contributions — those by Julia Gaisser, Patricia Osmond, and Robert W. Ulery, Jr. — represent revised and expanded versions of papers first presented at the Annual Meeting of the Renaissance Society of America, Chicago, March 29–31, 2001, during the panel "Identifying a Renaissance Commentary: Three Case Studies," organized by Osmond and Ulery and chaired by James Hankins. All of the essays deal with different commentaries written, or rewritten, in the fifteenth century on different authors (Sallust, Virgil, Martial, Pliny the Elder, Dioscorides and Apuleius), thus reflecting a wide variety of material and arguments. Yet each essay attempts to situate the particular commentary in the contemporary context of classical studies and to address a question that has important implications for the history of humanist teaching and hermeneutics: Is there a *Renaissance* commentary?

This question was raised by James Hankins at an earlier conference held at Villa I Tatti, The Harvard University Center for Italian Renaissance Studies in Florence, June 9–11, 1999, "The Italian Renaissance in the Twentieth Century." In the course of a discussion following the panel "Antiquity and Recovery," chaired by Anthony Grafton and including papers by Phyllis Bober, Julia Gaisser, and Ingrid Rowland, Hankins challenged the participants to identify a Renaissance (as opposed to a medieval) commentary, to distinguish, that is, those elements of content or method that might characterize a commentary as a work of Renaissance pedagogy or scholarship. The lively debate that ensued — and promises to continue — was thus the origin and inspiration of the theme chosen for the RSA panel and IANLS session and of the six case studies now published in *Noctes neolatinae*.

The contributors of this volume are grateful to the editorial board of the *Noctes neolatinae* who offered us the possibility to publish these six essays in the series.

Munich, July 2004   Marianne Pade

Sallust's *Bellum Catilinae* in the Edition of Venice, 1500: the Medieval Commentary and the Renaissance Reader*

ROBERT W. ULERY, JR.

The Roman historian C. Sallustius Crispus had a two–fold *fortuna* in the passage from late antiquity to the Middle Ages and the Renaissance: his monographs *Bellum Catilinae* and *Bellum Iugurthinum* survived in the curricula of the schools and have a rich manuscript tradition, while his *Historiae* survived only until the fifth century before being reduced to excerpts (speeches and letters) and a few scraps. The manuscripts of the two *Bella* have in many cases a great deal of marginal annotation, and in a few cases a full commentary is found. One of these is found in a manuscript of the twelfth–thirteenth century (Bern, Burgerbibl. ms. 411), but before it came to receive new attention as evidence was collected for the article on Sallust in the *Catalogus Translationum et Commentariorum*, it was known from its publication in Venice in 1500, with attribution to a noted Renaissance teacher of Vicenza, Omnibonus Leonicenus (Ognibene Bonisoli da Lonigo).[1]

The presence of Sallust in the canon of the revived classical curriculum of the medieval arts course is amply documented.[2] It comes to full fruition in the twelfth century, and coincides with fullest use of Sallust by writers, especially of history. The commentaries and the widespread *accessus* tradition from this period can show us the way in which the Sallustian monographs were read in some medieval schools, and the publication of one of the medieval commentaries in the context of Renaissance schooling and readership raises several questions: is this another example of the pseudepigrapha that were printed under the name of Ognibene after his death (c. 1476)?[3] Is it (also) possible, from what we know of his teaching of classical authors, that Ognibene may have used what was evidently a widely circulated school commentary in his own classes, slightly altering or interpolating here and there a few notes and

---

* Earlier versions of this article were presented at the meetings of the Renaissance Society of America, Chicago IL, 2001, and the International Association for Neo–Latin Studies, Bonn, 2003. I am grateful to my colleague Patricia J. Osmond, and to members of those audiences, for many helpful suggestions.

[1] See Patricia J. Osmond and Robert W. Ulery, Jr., "Sallustius Crispus, Gaius," in *Catalogus Translationum et Commentariorum*, vol. 8, ed. Virginia Brown (Washington DC, 2003), 183–326, esp. pp. 225–27. I am grateful to the Burgerbibliothek Bern for permission to quote from ms. 411.

[2] See Osmond and Ulery, 192–196, and the bibliography on pp. 218–20.

[3] See John Monfasani, "Calfurnio's Identification of Pseudepigrapha of Ognibene, Fenestella and Trebizond, and His Attack on Renaissance Commentaries," Renaissance Quarterly 41 (1988), 32–43.

hence associating his name and his teaching with the commentary? Does the commentary betray a new Renaissance interest in the text?

The general issues behind the study of commentaries in any period have been well outlined recently by Glenn W. Most.[4] For example, he suggests that we think of the commentary as empowering the reader, "because it puts materials at his disposal which help him not only to understand that text in ways that the commentator wants him to believe the author to have intended, but also other texts..."; and he asks us to consider the reciprocal effects of school practices and commentaries. In the present investigation, the principal concern is the nature of this commentary in the context of the new enthusiasm for classical Latin texts, and the effect of the commentary upon the view of the author and the developing Latinity of the time. The examples that follow are intended to demonstrate the curious instance of a medieval explication of a classical text, published as the work of a teacher of the revived classical learning at the end of the fifteenth century. The older habits of style exhibited in the commentary ill befit the stylistic elegance both of the historical narrative and of the emerging humanist Neo–Latin style; and there is little in the content that matches the interests of the age.

Ognibene Bonisoli da Lonigo (Omnibonus Leonicenus) lived and worked in and near his native Vicenza in North Italy from 1412 to 1474; he was a student of Vittorino da Feltre, whom he succeeded at the Giocosa in Mantua for seven years in mid–century, and taught privately at Treviso and at Vicenza, where he also held a public professorship from 1453 until his death. His commentaries include those on Juvenal, Persius and Cicero's dialogues; other commentaries on Lucan and Valerius Maximus are attributed to him; and he wrote treatises on grammar, rhetoric and education.[5]

The judgment of Giovanni Calfurnio, that the commentaries on Lucan and Valerius Maximus were falsely attributed to Ognibene, has been brought to our attention by John Monfasani.[6] This was apparently common in Venice after the scholar's death and gives an indication of the prestige of his name. To the question of the grounds on which Calfurnio based his judgment, Monfasani gives as the commonsensical answer that

> the works must have struck Calfurnio as uncharacteristic of their supposed author[s]. The commentaries simply were not worthy of Ognibene

---

[4] See his "Preface," in Commentaries = Kommentare (Göttingen, 1999), vii–xv.
[5] Osmond and Ulery (above, n. 1), 227, with bibliography; G. Ballistreri, "Bonisoli, Ognibene," in Dizionario Biogtafico degli Italiani 12 (1970), 234–36, with bibliography.
[6] Monfasani (above, n. 3); see also Dorothy M. Schullian, "Valerius Maximus," in *Catalogus Translationum et Commentariorum*, vol. 5, ed. F. E. Cranz (Washington DC, 1984), 360–62.

... and did not reflect the way [he was] known to treat classical texts. Considerations of style seem not to have played a decisive role in Calfurnio's opinion; or, at least, he did not think such considerations worth mentioning ...[7]

To the question of the characteristic content of a truly Omnibonensian commentary, one may begin with the general view of Ballistreri, that Ognibene was the most faithful heir to the moral figure of his teacher Vittorino da Feltre; but that the example of Guarino and the changed exigencies of the times drove him to abandon the *quadrivium* and to center his teaching on rhetoric, although the encyclopedic tradition of the Giocosa is recognizable in his extensive curriculum, comprising historians, poets, orators, philosophers, and Church Fathers.[8] Sanford writes this of Ognibene's Juvenal commentary:

> Both *accessus* and notes are based primarily on [a particular branch of the earlier anonymous commentary tradition]; Ognibene's additions emphasize rhetoric, grammar, and ethical values, and show a strong pedagogical interest. Paraphrase is often used; alternative explanations are usually given with an indication of preference. Points of Roman history, law, and antiquities are carefully explained, with especial reference to Suetonius, Lucan and Augustine. Fables are either briefly summarized or omitted as familiar ... His commentaries were chiefly composed after 1457.[9]

And later Robathan added, on the Persius commentary:

> Ognibene's commentary on Persius was written before 1460. In contrast to the wide diffusion of his commentary on Juvenal, the Persius commentary survives in only one manuscript... The commentary is on an elementary level; many scholia are taken word–for–word from the 'Vulgate'; and a few Greek words are found. There is no indication of other sources, nor does this commentary appear to be related to any other of the humanist commentaries I have studied.[10]

It may be noted that the introduction to the Persius commentary follows precisely the *accessus* format familiar from the medieval period: *In principio huius*

---

[7] Monfasani, 37; from the text given by him in the Appendix, 42: *16. Manes certe Omniboni me orant, obsecrant ut illum a tanta contumelia vindicem. 17. Nonne ego Omnibonum intus et in cute novi? 18. Nunquam has ineptias effudit. 19. Immo tanti viri animus a nulla re magis alienus erat quam ab huiuscemodi commentatiunculis.*
[8] Ballistreri (above, n. 5), 234.
[9] Eva M. Sanford, "Juvenalis," in *Catalogus Translationum et Commentariorum*, vol. 1, ed. P. O. Kristeller (Washington DC, 1960), 208.
[10] Dorothy M. Robathan, "Persius," *ibid.* vol. 3, ed. F. E. Cranz (1976), 257.

operis breviter quaerendum est quae materia quae intentio quae utilitas quae causa quis titulus cui parti philosophiae supponatur. Materia huius operis ...[11]

The attribution to Ognibene of the Sallust commentary has never been questioned; it is found in continuous form in a manuscript (Bern, Burgerbibliothek, 411) dated s. XII–XIII, as well as in several manuscripts s. XIV–XV:

- Biblioteca Apostolica Vaticana, Ottob. lat. 3291, s. XIV, with commentaries on the *Poetria nova* of Geoffroy of Vinsauf, and on Martianus Capella;

- Assisi, Biblioteca e Centro Documentazione Francescana (Sacro Convento), 303, s. XIV–XV, with commentaries on Valerius Maximus, Pomponius Mela, Persius, Horace and Virgil;

- Munich, Staatsbibliothek, Clm 7612, s. XV, with a collection of orations and letters;

- Padua, Biblioteca del Seminario, 142, s. XV, with Guarino's commentary on Valerius Maximus, and others on Terence, Virgil's *Georgics*, Cicero, Aesop, Avienus, and Ovid;

- Rome, Biblioteca Corsiniana, Cors. 1836 (43 F 11), s. XV;

- and, as one of the sources of marginal annotation in at least one other s. XV manuscript [Yale ms. 358, s. XV; see also Augsburg, Staats– und Stadtbibliothek, 2° Cod. 305, s. XVI].[12]

Though the exact textual relationship between these manuscripts and the printed edition of 1500 is not yet clear, it would appear that the later manuscripts from south Germany and Italy are rather closer to the edition of 1500, while the fifteenth–century Yale manuscript (from northern France) is drawn from a text closer to that of the Bern ms., itself of French origin.

That the Bern manuscript is not the source of the printed edition is effectively shown by more than one passage where a line has been omitted in copying, in one case leaving the ending of a verb, and the printed edition shows no sign of an omission or of its being "corrected", e.g.:

> (ms.) Namque ava(ritia) *ubi pro hiis uirtutibus s(cilicet) i(ta) avaritia uirtutes subverat* [sic]. *et* ambitio *non minus rebat s. affectus interius amarissimus erat.*
> (ed.) NAMque: *avaritia etc. pro his virtutibus scil. ista avaritia virtutes subvertit et* ambitio **vere** *non minus.* [page–end but not line–end] **NON ex re** *i.e.* **ex rei**

---

[11] On the *accessus* tradition see, e.g., Gunther Glauche, s.v. *Accessus ad auctores*, in Lexikon des Mittelalters, vol. 1 (Munich and Zurich, 1980), cols. 71–72.
[12] Osmond and Ulery (above, n. 1), 226–27.

veritate magis quam bonum vultum quam ingenium. VULtus i.e. exterius benignus apparebat sed affectus interius amarissimus erat.

In addition, we may note that there is little evidence of any additions or corrections to the commentary between the manuscript and the printed edition; indeed, the printed edition contains just as many errors of basic Latinity as the medieval manuscript, and it would appear to have had little or no copyediting in preparation for the press. Some examples of this will be given below.

The Bern manuscript contains commentaries or *Glosulae* on the *Catilina* and *Jugurtha,* and several on other standard school authors of the mainstream European tradition: Lucan, Virgil, Sallust, Terence.[13] Berthe Marti gave a late thirteenth–c. date to the portion of the manuscript containing Arnulf's commentary on Lucan.[14] But the hand of the Sallust portion appears to be different and perhaps earlier. The script is extremely small and the notes are arranged in double columns, as in the other portions of the manuscript; the commentary covers both monographs and yet is contained in just nine folios.

The printed version, of only the *Catilina* commentary, is found in the following editions:

- 1500.7, Venetiis (Venice): opera et impensa... Ioannis Tacuini de Tridino. The *Opera* (ed. P. Laetus, rev. Joh. Britannicus) with the *commentarii* of L. Valla and of Omnibonus Leonicenus on the *Catilina* and the *expositio* of Soldus on the *Iugurtha.* Flodr S 52; IIC 14233; IGIBI 8560; NUC. Vatican Library; (DLC).

- 1502, Venetiis (Venice): opera et impensa... Ioannis Tacuini de Tridino. NUC; Schweiger 2.867; Rome, Cors.; (CtY; MH).

- 1506, Venetiis (Venice). NUC. (CtY; NcU).

There it was added as a second commentary surrounding the text of the *Catilina,* with the commentary attributed to Lorenzo Valla at the top and this commentary at the bottom. The "Valla" commentary had first appeared in print in 1491:

> 1491.5, Venetiis (Venice): arte et ingenio Philippi Pincii de Caneto. The *Opera* of Sallust (ed. Pomponius Laetus) with the *commentarii* of Laurentius Valla on the *Catilina.* (This edition also contains Ps.–Cicero, *In Sallustium* and Ps.–Latro, *Declamatio in Catilinam.*) Flodr S 36; HC 14222; IGIBI 8551; NUC. BN; Rome, Cors.; Vatican Library; (ICN; NNC).

---

[13] Professor Frank Coulson informs me that the commentary on Ovid's *Ibis* in the Bern manuscript was printed in 1569 as anonymous.

[14] Berthe Marti, ed., *Arnulfi Aurelianensis Glosule super Lucanum* (Rome, 1958), LXIV–LXV.

To the question why Ognibene's name was put to this medieval commentary, perhaps the pairing with Valla is a sufficient answer, for both are representatives of the immediately preceding generation of humanist teachers. The other question is not so readily answered: why was there no recognition that this was not a Renaissance teacher's commentary? It may simply be a matter of the intended readers being students at the lower end of the curriculum, who need no great sophistication of philological argument or textual correction, only the glossing and paraphrase of a tradition that had not changed over the course of the last few centuries. This is the thesis that will be explored in some selected passages of the commentary.

The passages chosen for detailed examination here are the notes on chapters 1–18 of the *Bellum Catilinae* (hereafter *BC*), comprising the proem, the character sketch of Catiline, the digression on the moral decline of Rome, and the beginning of the account of the conspiracy; 31–37, comprising the confrontation between Catiline and Cicero, Catiline's departure to join his army, the message of Manlius to Marcius Rex, and the letter of Catiline to Catulus; and 51, the speech of Caesar on the punishment of the captured conspirators.

The commentary is introduced by an *accessus* beginning with a discussion of the *ordo librorum* (in this case of the two monographs) and proceeding with the full list of topics save for *cui parti philosophiae supponitur*.[15] This *accessus* then leads into a discussion of the prologue of the *BC* and from there to the explication of the first words of the narrative. The annotations cover the entire text of the *BC*, paraphrasing individual words and phrases and attempting to explain the logical connections in the narrative, but without attending to every possible difficulty, and only occasionally explaining simple points of grammar, rhetoric and ancient history.

The *accessus* in the 1500 ed. is essentially unchanged from that found in the Bern manuscript. It is somewhat unusual for a medieval Sallust *accessus* in that it does not begin with a summary statement of the requirements of an *accessus*, or directly with the *materia*, but rather with a brief explanation of the difference between the order of composition of the two monographs and the chronological order of their subjects:[16]

> *Salustius Crispus diversas diversorum temporum historias tractaturus, iugurtinam videlicet, cuius memoriam antiquitatis diuturnitate uix retinebat, sed et catelinariam cuius seuicia suo tempore exarserat, posteriorem praeposterando praemittit. Vbi bene*

---

[15] See Glauche (above, n. 11) for the traditional *schema*.
[16] Text is quoted from Bern ms. 411, expanding abbreviations but retaining spelling and punctuation.

prosecuta historia cuius certitudinis conscius erat, in prosecutione alterius historie quam non ita firmiter tenebat facilius et compertius sibi lector adquiescat.

This is called the *causa praeposterationis*, and the reader is then invited to cross over to the *materia* etc., that is to the traditional set of topics; in this case they are: *materia, intentio, causa intentionis, utilitas, titulus, (ordo), (nomen auctoris), prologus.* The *intentio* and its *causa* receive an extensive discussion:

> **Intentio** *eius est redarguere impugnantes patriam, sed quia cause impugnationis patrie sunt diverse, alii enim per ambitionem alii per auaritiam patriam impugnant, uidendum est quam causam impugnationis auctor iste intendat redarguere. Hic itaque intendit redarguere impugnantes patriam per ambitionem e contrario intendit laudare defendentes patriam, per bonam consultationem.* **Causa** *huius intentionis talis est. Viderat enim auctor iste quosdam frui temporis fraudulentos patrie impugnande sollicitos ad quorum dehortationem. Insta~ proponere historiam et hoc facit. duos inducendo in exemplum: Catelinam et Ciceronem. Alter quorum, scilicet Catilina, a nobilitate detrusus est ad ignobilitatem, utpote qui merito factis suis dignum uite inuenit exitum; alter uero Cicero uidelicet ab ignobilitate conscendit ad nobilitatem, utpote qui merito bone consulationis sue de rhetore factus est consul et pater patrie meruit appellari. Vnde IVVENALIS. Roma parentem Romam patrem patrie Ciceronem libera dixit. In iugurtina historia redarguit impugnantes patriam per auaritiam. Non Iugurtham neque suos. Roma enim non erat patria iugurte. sed illos romanos qui corrupti muneribus iugurte scelera eius non solum non puniebant sed impudenti declamatione ipsum in capitolio defendebant.*

Note the (here unnecessary) inclusion of the *Jugurtha*, an indication (like the opening of the *accessus*) that this discussion was originally an introduction to both works. The discussion of the *titulus* includes a further reference to the *ordo librorum* and the *nomen auctoris* before passing to the *prologus* by way of a pedagogically appropriate transition:

> *Et sciendum quia quidam auctores suis operibus titulum tantum praescribunt ut hortatius* [sic]. *Quidam titulum et proemium. et argumentum ut terentius. Quidam titulum et proemium ut auctor iste. Post titulum itaque prologum submittit, in quo tria facit. nam et inuidos confutat et negotium suum extollit. et materiam praelibat.*

A mixture of infelicities and improvements are found in the Latin of the 1500/1502 edition over against the text of the commentary found in the Bern manuscript:

> ms.: *cuius memoriam antiquitatis diuturnitate uix retinebat*
> ed.: *Cuius memoriam* **antiquitate diuturnitas iusta** *retinebat*
> ms.: *posteriorem praeposterando praemittit*
> ed.: *posteriorem* **praeponendam** *praemittit*

ms.: *facilius et compertius sibi lector adquiescat*
ed.: *facilius & **aptius** sibi lector acquiescat* (a s. XV ms. reads *apertius* here)
ms.: *de quorum uitiis et uirtutibus tractatus iste const~it~* (*construitur*? sic ms. Yale 358)
ed.: **Ex** *quorum uitiis & uirtutibus* **constat iste tractatus**
ms.: *merito factis suis dignum uite inuenit exitum*
ed.: *merito factis suis dignum uitae* **meruit** *exitum*
ms.: *ut uiso quid contigerit Catiline ex patrie impugnatione. patriam non impugnemus. Viso quid contigerit Ciceroni ex patrie defensione patriam defendamus*
ed.: *... defendimus*
ms.: *ubi n [enim] non est numerus, nec ordo*
ed.: *ubi* **deest** *numerus & ordo*
ms.: *Vbi dicit Sa. Cris. nomen designatur auctoris. Vbi de catilinario bello, materia declaratur subsequentis operis*
ed.: *... ubi* **dicit** *de catilinario bello* **materiam declarat** *subsequentis operis*
ms.: *Qui quod salustius a militari negotio ad literatoriam regressus fuerat professionem, desidie et inertie ascribebant*
ed.: *quod quidem Salustius a militario negotio ad litteraturam regressus fuerat: professionem desidiae & inertiae describebant*

The discussion of the prologue leads then into the commentary proper:

> *Inuidos confutat, nam erant quidam qui sibi misere inuidebant, et bone et solide ipsius conscientie dente detrectationis illidere tendebant. Qui quod salustius a militari negotio ad literatoriam regressus fuerat professionem, desidie et inercie ascribebant, utpote qui uim corporis ui animi praeferebant. Contra quos prologum confutationis praemittit in quo uim animi ui corporis esse praeferenda dicit sic incipiens:* <u>Omnis homines</u>. *quasi dicat: sententiam animi mei de quo me uituperant mutaui, quia nolebam uitam sub silentio transire. ad quod decet omnes niti et elabore [sic ex elebore?] et ab hoc puncto incipit:* <u>omnis homines</u> ...

And thus the commentary begins, with an explanation of the form *omnis* (citing Servius), a definition of *studere*, an explanation of the form *sese*, and a definition of *praestare* (expanded with a "scholastic" array of causes); the opening grammatical notes give a misleading impression of an essentially grammatical commentary, but those notes are exceedingly rare, and the paraphrase (beginning already here with *Intendit itaque Sallustius*) is more indicative of the basic type to which the commentary belongs:[17]

---

[17] The text of Sallust is quoted from the ed. of L.D. Reynolds (Oxford, 1991).

(Sallust, *BC* 1) *Omnis homines, qui sese student praestare ceteris animalibus, summa ope niti decet, ne vitam silentio transeant veluti pecora ...*

(Commentary) omnis homines: *accusatiuus pluralis est. dicit enim Seruius omnia nomina quorum genetiuus pluralis in –ium terminatur tam in –is quam in –es accusatiuos plurales terminare.* student: *studere est animum circa aliquam rem assidue cum magna uoluntate applicare.* sese: *Nota quod me et te et se ipsam substantiam significant. quae quia quadam uelocitate pronuntiantur ideo geminantur, ut significatum impensius et expressius intendatur.* Praestare:*.i. praeesse et praeualere. praeest aliquid alicui tum pulchritudine, tum donis fortunae, tum uiribus corporis, tum uirtutibus animi, tum creatione. Intendit itaque Sallustius hic persuadere mortalibus ut quemadmodum dignioris sunt creationis ceteris animalibus, sic eisdem praeesse laborent animi uirtutibus.*

[ed. 1502: *dicit enim seruius:* **quod** *omnia nomina quorum genetivus pluralis terminatur in –ium tam in –is quam in –es accusatiuos plurales* **terminant** *... Intendit itaque* **hinc** *Salustius persuadere* **moralibus s(cilicet) hominibus**]

Nothing here could seem to breathe the new air of Renaissance learning.

For a characteristically Renaissance comment on this passage we may turn to that of Badius Ascensius in 1504:[18]

Quantum uero ad uerborum elegantiam et sermonis leporem in quo iuuenibus plurimum immorandum est: Sciant primum omneis accusatiuum esse Latinum qui a priscis Latinis per ei diphthongon scribi consueuit ne in es finitus cum nominatiuo et accusatiuo pluralibus: et in is cum eiusdem singularibus consonet: simulque quod concinnius sonet accusativus in is: licet eis scribatur sequente praesertim es: ut hoc loco. Omnis homines. Nota est autem seruiana regula quod quotiens genitiuus pluralis in ium finitur accusatiuus in is aut in eis exeat. Notum est etiam Augustini dati de situ uocabulorum praeceptum quod hic quoque obseruatur: nam ab aliquo incepta est oratio. Praestare in diuerso significato rite datiuo & accusatiuo praestruitur. Nam praesto tibi est melior te sum quasi prae id est ante stans: ut hic praesto te.i. exhibeo aut represento: ut apud Maronem. Ibo animis contra uel magnum praestet achillem. Praesto autem tibi hanc rem est: aut in hac melior sum: ut in comico. Homo quid homini praestat: aut eam tibi commendo. Ratione etiam excessus dicimus multo non multum praestat.

Here the emphasis on the development of style and the array of authorities and examples are clear signs of a new command of everything needed for the interpretation of the text.

---

[18] See Osmond and Ulery (above, n. 1), 245–248; the text is quoted from the edition of Venice, 1513.

In contrast with Sanford's characterization of Ognibene's commentary on Juvenal, this earlier commentary is dominated by paraphrase, and any emphasis on rhetoric, grammar, and ethical values is very sporadic; the paraphrase is in what may be called the pedagogical manner, where the commentator speaks to the reader, occasionally in the voice of the author. Alternative explanations are only sometimes given, and very seldom with an indication of preference. Points of Roman history, law, and antiquities are rarely and imaginatively explained, usually wrongly, and with no citation of ancient authorities.

Here is the remainder of the comment on Sallust's opening paragraph:

> <u>decet</u>: *decens est honestum.* <u>summa ope</u>: *i.e. summo nisu. ad hoc inquam decet eniti.* <u>ne uitam silentio transeant</u>: *Vitam cum silentio transit qui uiuendo nihil memoria dignum agit.* <u>uelut pecora</u>: *sic enim pecora uitam transeunt, ut nec post mortem de illis mentio fiat.* <u>Quae</u>: *hic quodam modo pecora excusat. quasi dicat: si pecora uitam cum silentio transeant. non est mirum* <u>que</u>: *quia illa. causa tamen est* <u>natura finxit</u>: *i.e. formauit.* <u>prona atque</u>: *pro id est i.e.* <u>uentri obedientia</u>: *expo(sitio) est. Unde Ouidius: cetera cum prona spectent animalia tantum. os hominis sublime dedit. celumque uidere iussit et erectos ad sidera tollere uultus.* <u>Sed omnis nostra uis</u>: *ita pecora sunt uentri obedientia. utpote simplicem uim habentia. sed humana uis duplex est, cum in corpore, tum in anima. et hoc est* <u>sed omnis nostra uis</u>: *distribute legatur i.e. nulla uis est in nobis quae ut sit animi uel corporis.* <u>animi imperio</u>: *humanam uim duplicem esse ostenderat; nunc autem ad modum boni praeceptoris ostendit qualiter sit uterque utendum, ita scil. ut animus imperet, corpus seruiat. et hoc est* <u>animi imperio</u>: *9to [continuatio?]: Vere humana uis est in animo posita quia ad imperandum; nam* <u>magis utimur</u>.*i. uti debemus animi imperio quam animi seruitio.* <u>corporis</u>: *9to: Vere humana uis sita est in corpore. quia ad seruiendum.* <u>magis utimur</u>: *corporis seruitio quam corporis imperio.* <u>alterum</u>: *duplicem quidem uim hominis. quare altera s. animi imperium nos conformat cum diis, altera scil. corporis seruitium nos conformat cum beluis. et hoc est* <u>Alterum</u> *etc.* <u>Quo</u>: *et quia carius est quod nos conformat cum diis, quam illud quod nos conformat cum beluis, igitur* <u>rectius uidetur</u>: *et est* <u>opibus ingeni</u>: *quantum ad animum* <u>uirium</u>: *quantum ad corpus* <u>et quoniam</u>: *bene dico ut gloriam adquiramus ut scil.* <u>memoriam nostram quam maxime</u>: *i.e. ualde longam post mortem efficiamus.* <u>Quoniam uita</u> *etc.* <u>Nam diuitiarum</u>: *Per uirtutem animi famam nostri longam efficere debemus. nam [sic; non?] per uires i.e. bona corporis. bona animi sunt uirtutes, quae eterne sunt. nam et anima eterna. bona corporis alia corporis in corpore, alia corporis extra corpus. bona corporis in corpore ut pulcra lineamenta membrorum. robur etc. in hunc modum. bona corporis extra corpus ut possessiones et deuitie [sic] haec autem bona omnia tam corporis in corpore quam corporis extra corpus fluxa sunt et fragilia.* <u>Virtus</u> *uero* <u>habetur clara</u>: *in praesen(s?) dum exercetur.* <u>et eterna</u>: *apud posteros per memoriam.*

This may serve to illustrate the paraphrastic nature of the commentary, for after two straightforward glosses (*decet, summa ope*), themselves paraphrastic, interpretive paraphrase begins with several characteristic formulas:

inquam
quasi dicat
non est mirum ... causa tamen est
et hoc est
ostenderat; nunc autem ... ostendit
Vere ... quia; may be preceded by
continuatio
et quia ... igitur
bene dico ... Quoniam

Of these the most common in the commentary are *et hoc est*, which marks the transition from paraphrase to the quotation of the next piece of text; and *continuatio* (if this is the correct expansion, following the printed edition, of the consistently used abbreviation [9to]), sometimes followed after a colon by *Vere ... quia*, which emphasizes the logical sequence of thought in the passage under discussion.[19] The paraphrase is much more detailed and complete here, where considerable time and emphasis was probably given in the classroom to the explication of the philosophical prologue; in later passages there is often a similarly more detailed treatment in more philosophical passages. The only other kind of comment in this first paragraph is the quotation of Ovid (Met. I.84–86, but reading *tantum* for *terram*, and *hominis* for *homini*, and with some change of word–order at the outset but without violating the metre), prompted by Sallust's phrase *prona atque uentri oboedientia*. It will perhaps not be rash to assert that this evokes and represents the manner of the teacher in the traditional classroom of the High Middle Ages. In some of the formulae there is a tendency of the expositor to identify himself with the author: *inquam, bene dico*. A particular characteristic is the scholastic tendency toward schematic definition, seen above in the gloss on *praestare*, here seen in the discussion of *bona animi et corporis*:

> *bona animi sunt uirtutes, quae eterne sunt. nam et anima eterna. bona corporis alia corporis in corpore, alia corporis extra corpus. bona corporis in corpore ut pulchra lineamenta membrorum. robur etc. in hunc modum. bona corporis extra corpus ut possessiones et deuicie*

---

[19] Auguste Pelzer, Abréviations Latines Médiévales, 2nd ed. (Louvain and Paris, 1966), 13 (conto., Ottob. Lat. 1389 *passim*); see also p. 15 (9to=commento, Vat. lat. 2184 f.2r [Aristotle, s. XIII–XIV]; Ottob. lat. 179, f.98r); a *continuatio* is a rhetorical period, philosophical concatenation (Oxford Latin Dictionary, s.v.).

For a further illustration of the type of paraphrase in this commentary, see the remarks on *BC* 5.1 where Sallust begins the description of Catiline's character:

(Sallust) *L. Catilina, nobili genere natus, fuit magna ui et animi et corporis, sed ingenio malo prauoque. huic ab adulescentia bella intestina caedes rapinae discordia ciuilis grata fuere, ibique iuuentutem suam exercuit. corpus patiens inediae algoris uigiliae, supra quam quoiquam credibile est. animus audax subdolus uarius, quoius rei lubet simulator ac dissimulator, alieni adpetens, sui profusus, ardens in cupiditatibus; satis eloquentiae, sapientiae parum. uastus animus inmoderata incredibilia nimis alta semper cupiebat.*

(Commentary) <u>Lucius Catilina</u>: *Ecce quod promisit persoluit. et eum nobilem ostendit si enim ignobilis esset numquam tantam rem praesumeret.* <u>Sed ingenio malo</u>: *Ne bonum [s.l. laus] uideretur quod dixerat magna ui animi subiungit* <u>Sed ingenio malo et prauo</u>. <u>malo</u>: *naturaliter. quod ipse deprauerat exercitio.* <u>huic adolescentia</u>: *probat ab effectu quod malum habuit ingenium. quia ab adolescentia ista ei placuerunt uitia.* <u>bella intestina</u>: *i.e. ciuilia, quasi intra testam, intra muros facta.* <u>patiens inedie</u>: *inedia dicitur penuria quae est in-edere.* <u>supra quam</u>: *i.e. plus quam. et hic probauit quod magna ui esset corporis. modo probat quod magna ui sit animi dicens* <u>animus audax</u> *i.e. temerarius, et* <u>subdolus</u>: *i.e. latenter dolosus. Vere subdolus quia* <u>uarius</u>: *i.e. leuis et inconstans et uere uarius quia* <u>simulator</u>: *rei quae non erat. et* <u>dissimulator</u>: *rei quae erat.* <u>alieni appetens</u>: *non auarus ut absconderet sed ut profunderet. unde subiungit* <u>sui profusus</u>: *i.e. prodigus. et quia profundebat ideo ardentius capiebat. et hoc est* <u>ardens in cupiditatibus</u>. <u>satis eloquentiae</u>: *erat ei, et* <u>parum sapientiae</u>: *Eloquentia autem sine sapientia multum obest, ut ait Tullius.* <u>animus uastus</u>: *i.e. tumidus.* <u>cupiebat immoderata</u>: *i.e. modum excellentia quantum ad se. et uere immoderata quia* <u>incredibilia</u>: *quantum ad alios. uere incredibilia quia* <u>nimis alta</u>: *quantum ad rem consideratam. uere nimis alta quia dominatione rei publicae.*

[ed. 1502: *Ne* **huius** *uideretur quod dixerat magnam vim animi subiungit.* **SED** *ingenio malo* **pravoque** *malo naturaliter.* **PRAvo:** *quod ipse depravaverat exercitio ...* **BELLA INTESTINA** *idest* **intra muros sit vel intrinseca.** **CAEDES** **Trucidationes** **RAPINAE:** *Depraedationes.* **CORPUS PATIENS** *inaediae inaedia dicitur penuria quae est* **in aede** *... om. Vere subdolus ...* **SUI** *profusus prodigus* **et disipator** *...* **ANImus** *vastus i.e.* **timidus. IMMO***derata* **in modo** *excellentia ...* **Quantum ad rem desideratam**]

The commentary begins here with paraphrase of the new section; then a scholastic explanation of the difference between *malo* and *pravo* (the same characteristic may be seen in *probat ex effectu*); two definitions, one using fanciful etymology, the second correct (abbreviation of *inedere* was misunderstood in the text represented by the printed edition); then gloss and paraphrase, sometimes linking the asyndetic list of traits (a problem of Sallustian *brevitas* neatly explained); a scholastic and true distinction between *simulator* and *dissimulator*; it then fills in an ellipsis, gives a citation of Cicero; and more glossing and paraphrase and linkage using a scholastic distinction, particularly on the triad *immoderata incredibilia nimis alta*.[20] This shows very clearly the way in which a highly elliptical passage packed with multiple characterizations in a tight series is opened out and explained in continuous paraphrase, a characteristic of the medieval commentary.

After the character sketch of Catiline in *BC* 5, there begins a digression on the moral decline of Rome which occupies sections 6–13:

(Sallust 5.9) *Res ipsa hortari uidetur, quoniam de moribus ciuitatis tempus admonuit, supra repetere ac paucis instituta maiorum domi militiaeque, quo modo rem publicam habuerint quantamque reliquerint, ut paulatim inmutata ex pulcherruma <atque optuma> pessuma ac flagitiosissuma facta sit, disserere.*

(6) *Vrbem Romam, sicuti ego accepi, condidere atque habuere initio Troiani qui Aenea duce profugi sedibus incertis uagabantur, cumque iis Aborigines, genus hominum agreste, sine legibus, sine imperio, liberum atque solutum. Hi postquam in una moenia conuenere, dispari genere, dissimili lingua, alius alio more uiuentes, incredibile memoratu est quam facile coaluerint; ita breui multitudo diuorsa atque uaga concordia ciuitas facta erat.*

(Commentary) *Res ipsa (5.9): quia dixerat mores ciuitatis corruptos. imperium autem romanum ubique erat dilatum, quod uidebatur contrarium. iccirco iuxta praeceptum Horatii ab oratione digreditur, ut ostenderet non per mores corruptos imperium creuisse. Sed imperio satis aucto, tunc mores corruptos esse. et est competens digressio, non pannus assutus [Hor. A.P. 16]. Ordo. Res:.i. ipsa rei utilitas. ut probabilis uideatur narratio, materia [m.a] uidetur hortari supra repetere:.i. alterius incipere. quae attinent de moribus ciuitatis ad amplificationem criminationis modernorum. ac paucis disserere:.i. dicere. domi:.i. in pace. militie:.i. in bello. et ut:.i. qualiter. R. p. paulatim q.rim [?]: et uere immutata quia ex pulcherrima:.i. ex optima. Vrbem Romam (6.1): Ecce incipit quod promisit et commendat uirtutem antiquorum ad exaggerationem criminum modernorum. sicut ego accepi:.i. audiui. diuersi enim de Romae conditoribus diuersa sensere. leuius enim dicit Troianos condidisse, Ennius Remum et Romulum, Virgilius Euandrum: Ac pater Euandrus Romanae conditor urbis [Aen. 8.313: Ac rex ... arcis]. potest autem sic solui, quod quidam fundauerunt et adauxerunt. Qui Aenea: Quia multi Troiani multis in locis remanserunt, de quibus dicat ostendit. Qui Aenea duce etc. Aborigines: Aborigenes dicuntur non qui omnino origine careant, sed quorum origo ignoratur. sine legibus: et ideo solutum. sine imperio: et ideo liberum. coaluerint:.i. simul creuerint.*

---

[20] Several of these distinctions are found elsewhere in the medieval tradition, e.g. in a Munich manuscript, Staatsbibl. Clm 19480; see Osmond and Ulery (above, n. 1), 229–30.

[ed. 1502: *non per mores corruptos* **Imperium creuisse. Sed imperio satis auc-to.tunc mores corruptos** *esse: & est competens digressio* ... *narratio in ea uidetur hortari supra repetere de moribus ciuitatis* ... *Paulatim & uere immutata. Quia ex* PUL*cherrima. Id est optima.* **PESSIMA ac flagitiosissima facta sit** ... **Liuius** *enim dicit* ... **unde et** *pater euandrus* ... *fundauerunt &* **alii auxerunt**]

The justification of the digression receives a reference to the authority of Horace in the paraphrase, and at the beginning of the digression proper a reference to Livy, Ennius and Vergil expands on Sallust's unspecific citation of his sources; the same information is given in the Munich manuscript (above, n. 20) and there is evidence that this is in the medieval tradition.[21] Simple glosses and paraphrase complete this section; the use of *Ordo* marks the passage from summary explication to individual words and phrases.

For a last continuous passage of paraphrase with an interesting historical *exemplum*, from *BC* 9:

(Sallust) *Igitur domi militiaeque boni mores colebantur; concordia maxuma, minuma auaritia erat; ius bonumque apud eos non legibus magis quam natura ualebat. Iurgia discordias simultates cum hostibus exercebant, ciues cum ciuibus de uirtute certabant. In suppliciis deorum magnifici, domi parci, in amicos fideles erant. Duabus his artibus, audacia in bello, ubi pax euenerat aequitate, seque remque publicam curabant. Quarum rerum ego maxuma documenta haec habeo, quod in bello saepius uindicatum est in eos qui contra imperium in hostem pugnauerant quique tardius reuocati proelio excesserant quam qui signa relinquere aut pulsi loco cedere ausi erant; in pace uero quod beneficiis quam metu imperium agitabant et accepta iniuria ignoscere quam persequi malebant.*

(Commentary) Igitur *(9.1): et quia malebant benefacere quam benefacta aliorum dicere,* igitur *etc.* non magis ualebat legibus quam ne *[sic]: Nam et si leges non essent, naturaliter ius legale seruare [sic].* discordias*: manifestas.* simultates*: latentia odia.* in suppliciis deorum*:.i. in supplicationibus. Supplicia pro supplicationibus ideo ponuntur quia moris erat antiquitus ut de rebus supplicum.i. damnatorum—qui enim damnatur supplex est et humilis—donaria.i. templa deorum ampliantur.* Magnifici*:.i. largi.* his duabus artibus*: scil. audacia in bello, et aequitate in pace.* Quarum rerum*: scil. quod r. p. et se audacia et aequitate curarent.* habeo haec documenta*:.i. argumenta. quod citius et grauius puniebantur qui contra praecepta militaris disciplinae in hostes irruebant, uel reuocati cessare nolebant, quam qui pulsi fugiebant. Unde de Manlii Torquati filio legitur [Livy 8.7], quia cum a Roma abesset Manlius, et ne aliquis*

---

[21] *Corpus Glossariorum Latinorum* V, 578,3: Excerpta ex cod. Cassin. 90 (saec. X) *Romae conditor certus nescitur. Salustius dicit initio troiani eam condidere. uergilius ab ebandro, ennius et alii a Romulo.* Cf. Servius Danielis in Aen. I 273: *Naeuius et Ennius Aeneae ex filia nepotem Romulum conditorem urbis tradunt.*

contra hostes exisset publico edicto prohibuisset, filius eius habita occasione contra hostes exiuit et eos deuicit. Reuersus pater probitatem quidem filii laudauit, sed tamen ipsum, quia contra imperium pugnauerat, occidi iussit. In pace uero hoc argumentum habet de equitate: quia <u>agitabant</u> magis <u>beneficiis quam</u> metu, quod erat aequum. <u>accepta iniuria</u>:.i. perpessa ab aliquo.

[ed. 1502: *Non magis legibus quam* **natura** *ualebat ... ius legale* **seruari non posset** [recte] *... om. Supplicia pro supplicationibus ...* **uel** *donaria.i. templa* **ampliarentur** *... QVArum rerum.s.* **reipu.** *& se ...* **quod cum a roma** *... probitatem filii (om. quidem) ... argumentum* **habeo**]

Notable here is the addition to the paraphrasing of an explanation of *supplicia* in which appears the infrequent technical term *donaria* (for the part of a temple in which offerings are kept), and the summary narration of the incident (best source in Livy 8.7) in which Manlius Torquatus slew his own son for countermanding orders, giving a specific historical reference for a generalizing statement in Sallust; the incident is of course briefly mentioned later in the text of Sallust, in the speech of Cato at 52.30–31.

As the digression on the moral decline of Rome continues in *BC* 10–13, the commentary's paraphrase dances rather lightly over a text packed with meaning, but it is also provided with some knowledge from outside the text: a citation of Lucan; approval of word *aemula* from knowledge of Rome's history with Carthage. The explanations include supplying missing referents or modifiers, and in one case seek to explain a manuscript misreading, with no happy result; the correct interpretation of historical infinitive is perhaps notable. The edition of 1500/1502 cannot be copied from the Bern manuscript, but somewhere in the parentage of its exemplar must be a manuscript abbreviated in much the same extreme way as that, to judge from its misreadings. On *BC* 11.4 the paraphrase incorporates a measure of historical knowledge concerning the dictatorship of Sulla, and offers one of the rare grammatical comments, on the ambiguity of the form *alius*, and the even more unusual rhetorical comment on *mirari* for *cupere*: *antecedens pro consequenti. Ea enim quae miramur cupimur.* The somewhat lurid account of the moral decline of Rome in *BC* 12 does not arouse any unusual interest in the commentator, aside from the need to introduce the odd words *ganea* and *propatulo*, the latter producing a pair of alternative explanations (which became garbled in the printed edition):

in <u>propatulo</u> (13.3).i. in aperto quasi dicat omnes pudice erant. non enim erat qui tangeret. uel <u>impro.a.</u> [sic].i. pro uili. quod enim commune est uile est et ipse pro uili pudicitiam habebant quia publice se offerebant.

[*ed. 1502: IN propatulo.i. in aperto.i.* **manifesto** *quasi dicat omnis* **impudice** *erant. Quod enim commune est uile est* **etiam** *& ips(a)e pro uili pudicitiam habebant quia* **pudicitiae** *se offerebant.*]

Historical infinitives continue to be interpreted correctly as imperfects, and some unnecessary distinctions are made in addition to simple glosses.

At *BC* 14 the transition from the digression to the narrative is noted as before, and *continuatio* again marks the beginning of a paraphrase. Notable here is the note on the source of the metaphor seen in the word *conflauerat*: *metaphora ducta a fusore*. The tendency to make distinctions is again seen in one made between *flagitium* and *facinus*, between *periurio* and *sanguine*:

> (on 14.1) *flagitium in dictis. facinus in factis ... <u>illi quos alebat manus et lingua periurio</u> (14.3): si falsum fecit testimonium. et hoc ad linguam. <u>aut sanguine ciuili</u>: si ciuem interfecit. et hoc ad manum.*

[*ed. 1502: et ad linguam hoc* **pertinet** *... se* **quem** *interfecit*]

Notable also is a multiple derivation of *parricida*, a comment on the appropriate use of the word *inciderat*, and a definition and derivation of *inlecebris*. In *BC* 15 is again seen a distinction made between *ius* and *fas*, and three alternative explanations of the author's speculation on causation, as well as alternative derivations of *excitam*. There follows, on *BC* 16, a dubious assertion that giving of false testimony was a capital crime for the Romans, a mistaken reading of *fidem* with *commodare* instead of *habere* (hence no understanding of *commodare* as historical infinitive, which is implied by the punctuation of the Oxford edition); but perhaps most notable is a series of *causae* and *opportunitates*, and a strange geographical note making Spain adjacent to Italy; also a false distinction between *tutae* and *tranquillae*. Interpreting *ipsi consulatum petenti* as referring to Pompey may be a forgivable lapse.

At *BC* 17 the commentary characteristically remarks on the rhetorical strategy of the author at the beginning of a new section:

> <u>Igitur circiter Kal.</u> etc. *(17.1): tempus determinat ut uideatur uerisimile quod dicit.* <u>L. Cae. et Gaio Figulo consulibus</u>: *consules ideo ponit ut eos insipientes intelligamus quorum tempore ausus est ista inchoare.*

[*ed. 1502: quorum* **ipse** *est ausus ista (om. tempore)*]

But no comment is made on any of the long list of names after the first. Careful definitions of *coloniae* and *municipia* may be drawn from Isidore. And no notice is taken of the question of Crassus' involvement in the conspiracy. In the following chapter (18) the attempt to provide historical information relevant to the interpretation of this passage is quite fanciful:

designati consules (18.2): nondum intronizati. duo comitia erant in anno, estiualia et hiemalia. aestiualia erant in Kalendis Iulii, in quibus designabantur et eligebantur consules. hiemalia erant in Kalendis Ianuarii, quando intronizabantur.i. in sede dignitatis eleuabantur. Isti autem duo antequam administrarent damnati fuerant. Interrogati legibus ambitus: una est dictio. Lex ambitus erat quae eos qui per pecuniam ad honorem uenerant damnabat. uel sint due dictiones. interrogati legibus:.i. secundum leges. dederant poenas:.i. pertulerant. poenas:.i. repulsam, qua nihil grauius. ambitus:.i. ambitionis sue. Isti qui pecuniam dederant repudiati sunt. sed Catilina: qui reddere non potuit quae debuit, prohibitus est petere. et hoc est paulo post: Causam subdit quare prohibitus sit, quia reus repetundarum eo quod intra legitimos dies profiteri nequiuerat: Mos erat Romae quod si quis deposuisset pecuniam alicui nec posset habere, ueniebat ad praetorem. Praetor uero mandabat debitorem, et constituens terminum quendam praecipiebat ut infra terminum illum pecuniam profiteretur. et tunc, ut ita dicam, dicebantur petundae. si uero debitor in termino non profiteretur, item depositor ueniens ad praetorem pecuniam repetebat. et inde dicebantur repetundae. Tunc uero debitor damnante praetore reus erat repetundarum.

[ed. 1502: & *aestiualia erant Calen. Iulii (om. in) ... quando* **in sede maiestates uel dignitates** *eleuabantur ... antequam* **admitterentur** *... DEDErant (om. poenas).i.* **substinuerant** *poenas: repulsam. quia nihil grauius ... repudiati (om. sunt) ... reddere non poterat ... quia prohibitus (om. sit) ... mandabat* **debitori** *... praecipiebat ei ... in* **terminum** *non profiteretur ... repetebat:* **unde** *dicebantur ...* **damnantem** *praetore*]

Notable is the mention of "winter and summer" *comitia*, of electoral defeat as the penalty for bribing the voters, and the linking of *res repetundae* and *profiteri* to ordinary debt instead of extortion in provincial administration and declaration of candidacy. Although the printed edition eliminates the medieval word *intronizare* and has a few better readings, it shows no advance in knowledge over the earlier manuscript.

To see how the commentary deals with the more straightforward narrative parts of the Sallustian monograph, an example may be cited from the famous confrontation of Cicero and Catiline in the Senate in *BC* 31. Added to the paraphrase here is a desperate attempt to explain the reference to the *lex Plautia* (*Plautitia* in some mss.) without any knowledge of the law in question:

lege Plautitia (31.4): lex Plautitia erat ut si aliquis suspectus esset aliquid machinari contra r.p., aliqua nobilis et praepotens persona ipsum super hoc interrogabat. et cogebatur uenire in capitolium et ibi negare uel affirmare.

[ed. 1502: *lege. PLAUtia: lex plautia erat*]

There are quite reasonable etymologies for *luculentam* and *inquilinus*; identification of the irony in Catiline's remark about the *bonum custodem*; and a good explanation of the famous threat of Catiline on that occasion. But there is no interest in the historical or oratorical aspects of the event reported.

The subsequent narrative elicits only minimal comment. At *BC* 33 the instructions of Manlius are in the form of a speech and so receive a rhetorical introduction and comment, along with an attempt to explain Roman law concerning debtors.

> <u>Deos hominesque</u> *(33.1): haec oratio Gaii Manlii partim est excusatoria, partim supplicatoria. Inprimis enim se excusat quod arma non ceperit ad r.p. impugnationem, sed ad corporis sui defensionem. postea supplicare intendit, ubi ab ipso consilium requirit. statim in principio captat ipsius beniuolentiam appellando eum a nomine dignitatis, dicens <u>imperator</u> etc. <u>quo</u>:.i. ut. <u>corpora nostra</u>.i. nostrum. nostrum dico, <u>qui miseri</u> etc. <u>Violentia atque crudelitate faeneratorum</u>: hic captat beniuolentiam a persona aduersariorum, ducendo eos in infestationem et odium per hoc, quod dicit eos uiolentos et crudeles. Utrumque probat.*

[ed. 1502: *non* **cepit** *ad reipublicae* **repugnationem** ... *statim et in principio* ... *om. appellando eum a nomine dignitatis* ....*i. nostrum dico (om. nostrum)* ... *in fe-* **stinationem** *et odium et per hoc dicit (om. quod)*]

At *BC* 34 there are glosses and paraphrase with a mistaken second definition of *consularis* and an interesting distinction between *exemplum* and *exemplar*, omitted from the printed edition perhaps because irrelevant: *Exemplum est quod sumitur, exemplar est unde sumitur.* The beginning of Catiline's letter at *BC* 35 is again given a rhetorical introduction as a speech:

> <u>Lucius catilina</u> *(35.1): in hac oratione intendit Catilina Q. Catulo Aureliam Orestillam commendare, et consilii sui ueritatem, quam aliis texerat, aperire. Prius autem captat ipsius beneuolentiam, dicens eius fidelitatem sibi firmiter esse expertam.*

[ed. 1502: *aliis* **tedat** *aperire prius* **enim** *captat*]

An attempt is made to explain the phrase *medius fidius*, and here the alternative explanation is given a stamp of approval:

> <u>medius fidius</u> *(35.2): aduerbium iurandi, a mediatore et fido,.i. per Mercurium, qui mediator est et fidus interpres deorum. uel, quod melius est, <u>medius fidius</u>:.i. mediante fide.*

[ed. 1502: *a mediatore &* **fidem**]

A distinction is made between *labor* and *industria*, a false explanation of *liberalitas* and an unneeded one for the intrusive gloss *mutuum*, along with an attempt to give the background of the mention of *nominibus* in connection with debt.

At *BC* 36 there is again a rare grammatical note, citing Priscian as authority (Sallust is quoted on this point several times in Priscian):

> (on 36.2) *liceret inquam omnibus praeter condemnatis. Priscianus hoc adducit in exemplum [GL 3.187–8]. quod praeter figuratiue [fr.te.] ablatiuo adiungitur, cum accusatiuo tantum debeat adiungi.*
>
> [ed. 1502: *Priscianus* **ad hoc abducit in exemplo**. *Quia praeter figuratiue*]

At the end of the chapter *tabes* is defined as *morbus porcorum* (printed edition has *prochorum*; in other medieval commentaries it is a *morbus pecorum* or even *paucorum*). Aside from a derivation of *petulantia*, a definition of *sentina* (partially omitted in the printed edition), and a faulty interpretation of *miles gregarius*, all is explanatory paraphrase; in the attempt to provide such for the transition to what the commentator regards as the beginning of the digression, a misunderstanding arises that shows again that the source of information is just the text itself:

> (on 37.11) <u>*ideo [sic mss.]*</u> *malum reuerterat antiquum est et bene dico reuerterat nomina [sic] prius extiterat ad quod ostendendum facit auctor digressionem. siquidem tribunicia potestas maxima esse solebat. tribunus enim quotiens uolebat plebem contra nobilitatem excitare poterat. sed iam longo tempore deperierat. Contigit autem* GNEIVM PONPEJVM. *et* MARCVM CRASSVM. *eodem tempore tribunos et consules esse qui quodam modo negleto [sic] consulatu tribunatum uoluerant in pristinum statum reuocare et ita plebem contra nobilitatem grauiter excitauere. et tunc aplebe grauisse [sic] atrita est nobilitas. Postea contigit pompeium contra regem ponti missum fuisse. et tunc opes plebis maxime sunt imminute. et sic econtrario plebs grauisse [sic] atrita est a nobilitate. et hoc exequitur auctor dicens* <u>Nam postquam</u> *(38.1) etc.*
>
> [ed. 1502: **nam** *prius extiterat ... grauiter* **excitare** *... grauissime* **astricta** *est ...* **grauissima astricta est nobilitate** *(om. a)*]

The introduction to the lengthy speech of Caesar in *BC* 51 provides a final example of an interest in rhetoric:

> (on 51) *In hac oratione C. Caesar intendit illis interceptis misericordiam impetrare a patribus conscriptis. et hoc facit improbando et destruendo sententiam Decii Sillani, qui eos iudicauerat at dignos interfeci [sic]. Agit autem rhetorice et utitur insinuatione. Multis enim in locis eos damnare et grauiter eos puniendo iudicat, ut scil. facilius ueniam et misericordiam impetrare ualeat. Ne autem uideretur aperte ipsos uelle defendere, hoc remouet, dicens se ab amicitia et misericordia et ceteris animi [ai] affectionibus uacuum esse. a quibus omnes iudices uacuos decet esse. et ab hoc puncto incipit dicens:* <u>Omnes homines</u> *etc. (51.1).* <u>patres conscripti</u>: *Ubi patres appellat eos ad misericordiam multum incuruat. quemadmodum enim pater super filio siquid peccaue-*

rit misericorditer debet commoueri. Sic et ipsi super ciuibus suis miserrimis, qui sunt quasi filii. conscripti *siquidem romulus secundum quosdam* XXX*ta secundum alios c. senatores qui res p. prouiderent elegit. et eorum nomina in aenea tabula. et aureis litteris conscripsit. in enea tabula propter designandam imperii perhennitatem. litteris aureis propter ipsorum dignitatem.*

[ed. 1502: **ut** *dignos* **interfici** ... *eo* **damnat** *et graviter puniendos* **indicat**: *ut ita facilius* ... *Ne autem* **viderentur** ... **hic** *remouet* ... *ceteris* **cum** *affectionibus* ... *super* **filios** *si quid* **peccauerunt** ... *litteris* **sciripsit**]

The oratorical approach is one that is found in many medieval commentaries: a statement of the orator's intention, and a broad characterization of the tactic of the speech. The explanation of the phrase *patres conscripti* focuses not upon its being the standard vocative phrase for addressing the Senate, but finds in the first word an oratorical ploy, and in the second gives a standard historical explanation from information readily available during the medieval period. At the end of this section it reverts to the kind of paraphrase approach already seen.

The only expansion of that paraphrase occurs as a quasi–scholastic discussion is given of the four emotions (*odium, amicitia, ira, misericordia*):

Omnes inquam omnes decet esse uacuos *(51.1): ab illis quattuor affectionibus, quarum due sunt de praesenti, due de praeterito; due nouicie, due uetuste; due de bono, due de malo. Odium est quaedam animi passio uetusta ad malum prona non subito sed ex deliberatione progenita. Amicitia est quaedam animi affectio uetusta ad bonum prona, non ex deliberatione progenita. Ira est quaedam animi passio nouicia ad malum prona, non ex deliberatione sed repentino animi impulsu progenita. Misericordia est quaedam animi affectio nouicia ad bonum prona, non ex deliberatione, sed subito et repentino animi impulsu progenita. Vere ab his affectionibus omnes iudices uacui esse debent, quia ubi iste adsunt, officiunt, et ubi officiunt, non ueritas facile prouidetur.*

[ed. 1502: *Odium* ... *animi passio* **uetusta**: **ad malum prona subito** *sed ex deliberatione progenita*]

The opening of Cato's speech is given a similar rhetorical introduction followed by paraphrase:

Longe mihi *(52.1): In hac oratione intendit Marcus Porcius Cato sententiam Caesaris obuiare [sic] et patres conscriptos ad interceptos grauiter et cito puniendos animare dicens* Longe mihi *etc. Quasi dicat cesar et alii eos non morte puniendos iudicauerunt.* Sed mihi longe alia mens est: *Beniuolentiam captat sicut cesar superius a nomine dignitatis. uocans eos patres conscriptos* cum considero res atque pericula nostra.*i. res nostras in maximo periculo sitas.*

But the method of the commentator is not otherwise affected by the extraordinary length of the paired speeches, nor by the distinctive *synkrisis* that follows them.

The characteristic nature of the commentary, a careful and methodical mixture of gloss and paraphrase, continues to the end of Sallust's narrative in *BC* 61:

> (Sallust) *Sed confecto proelio, tum uero cerneres quanta audacia quantaque animi uis fuisset in exercitu Catilinae. Nam fere quem quisque uiuos pugnando locum ceperat, eum amissa anima corpore tegebat. Pauci autem, quos medios cohors praetoria disiecerat, paulo diuorsius, sed omnes tamen aduorsis uolneribus conciderant. Catilina uero longe a suis inter hostium cadauera repertus est, paululum etiam spirans ferociamque animi quam habuerat uiuos in uoltu retinens. Postremo ex omni copia neque in proelio neque in fuga quisquam ciuis ingenuos captus est: ita cuncti suae hostiumque uitae iuxta pepercerant. Neque tamen exercitus populi Romani laetam aut incruentam uictoriam adeptus erat; nam strenuissumus quisque aut occiderat in proelio aut grauiter uolneratus discesserat. Multi autem, qui e castris uisundi aut spoliandi gratia processerant, uoluentes hostilia cadauera amicum alii, pars hospitem aut cognatum reperiebant; fuere item qui inimicos suos cognoscerent. Ita uarie per omnem exercitum laetitia maeror, luctus atque gaudia agitabantur.*
>
> (Commentary) <u>sed confecto</u> *(61.1)*: *dum pugnantes steterunt maxima uirtus in Catilinariis potuit notare, sed etiam postquam ceciderunt. et hoc est* <u>sed confecto proelio</u> *etc.* <u>tegebat</u>: *mortuus scil. eundem locum quem quisque uiuus occupauerat.* <u>aduersis uulneribus</u>:*.i. oppositis. a pectore enim fixi erant, a tergo.* <u>spirans</u>: *spiritum ducens.* <u>iuxta</u>:*.i. aequaliter.* <u>pepercerant suae uitae et hostium</u>: *quia neque sue neque hostium uite pepercerunt.* <u>Neque tamen</u>: *Sic se ex utraque parte habuerunt, et tandem Romani uictoriam obtinuerunt, non tamen lentam [sic], sed cruentam et luctosam [sic]. multi autem illorum qui ex castris profecti sunt alii letabuntur [sic], alii tristabuntur [sic]. alii tristebantur [sic] et hoc est* <u>leticia</u>: *in uultum [sic] pro hostibus inuentis, et gaudium in corde, iterum pro hostibus.* <u>Meror</u>: *in corde pro amicis.* <u>Luctus</u>: *in uultu pro amicis.*
>
> [ed. 1502: **non** *a tergo (recte) ... habuerunt.* **quia** *tandem ... non tamen* **laetam** *(recte) ... luctuosam (recte) ... ex castris* **perfecti** *... laetabantur (recte) alii tristabantur & * **hic** *est laetitia in* **uultu** *(recte) ... luctus in uultu* **iterum** *pro amicis*]

It may be said, as presumably Calfurnio would say, that this work strikes the reader as uncharacteristic of its supposed author, that it simply is not worthy of Ognibene or the way he and other Renaissance commentators are known to treat classical texts. Even if there were no witnesses to this text prior to its appearance in print in 1500, it could be said that it lacks the characteristic spirit of a Renaissance reading of Sallust's text, that it lacks any marks of the new sources of information about the classical past, its history and its language. Nor is there any criticism of the received vulgate text, any attempt to create a new edition. Even if intended only for the instruction of young beginners, it breathes throughout the air of the classroom of an earlier period. In addition, it seems hardly to be the case that the commentary as printed in 1500 is a reworking by Ognibene of the medieval manuscript commentary, for the text is not at all improved and seems quite ignorantly set up for printing. Nor, despite the presence of paraphrase, rhetorical criticism, grammatical points, and ethical statements in its pedagogical approach, can we see the manner of that or perhaps any other teacher of the period. It may be relevant to note that, besides the question of the age of intended readers, Sallust was an old friend, not a new interest, even though there was more to be learned from his text than the earlier tradition had learned.

The printers were, it appears, anxious to provide a text of Sallust with two different commentaries, approximating in print form what was desired by school readers of ancient texts, as opposed to wealthy patrons, namely a text enriched with interpretive comment by those who had previously worked on it. They chose the well-known name of Omnibonus Leonicenus to make their product more attractive to their prospective market. In juxtaposing on the page the commentary of the new age alongside a traditional medieval commentary, they may seem to have given, in the attribution of the latter to Ognibene, another example of the continuity between medieval and Renaissance scholarship.

Robert W. Ulery, Jr.   Wake Forest University

The Valla Commentary on Sallust's *Bellum Catilinae*: Questions of Authenticity and Reception*

PATRICIA J. OSMOND

In 1491 an edition of Sallust's *opera*, with texts edited by Pomponio Leto and a commentary on the *Bellum Catilinarium* attributed to Lorenzo Valla, was printed in Venice by Filippo Pinzi.[1] Pomponio's edition of the *opera* had already been published in Rome the preceding year by Eucario Silber, but the 1491 Venice imprint marked the *editio princeps* of the Valla commentary; in fact, it was the first commentary on any of Sallust's works to appear in print.

The authorship of this commentary is still disputed, and whether it is a genuine work of Valla, a set of notes compiled by one or more of his pupils, a case of forgery, or simply an unintended misattribution, remains a *vexatissima quaestio*. In her article "Per il *Commento* a Sallustio di Lorenzo Valla," in Res publica litterarum 14 (1991), Mariarosa Cortesi reviewed the arguments for and against Valla's authorship and, more recently, Robert W. Ulery and I have summarized them in our introduction to the Valla commentary in "Sallustius Crispus, Gaius," *Catalogus translationum et commentariorum*, vol. 8 (2003).[2]

On the one hand, the proem (or *vita Sallustii*) introducing the commentary (see Appendix) shows a number of correspondences with ideas and themes familiar in Valla's known writings. The dismay at the destruction wrought by the Goths, the lament for the lost portions of Sallust's *Historiae*, and the appeal to preserve, study, and disseminate as widely as possible whatever has survived of Sallust's writings (... *summa nos ope niti decet ut praeclara eius monumenta, si qua adhuc restant, non tantum ipsi studio condiscamus sed, si fieri etiam possit, quam plurimis nostra industria omni sint ex parte conspicua*) recall his prefaces to the *Elegantiae*

---

* I would like to thank the editor, Marianne Pade, and the readers, especially Craig Kallendorf and Robert Ulery, for their comments on and contributions to the revised version of this paper.

[1] *Laurentii Vallensis in C. Crispi Salustii Catilinarium Commentarii*, in C. Sallustius Crispus, *Opera* (Impressum Venetiis ... arte et ingenio Philippi Pincii de Caneto, 1491). The title page of the 1491 edition has *C. Crispi Sallustii bellum catilinarium cum commento Laurentii uallensis*.

[2] Mariarosa Cortesi, "Per il *Commento* a Sallustio di Lorenzo Valla," Res publica litterarum 14 (1991), 49–59. Cortesi reviews the bibliography to date (including Gianni Zippel, "Lorenzo Valla e le origini della storiografia umanistica a Venezia," Rinascimento 7 [1956], 93–133), points out a number of the thematic correspondences between the proem and other writings of Valla summarized below, and cites examples of the historical, grammatical and stylistic notes. The two versions ("A" and "B") of the proem and of the *incipit* and *explicit* of the commentary, as well as a summary of the textual tradition, are given in the entry "Laurentius Valla (?)" in Patricia J. Osmond and Robert W. Ulery, Jr., "Sallustius Crispus, Gaius," CTC (see note to the Appendix below), 237–43.

(c.1435–44)[3] as well as his exhortations in the *Oratio in principio studii* (1455)[4] to recover and restore the Latin language. Quintilian's comparison of Sallust with Thucydides (*Inst.* 10.1.101) is suggested in a passage of Valla's dedicatory letter to Nicholas V accompanying his translation of Thucydides (1452), for which he had relied upon Sallust's own imitation of the Greek historian for his Latin rendering.[5] The praise of history in teaching *ciuilis sapientia* and of the historian's role in serving the *res publica* — *quia praeclara ingenia aut domi consulendo suorumque facta illustrando aut foris rem publicam administrando patriae uideri possunt utilia* (*cf. Bellum Catilinae* 3.1) — also appears in Valla's proem to the *Gesta Ferdinandi regis Aragonum* (1445),[6] and a nostalgic allusion to the *optimatium administratio* recalls his words of admiration for the conservative faction of the Roman senatorial class in his *Declamatio* on the false Donation of Constantine (1440)[7]. Moreover, while the author of a medieval *accessus* tended to view the classical text he was introducing *sub specie aeternitatis*, the author of the proem to the Valla commentary was attempting to locate Sallust's work in the historical context of ancient Rome and in the framework of ancient literary criticism.

The annotations to the text, however, have a different character. Here we find a line–by–line, often word–by–word, commentary giving synonyms and paraphrases, illustrating basic rules of grammar and syntax, rhetorical constructions, and figures of speech, and briefly explaining Roman laws, magistracies, and institutions mentioned in the text. A glance at the first notes to the *Catilina* shows the simple pedagogical approach: the use of *praesto* with both the

---

[3] *Laurentii Vallensis de elegantia lingue latine proemium primum* 22–23 and 29ff., ed. Mariangela Regoliosi, in Regoliosi, Nel cantiere del Valla. Elaborazione e montaggio delle "Elegantie" (Rome, 1993), Appendice, 117–25. Valla renews his attack on the Goths in his preface to book three of the *Elegantiae* (Cortesi, ibid., 57).

[4] "Oratio in principio studii," in Lorenzo Valla: Orazione per l'inaugurazione dell'anno accademico 1455–56: Atti di un seminario di filologia umanistica, ed. Silvia Rizzo (Rome, 1994), 192–201, on which see Rizzo, "L'*Oratio* nella riflessione del Valla sulla lingua latina," ibid., 73–85.

[5] Vatican City, Biblioteca Apostolica Vaticana, Ms. Vat. lat. 1801, f. 2r. See Marianne Pade, "Valla's Thucydides: Theory and Practice in a Renaissance Translation," Classica et mediaevalia 36 (1985), 275–301, at 288.

[6] *Laurentii Valle Gesta Ferdinandi regis Aragonum*, Proemium 11, ed. Ottavio Besomi (Padua, 1973), 6.

[7] Laurentius Valla, *De falso credita et ementita Constantini donatione*, 40, ed. Wolfram Setz (Weimar, 1976), 322. See Pade, ibid., 290–91, on Valla's use of *populares* and *optimates* in his translation of Thucydides. On his sympathy for the *optimates*, see also Cortesi, ibid., 57 and Salvatore I. Camporeale, Lorenzo Valla. Umanesimo e teologia (Florence, 1972), 438–39 in reference to Giovanni da Tivoli and Valla's notes on Sallust.

dative and accusative; the meaning of *animantibus*, and the significance of *opis* in Virgil's *Aeneid* 1.600–601:

> *Praestare [1.1]: datiuo & accusatiuo iungitur, ut praesto illi & praesto illum. Praestare excellere. Caeteris animantibus: scilicet brutis animalibus. Summa ope: summa possibilitate & uiribus summis. Nam opis significat possibilitatem. Virgilii Aeneidos libro primo: Grates persoluere dignas Non opis est nostrae, Dido, id est, possibilitatis.*

Other ancient authors cited as sources of historical information or moral lessons and *exempla*, or as authorities on grammar and rhetoric, include Servius on rules for nouns of the third declension, Valerius Maximus on the sayings of Appius Claudius, Livy, and Plutarch on the story of the foundation of Rome, and Cicero on the forms of *narratio* (*Ars vetus*, i.e., *De inuentione*). The citation of classical authors is not frequent, however, and there are no instances of textual emendation or variant readings. To be sure, there is a certain sensitivity to Sallust's word choice and definition — what the author of the commentary in a note to *BC* 2.5 calls his *uocabulorum proprietas* — and an appreciation of the distinctive features of Sallust's style. But there is no attempt to elaborate upon the themes of the preface, to consider Quintilian's judgments on Sallust as historian or orator, or even to mention Quintilian again in the course of the commentary. Nor is there any trace of the critical, polemical spirit that characterized many of Valla's philological writings.[8] Occasional errors of historical fact and misunderstandings of the Latin also occur: for example, *tabulae nouae* (*BC* 21.2), described as paintings in the notes on this passage, have evidently been confused with the meaning of *tabulae* in the preceding chapter, 20.12 (*Quom tabulas signa toreumata emunt, noua diruunt* ...), and even in the proem, where we see a closer affinity with Valla's known work, Sallust, who was born in the municipal town of Amiternum to a family of the equestrian order, is described as *patritia gente Romae natus*. Certain phrases introducing the notes, such as *ergo constat, reddit rationem cur, ad propositum reddit, quasi dicat, nota ergo*, etc., also have a seemingly scholastic air.

The circumstances surrounding the printing of the commentary in Venice in 1491 by Filippo Pinzi are still a mystery. A number of manuscripts containing the proem and commentary (in different versions) were circulating in Italy

---

[8] This is evident not only in his *Declamatio* but also in his emendations of Livy, on which see Regoliosi, "Le congetture a Livio del Valla: metodo e problemi," Lorenzo Valla e l'umanesimo italiano. Atti del convegno internazionale di studi umanistici, Parma, 18–19 ottobre, 1984, eds. Ottavio Besomi and Mariangela Regoliosi (Padua, 1986), 51–71; on Valla as *reformator grammaticus* and polemicist, see also Christopher S. Celenza, "Renaissance Humanism and the New Testament: Lorenzo Valla's Annotations to the Vulgate," Journal of Medieval and Renaissance Studies 24 (1994), 33–52.

from the middle, or at least the third quarter,[9] of the fifteenth century, and to judge from the notes, it must have been destined for use in the schools, perhaps in Venice itself. But we do not have the exemplar used for the *editio princeps* or know how it was obtained by the printer, and the relationship between the extant manuscripts and the printed edition is not clear. One name, however, does stand out: that of Antonio Moreto (or Moretto), a Brescian humanist who was active in Padua and in Venice from c.1470 to the early 1500s as bookseller and consultant to authors and printers. In the dedicatory letter of Pomponio Leto to Agostino Maffei, first printed in Pomponio's Rome edition of Sallust's *opera* in 1490, then reprinted in the Venice 1491 edition of the *opera* with the addition of the Valla commentary, Moreto's name was substituted for that of Giovanni da Reggio, Pomponio's publisher–bookseller in Rome. It is likely, therefore, that Moreto played a significant role in financing, editing, and/or promoting the 1491 edition.[10]

* * *

The purpose of this paper, however, is not to determine whether the commentary printed in 1491 was, or was not, a *genuine* work by Valla, but rather to look at the question of its authenticity as a criterion for identifying a Renaissance commentary. My discussion centers, therefore, on what was said, or not said, about the attribution of the commentary. (I am reminded of the words of the seventeenth–century skeptic Pierre Bayle, who declared: "je ne lis presque jamais les Historiens dans la vue de m'instruire des choses qui se sont passées, mais seulement pour savoir ce que l'on dit dans chaque Nation & dans chaque parti, sur les choses qui se sont passées.")[11] Was this commentary on Sallust's *Bellum Catilinae*, in the opinion of teachers and scholars of the late 1400s and

---

[9] The manuscripts, containing all or parts of the proem and/or commentary, which (on the basis of our tentative dating) were written earlier than 1491 (the date of the first printed edition) are listed in Osmond and Ulery, "Sallustius," 8.238 and 241 (with further bibliography): (Version A) Munich, Universitätsbibliothek, 2° Cod. Ms. 548, s. XV, fols. 1r–35v; and (Version B): Modena, Biblioteca Estense, Est. lat 306 (alpha W.4.13), s. XV, fols. 228r–252v; Munich, Bayerische Staatsbibliothek, Clm 7612, s. XV, fols. 101r, 127v–131r; Venice, Biblioteca Nazionale Marciana, lat. XIV 179 (4488) (miscellany), s. XV, fols. 149r–158v; Naples, Biblioteca Nazionale, IV C 3, s.XV, fols. 1r–37v.

[10] On Moreto, see John Monfasani, "The First Call for Press Censorship: Niccolò Perotti, Giovanni Andrea Bussi, Antonio Moreto, and the Editing of Pliny's Natural History," Renaissance Quarterly 41 (1988), 1–31, and Angela Nuovo and Ennio Sandal, Il libro nell'Italia del Rinascimento (Brescia, 1998), 51 and 172–73. Cortesi, "Per il *Commento*," 50–51, mentions Moreto's likely role in publishing the Valla commentary.

[11] Pierre Bayle, "Critique générale de L'Histoire du Calvinisme de M. Maimbourg," Oeuvres Diverses (The Hague, 1727), II.10. The words are quoted in an English translation by Jacques Barzun and Henry F. Graff, The Modern Researcher, 3rd ed. (New York, 1977), 157.

first half of the 1500s, a work that could have been written by Valla? Was it *worthy* of one of the most distinguished philologists of the fifteenth century, appropriate to the reputation of a scholar who had passionately and persuasively set forth the goals of linguistic and cultural reform in his prefaces to the *Elegantiae*?[12] Was it eligible, in other words, as a Renaissance commentary, not in the sense that it was written and read in an era we are accustomed to call the Renaissance, but insofar as it embodied the spirit and aims of *renovatio litterarum* that Valla's scholarship had come to represent?

The question of authenticity is linked, in turn, to the broader issue of reception history, to the reception of Valla's own work, and in particular to the *fortuna* of the *Elegantiae*. The subject, of course, is vast and would require an investigation far wider than can be attempted in this paper. I shall focus, however, on certain aspects of the issue and raise a few general questions. What elements in the commentary, for instance, were selected or privileged as evidence for or against Valla's authorship? What attitudes and interests, reflecting the teaching traditions and interpretive communities in which the commentary was studied or the social–economic milieux of printers, publishers, and booksellers, could support arguments in favor of Valla's authorship or, on the contrary, challenge the attribution? What do we know of the ways in which Valla's philological writings were circulated and read in the last decades of the fifteenth century and in the first decades of the sixteenth century within Italy and North of the Alps?

Italy 1491–1500

In Italy in the last years of the fifteenth century — to judge from both the immediate success of the edition and the absence of any controversy over the authorship — it appears that the commentary of 1491 was at least tacitly accepted as Valla's work. Between 1491 and 1494, it was reprinted at least six times: four times in Venice, once in Milan, and once in Turin (and perhaps once also in Lyons). To these 'pirated' editions, copied from Filippo Pinzi's *editio princeps*, we can then add the variorum editions that began to appear in the following years: the *opera* of Sallust edited by Giovanni Britannico with the commentary of Johannes Chrysostomus Soldus (Giovanni Crisostomo Soldi) of Brescia (1495), reprinted at least four times between Venice, Paris, Zwolle, and Milan in the space of three years (1495–98) and an edition of Venice 1501

---

[12] For modern scholarship on Valla's *Elegantiae*, and other works, see Regoliosi, Nel cantiere del Valla, with discussion of the first proem, p. 63ff. and bibliography. See also Elisabet Sandström, ed., Laurentius Valla. *De reciprocatione 'sui' et 'suus'* (Göteborg, Acta Universitatis Gothoburgensis, 1998), with further bibliography including, in addition to works cited below, other relevant studies by Vittorio De Caprio, Franco Gaeta, Joseph IJsewijn, and Gilbert Tournoy.

containing a second commentary on the *Bellum Catilinae*, attributed to Omnibonus Leonicenus (Ognibene da Lonigo).[13] Between 1504 and 1590 the Valla commentary appeared in at least another ten, increasingly large, composite editions, along with notes not only by Soldus and Omnibonus but also (in different combinations) by Jodocus Badius Ascensius, Bartholomaeus Marlianus, Henricus Glareanus, Johannes Rivius, Franciscus Sylvius, Jacobus Crucius Bononiensis, Bartholomaeus Zanchus, and Vincentius Castellanus. If there had been any suspicion that the Valla Commentary was a forgery (or simply a mis–attribution), we might expect that some enterprising scholar would have been quick to expose it. In 1476 Giovanni Calfurnio had written a scathing attack on profit–hungry printers who had been publishing editions under the names of famous authors.[14] In 1494 a new edition of Quintilian's *Institutio oratoria* with notes ascribed to Valla was published in reaction to the appearance the previous year of a commentary by Raffaele Regio dismissing these same notes as a forgery.[15] And yet, in the case of the 1491 commentary on the *Bellum Catilinae*, Italian humanists familiar with Valla's work, including Pomponio Leto himself, apparently raised no cries of protest. As far as we know, no accusations were made against Pinzi or Moreto for perpetrating a fraud. In fact, about four years later, Pinzi, whose house and shop had recently been destroyed by a fire, applied for a privilege to reprint the Valla commentary, along with another commentary on Sallust (no longer extant) by Battista Guarini.[16]

The absence of controversy is arguably no proof of authenticity, but it does suggest that readers were at least disposed to accept the commentary as authentic or, conversely, unwilling to challenge it. It is possible, for instance, that the very absence of fanfare, which usually accompanied the publication of a major author and especially a newly–discovered text,[17] concealed a certain

---

[13] See the article in this volume by Robert W. Ulery, Jr. on the commentary attributed to Omnibonus Leonicenus.

[14] John Monfasani, "Calfurnio's Identification of Pseudepigrapha of Ognibene, Fenestella, and Trebizond, and His Attack on Renaissance Commentaries," Renaissance Quarterly, 41 (1988), 32–43, at p. 34 and Appendix, 41–43, at sent. 15ff.

[15] Alessandro Perosa, "L'edizione veneta di Quintiliano coi commenti del Valla, di Pomponio Leto e di Sulpizio da Veroli," in Miscellanea Augusto Campana, 2 vols., (Padua, 1981), 2. 575–610, at 602–04. On charges and countercharges of forgery involving Raffaele Regio, see also Monfasani, "Calfurnio's Identification of Pseudepigrapha."

[16] Rinaldo Fulin, "Documenti per servire alla storia della tipografia veneziana," Archivio Veneto 23 (1882) 84–212, no. 36 at p. 118, referring to January 20, 1494 m.v. (=1495). No such edition has been found, and the reference in Hain (no. 14231) cited by Fulin is probably to be identified with the c.1496–97 edition of Sallust with commentaries of Valla on the *Catilina* and of Soldus on the *Iugurtha* printed in Venice by Cristoforo de Pensis.

[17] If the commentary had been considered the work of Valla 'without the shadow of doubt', or if, on the contrary, the publishers had attempted to foist a forgery on the public, one

embarrassment, or simply caution: an attempt, perhaps, to avoid a possibly compromising statement, one way or the other. A number of previously unknown works by Valla were turning up in Venice in these very years, and it was not always easy to distinguish between the genuine and the false. In the case of the notes on Quintilian, Raffaele Regio had expressed his doubts about Valla's authorship, but had turned out to be wrong. The debate over the authorship of various *opuscula* attributed to Valla, reportedly found in Naples or Rome by a certain Benedictus Presbyter and published in Venice in 1503 by Cristoforo de Pensis, including the *De conficiendis epistolis* and the *Emendationes quorundam locorum ex Alexandro ad Alphonsum primum Aragonum regem*, is a debate that continues even today.[18]

For printers and publishers, there were certainly practical, economic reasons for promoting, or accepting, the attribution of the commentary to an illustrious name. Not only Moreto and Pinzi, but all those who in the 1490s rushed the Valla commentary on the *Bellum Catilinae* through the press could expect to reap large profits and publicity — neither of which they would want to jeopardize by questioning Valla's authorship. For a newcomer to Venice like Filippo Pinzi of Mantua, the triad of Sallust, Leto, and Valla served to launch his press.[19] It is likely, in other words, that printers, patrons, and booksellers saw the prospects of good sales and seized the opportunity to publish, or republish, a popular text — no questions asked.

Teachers in the humanist schools must also have welcomed a new, authoritative edition that combined under the same cover the texts of Sallust edited by Pomponio Leto and a commentary by Lorenzo Valla.[20] Sallust had been a staple of the arts curriculum, a fixture in the canon of Latin authors, for centuries, and the publication of text and commentary would satisfy not only a

---

might expect that they would have surrounded their 'discovery' with some fanfare (Anthony Grafton, Forgers and Critics: creativity and duplicity in Western scholarship [Princeton, NJ, 1990], especially 62–67). Antonio Moreto, in fact, regularly used the prefaces to his editions to advertise his connections with the world of humanist scholarship (Monfasani, "First Call for Press Censorship," 15).

[18] Opuscula quaedam nuper in lucem edita (Venice, 1503). See *Laurentii Valle Epistole*, eds. Ottavio Besomi and Mariangela Regoliosi (Padua, 1984), 17–19, and, on the authorship of certain treatises in this collection, John Monfasani, "Three Notes on Renaissance Rhetoric," Rhetorica 5 (1987), 107–18, at 108–10, reprinted in Language and Literature in Renaissance Italy (Aldershot, Hampshire, Great Britain, 1996).

[19] See n. 16 above. In 1495 Pinzi applied for a "privilege" to reprint the Valla commentary, counting on the protection of a 'copyright' and profits from good sales to restore his finances after a fire had destroyed his shop.

[20] Martin Lowry described Pomponio as "the arbiter of correct Latin usage" in Nicholas Jenson and the rise of Venetian publishing in Renaissance Europe (Oxford, 1991), 118.

continuing but, by now, growing demand for his work. Even if most of the commentary on the *Bellum Catilinae* dealt with the essentials of vocabulary and grammar, or simple aspects of Roman history and institutions, features that could also be found in earlier commentaries, we know that teaching practices, especially at the lower end of the curriculum, tended to be conservative.[21] Moreover, in the humanist schools of Venice, training in grammar and rhetoric, instruction in the essentials of Roman political history (with comparisons of Roman and Venetian institutions), and inculcation of moral precepts and *exempla* provided a solid education for the future leaders of the Venetian Republic.[22] The reference to the *optimates* in the proem — besides the praise of *concordia* and the condemnation of conspiracy implicit in the very choice of Sallust's monograph — had a special appeal to the Venetian patriciate, and a note on *BC* 17.4 explaining the difference between *coloniae* and *municipia* with reference to Vicenza as a *colonia* of Venice would flatter the pride of the Venetian governing class.

Valla himself had enjoyed a strong and loyal following in Venice since the early 1450s,[23] thanks especially to the efforts of Gian Pietro da Lucca and Francesco Diana, teachers at the Chancery School in Venice, to disseminate his writings and to carry on his mission of linguistic reform and cultural renovation through a careful, detailed study of the ancient authors. In a letter to Valla of 1452, Gian Pietro paid tribute to his role in restoring the elegance of the Latin language and the knowledge of the liberal arts, in words that remind us of Valla's preface to Book One of the *Elegantiae*: *tu enim longo interuallo me in patriam reuocasti, tu mihi sermonem patrium restituisti, tu denique omnes liberales artes corruptas ac penitus euersas ad pristinam sinceritatem ac ueritatem deprauatas ac funditus deletas reuocasti atque recreasti.*[24]

---

[21] Robert Black sums up this point in his Humanism and Education in Medieval and Renaissance Italy: Tradition and Innovation in Latin Schools from the Twelfth to the Fifteenth Century (Cambridge, 2001), 11. See also Anthony Grafton and Lisa Jardine, From Humanism to the Humanities: Education and the Liberal Arts in Fifteenth– and Sixteenth–century Europe (Cambridge, MA, 1986), and Paul F. Grendler, Schooling in Renaissance Italy: Literacy and Learning, 1300–1600 (Baltimore, MD, 1989).

[22] James Bruce Ross, "Venetian Schools and Teachers Fourteenth to Early Sixteenth Century: A Survey and a Study of Giovanni Battista Egnazio," Renaissance Quarterly, 29 (1976), 521–66. See also Margaret King, Venetian Humanism in an Age of Patrician Dominance (Princeton, 1986), with profiles of Venetian humanists and further bibliography.

[23] On the ambiente veneziano of Valla, see Cortesi, "Gli scritti del Valla tra Veneto e Germania," in Lorenzo Valla e l'Umanesimo italiano, 365–98, with further bibliography, including works by Gianni Zippel, Salvatore I. Camporeale, and Franco Gaeta.

[24] The letter praising Valla's work, which was subsequently included in Valla's *Antidotum in Pogium II*, concludes with the words: "ut cum sermo patrius ac lingua latina per eum nobis reddita ac restituta fuerit, tum demum imperium ac summa rerum in Italiam redeat." *Lau-*

With the advent of printing Valla's works were even more widely diffused. More than thirty editions (or imprints) of the *Elegantiae* were published between 1471 and 1500, including an edition that issued from Filippo Pinzi's press in 1492, a year after his printing of the Valla commentary.[25] In the same year (1492), Pinzi also published a popular *Epitome* of the *Elegantiae*, summarizing the grammatical rules in alphabetical order, and a brief critical analysis or *Lima in Vallam*, composed by Antonio Mancinelli (who subsequently edited Valla's Latin translation of Herodotus for the De Gregori press in 1494 and a new edition published by Antonio Moreto in 1495). These are the years, too, in which the name of Valla was being taken up as standard–bearer in the Venetian campaign of *renovatio litterarum*, aimed at placing Venice at the forefront of the humanist movement. In Marcantonio Sabellico's *De latinae linguae reparatione dialogus* (c.1490), Valla was hailed as the "new Camillus," who had expelled the Gauls from Rome and restored the *sermo latinus*: words that again echo his own preface to the *Elegantiae*, while recalling, at the same time, the preface to the commentary on the *Bellum Catilinae* with its appeal to study and propagate Sallust's surviving works.[26] In fact, while the grammatical and historical notes of the commentary could satisfy the practical exigencies of the school curriculum, the proem, with its more philosophical appeal, elevated the tone and gave it a programmatic importance. It is interesting, moreover, that one of the interlocutors in Sabellico's dialogue, Benedetto Brugnoli, teacher at the Chancery school, must have devoted considerable attention to Sallust, for a distinguished pupil of his, the patrician Bernardo Giustiniani, drew upon the scheme of the rise and decline of the Roman Republic in *Bellum Catilinae* 6–13 to portray the virtues of the early Venetians in his *De origine urbis Venetiarum* (1492) — and to warn his fellow nobles of the corrupting effects of ambition

---

rentii Vallae Epistole, ed. Besomi and Regoliosi, letter 50b, 378; see also 360–61. It is quoted by Salvatore I. Camporeale, Lorenzo Valla. Umanesimo e teologia (Florence, 1972), 382–83. Cf. Cortesi, "Scritti di Lorenzo Valla," 369.

[25] For a census of the editions of the *Elegantiae*, see Jozef IJsewijn and Gilbert Tournoy, "Un primo censimento dei manoscritti e delle edizioni a stampa degli "Elegantiarum linguae latinae libri sex" di Lorenzo Valla," Humanistica Lovaniensia, 18 (1969), 25–41, and 'Nuovi contributi per l'elenco dei manoscritti e delle edizioni delle *Elegantiae* di Lorenzo Valla," ibid., 20 (1971), 1–3.

[26] Francesco Tateo, "Marcantonio Sabellico e la svolta del classicismo quattrocentesco," in La storiografia umanistica. Convegno Internazionale di Studi, Messina 22–25 ottobre 1987, 2 vols, eds. Anita Di Stefano [et al.] (Messina, 1992), 1.41–63. See also Guglielmo Bottari, Marcantonio Sabellico, *De latinae linguae reparatione*, a critical edition of Sabellico's dialogue with "Introduzione", 7–67 (Messina, 1999). Marianne Pade refers to Valla's military imagery in "La fortuna della traduzione di Tucidide," p. 291, and in her article in this volume, "Niccolò Perotti's *Cornu copiae*: Commentary on Martial and Encyclopedia," she points out that Perotti adopted this imagery to signal his own rivalry with his former *maestro*.

and avarice. A request for a privilege in 1504 refers to a commentary (now lost), the *Commentum magistri Benedicto Brugnolo super Sallustium numquam impressum*.[27]

In short, Sallust and Valla proved a winning combination, a packaging success: Sallust, a source of *doctrina* and *elegantia*, champion of the *mos maiorum*, and defender of *concordia*; Valla, an advocate of conservative social and cultural values and arbiter of Latin usage, an author whose name could advance the careers of editors and printers, promote the *studia humanitatis*, and exalt the image of the Venetian republic as heir to ancient Rome and custodian of Rome's literary, moral and political heritage. The 1490 edition of Sallust's texts by Pomponio Leto, reprinted in 1491 with the Valla commentary, provided an additional seal of approval, a guarantee of careful scholarship and — given the fact that Pomponio had studied with Valla in Rome — a (tacit) link to Valla himself. In such an environment there could have been little incentive to question Valla's authorship. Even if one did harbor doubts, it may have been more expedient to keep silent.

Northern Humanists

In northern Europe, Valla's grammatical work was also considered an indispensable part of the intellectual formation of the new generation of humanists, and especially in Germany a number of annotated manuscripts and compendia testify to the efforts of the more innovative teachers to substitute the *Elegantiae*, or abridged versions of it, for the conventional textbooks.[28] In the sixteenth century, many of Valla's writings, and especially the *Elegantiae*, were printed in Paris, Lyons, Basel, Strasbourg, Cologne, and elsewhere; in fact, about eighty percent of the imprints of the *Elegantiae* now came from presses in France, Germany, and Switzerland.

---

[27] This title is given by Fulin in "Documenti," no. 138 pp. 153–54: 1504, 25 Febbraio (1503 m.v.) (N.C.). We know that Brugnoli also collaborated with Filippo Pinzi as corrector for his press. On Bernardo Giustiniani see Patricia Labalme, Bernardo Giustiniani: A Venetian of the Quattrocento (Rome, 1969), especially 282–91 for a translation and discussion of Giustiniani's "The golden age of Venice" and "Nobility and order" in which one finds significant echoes of Sallust.

[28] Carlo Vecce, "Tradizioni valliane tra Parigi e Le Fiandre dal Cusano ad Erasmo," Lorenzo Valla e l'Umanesimo italiano, 399–408, at 399. For the diffusion of Valla's writings north of the Alps, see Jacques Chomarat, "Erasme lecteur des *Elegantiae* de Valla," in P. Tynman, G. C. Kuiper, and E. Kessler, eds., *Actus Conventus Neo–Latini Amstelodamensis*: Proceedings of the Second International Congress of Neo–Latin Studies, Amsterdam, 19–24 August 1973; Agostino Sottili, "Notizie sul 'Nachleben' di Valla tra Umanesimo e Riforma," in ibid., 329–64; and Cortesi, "Scritti di Lorenzo Valla tra Veneto e Germania," ibid., 365–98.

Northern humanists, however, seem to have taken a more detached, critical approach to the Valla commentary than their Italian contemporaries or predecessors.[29] To begin with, other commentaries on Sallust were being composed and/or printed, and other features of his writing, or the textual transmission of his works, were attracting attention. Jodocus Badius's *Familiaris explanatio* (or *interpretatio*) on all the texts in the Sallustian corpus, printed in Paris in 1504, supplied an alternative to the commentaries of Valla and Omnibonus (on the *Bellum Catilinae*) and to that of Johannes Chrysostomus Soldus (on the *Bellum Iugurthinum*). In 1529 the *Scholia* of Philipp Melanchthon appeared; in 1538 the *Adnotationes* of Henricus Glareanus, and in the following year the *Castigationes* of Johannes Rivius. By this time, too, the notes and emendations of Glareanus and Rivius reveal the shift from the beginning–level school commentaries (of Valla, Soldus, and Omnibonus) to more sophisticated textual and philological analysis and to greater emphasis on historical, geographical and antiquarian topics, especially among the Swiss and German scholars.[30] The large number of printed editions of Sallust, the most popular of Roman historians throughout the Renaissance,[31] made it increasingly important (if certainly no easier) to correct the text, and the spirit of rivalry with Italian humanists must have stimulated debate.

The first scholar to question Valla's authorship of the commentary was, as far as I know, the Flemish humanist, Jodocus Badius Ascensius (Josse Bade), who in 1504 published at his new press in Paris an edition of Sallust with his *Familiaris explanatio*, probably written in the late 1490s while teaching in Lyons.[32] In

---

[29] For examples in Italy of the influence of Valla's methodology, see David Marsh, "Grammar, Method, and Polemic in Lorenzo Valla's *Elegantiae*," Rinascimento, 19 (1979), 91–116, who cites Giovanni Pontano's "correction of Valla on Valla's own terms" (116); W. Keith Percival, "Lorenzo Valla and the Criterion of Exemplary Usage," Res publica litterarum, 19 (1996), 133–52, at 144–45 on Perotti and other grammarians; M. Pade, "Valla e Perotti," Studi umanistici Piceni, 20 (2000), 72–85, on Perotti's extensive use of Valla's linguistic works; and Simona Gavinelli, "Teorie grammaticali nelle 'Elegantie' e la tradizione scolastica del tardo umanesimo," Rinascimento, 2nd ser., 31 (1991), 155–81.
[30] On the changing trends in commentaries on Sallust, see Osmond and Ulery, "Fortuna," "Sallustius," CTC 8. 186–217, especially 204–08, with further bibliography.
[31] The publication data for printed editions of and commentaries on Sallust's work between 1470 and 1600 and a comparison of the data with the edition statistics for other Roman and Greek historians are given in Patricia J. Osmond, "*Princeps Historiae Romanae*: Sallust in Renaissance Political Thought," Memoirs of the American Academy in Rome, 40 (1995), 101–43, at 132–39.
[32] *C. Crispi Salustii Coniuratio et bellum Catilinarium ... Bellum Iugurthinum* [etc.] (Parrhisiis: Iehan Petit [and Ascensius], 1504), with Badius's *Familiaris explanatio* on the *opera*. See Osmond and Ulery, "Sallustius," CTC 8.245–48.

a note on *Bellum Catilinae* 3.1 Badius warned his students that in the case of *benefacere*:

> *una est dictio, sed bene dicere Valla duas uult, quod hic uerum est, neque tacuisset si commentarios eos qui ipsi ascribuntur fecisset.*[33]

While Valla had written *bene* and *dicere* as separate words, the author of the 1491 Venice commentary on Sallust had written them as one:

> *Benefacere reipublicae: ecce quantum ad res gestas. Benedicere: quantum ad bonas artes, quia de aliqua re scribere, quam aliquis gesserit, laudabile est atque probatum.*

Elsewhere, too, Badius brought to the attention of his readers the discrepancies between the readings in the Valla commentary on the *Bellum Catilinae* and the same passages from Sallust's monograph that were cited in Valla's *Elegantiae*. While the Commentary, for example, ignored the reading *strenuissimus quisque* (61.7) cited in *Elegantiae* I.XIV (and found in certain Sallust manuscripts), and did not touch upon the grammatical rules involving the superlative and positive forms of an adjective with *quisque*, Badius observed:

> *Neque tamen exercitus populi Romani erat adeptus uictoriam laetam aut incruentam. Nam strennuus aut strennuissimus* [sic] *quisque (dubitat enim Valla utrum legendum sit) aut occiderat in praelio aut discesserat uulneratus grauiter.*[34]

Badius, who had studied in Ferrara under Battista Guarini and whose own commentaries aimed at the teaching of better Latinity, was particularly attentive to questions of word choice and formation, grammar, and syntax, as well

---

[33] "The word [*benefacere*] is one, but Valla wants *benedicere* [to be] two, ... nor would he have kept silent if he had written those commentaries which were ascribed to him." Badius is probably referring to *Elegantiae*, III.LXXXVII, "De 'bene' & 'male', cum uerbis" on *male dicendo* and/or to *Elegantiae* I.X, "De nominibus in '–icus'" on *benedicus, benedico*, etc. References are to the edition of *Elegantiarum libri VI*, in *Laurentii Vallae Opera* (Basel, 1540) reprinted in Laurentius Valla, *Opera omnia*, ed. Eugenio Garin (Turin, 1962), vol. 1. (The Oxford text of the *Catilina* edited by L. D. Reynolds [1991] reads: *Pulchrum est bene facere rei publicae, etiam bene dicere haud absurdum est.*)

[34] "Nor, however, did the army of the Roman people win a joyful or bloodless victory. For every vigorous or very vigorous man (for Valla doubts which is to be read, [i.e. *strenuus* or *strenuissimus*]) either had been killed in battle or had departed gravely wounded." The passage in the *Elegantiae*, I. XIV (ed. Garin), "De natura superlatiui", reads: *Sallustius in Catilinario: Nam strenuus quisque aut occiderat in praelio, aut grauiter uulneratus discesserat. Ipse mallem dicere strenuissimus quisque, piissimus quisque. Quidam tamen Sallustiani codices scriptum habent strenuissimus.* (The 1991 Oxford edition has *nam strenuissumus quisque.*) I thank Robert Ulery for his contributions to the English translations of the Latin passages here and below.

as to the ethical, or imitative, uses of classical texts.[35] He was also one of the major publishers and promoters of Valla's writings.[36] Between 1497 and 1535, more than twenty of his editions or reprints of the *De latinae linguae elegantia* appeared, as well as several editions of other works by Valla: *In latinam noui testamenti interpretationem* (1505), *Reconcinnatio totius Dialecticae* (1509), *De uoluptate ac vero bono* (1512), *In Benedictum Morandum et Bartolomaeum Facium*, to which were appended Valla's emendations of Livy (1528), *De rebus a Ferdinando gestis* (1528), and Valla's translation of Herodotus (1528).[37] Accompanying most of the editions of the *Elegantiae* (and also published separately) were his own *epitomes*, which summarized each chapter, and his *explanationes*, which clarified Valla's grammatical rules, cited passages from Antonio Mancinelli's *Lima in Laurentium Vallam*, and added further illustrations from both the practice of ancient authors and from Valla's other writings. Moreover, in notes to his edition of Quintilian's *Institutio oratoria* (Paris, 1516), also accompanied by the commentaries of Raffaele Regio and Giorgio Merula, Badius charged Regio with having appropriated Valla's annotations (at the same time as the latter had rejected Valla's authorship of them).[38] The Commentary on Sallust's *Bellum Catilinae*, however, was a different story, for the examples and explanations were not consistent, Badius felt, with what he knew from the *Elegantiae*; they simply did not measure up to the rigorous lexical and grammatical analysis that he took to be the hallmark of Valla's method.

In 1538 another humanist, the Swiss scholar Heinrich Loriti or Glareanus, also raised doubts about Valla's authorship of the commentary. In the dedicatory letter to Johannes Wernherus von Rischach of Freiburg, accompanying his notes on Sallust's *Opera* (Basel, 1538), Glareanus complained that despite the efforts to produce better texts of many classical authors, including Livy, Cicero, and Pliny, no one had devoted much attention to Sallust:

> *Cum hac nostra aetate in emendandis optimis auctoribus doctissimi quique in omni arte uiri certatim satagant, laborent, desudent, quod germana lectio eorundem indigna temporum iniuria deprauata tandem priscam recipiat lucem ac in integrum restituatur, quod in Livio, Cicerone, Plinio aliisque multis et fecimus ipsi et alios fecisse uidemus, nequeo hercle satis admirari cur in Sallustium tam ueterem, tam frugiferum, tantae*

---

[35] Peter Gerhard Schmidt, "Jodocus Badius Ascensius als Kommentator," in A. Buck and O. Herding, eds., Der Kommentar in der Renaissance (Deutsche Forschungsgemeinschaft: Boppard, 1975), 63–72.
[36] As Carlo Vecce observes in "Tradizioni," 399–400: "A Bade possiamo ascrivere in effetti un vero e proprio programma d'edizioni del *corpus* valliano."
[37] Philippe Renouard, Bibliographie des impressions et des oeuvres de Josse Badius Ascensius Imprimeur et Humaniste 1462–1535 (Paris, 1908; reprinted, New York [1967]), 3.325–48.
[38] Perosa, "L'edizione veneta di Quintiliano," 603–04.

> *postremo existimationis apud omnes classicos auctorem ut Quintilianus Thucydidae comparare non dubitarit [Inst. 10.1.101], nemo hodie dignum lectu quod sciam quicquam tentarit, quo sanaret tot uulneribus a barbarie diutina confossum, tam mutilum, tam lacerum ut, si a mortuis hodie resurgat, suorum scriptorum fragmenta agniturus quidem fuerit sed haud absque lacrimis inspecturus. ... Quapropter, quando in aliis auctoribus nunc saepe id laboris haud grauate susceperim, nec eius rei hactenus paenituerit; etiam hic me studiosis operae pretium facturum existimaui si quae in hoc auctore sciolorum ignorantia et longa uetustas deprauarit pro uirili restitueremus. Ad quae non nudam dumtaxat coniecturam adferimus, sed historiae apud alios auctores collationem codicumque ueterum fidem. Inter quos peruetustus unus Iulii Gothi, adolescentis eximiae spei et nobis in primis familiaris, fuit, quem ipse e Biturigibus, cum illic sub Alciato, doctissimo uiro, iuris prudentiae strenue operam nauaret, huc attulerat, ex Italia tamen antea in Galliam delatum.*[39]

According to Glareanus, all the editions and commentaries produced thus far, including the annotations on the *Catilina* attributed to Valla, were practically worthless. Adopting the Latin locution *tantum abest*, to which Valla himself had devoted a chapter in his *Elegantiae*, to underscore his point, he dismissed the commentary as something far removed from anything that Valla could possibly have written.

> *Idem dico de Commentario in Catilinam, qui initio quidem splendide nec absurde rhetoricatur, ut existimes propemodum uel Vallae uel non indoctioris esse; at in posterioribus deinde commentationibus uix alicuius docti uiri putabis, tantum abest ut Vallae uideri possit.*[40]

---

[39] In *C. Crispi Sallustii historici clarissimi quae adhuc extant historiarum fragmenta Henricii Glareani Helvetii Annotationes* (Basileae: apud Andream Cratandrum, 1538). See Osmond and Ulery, CTC 8.253–55. "Since in this age of ours all the most learned men in every discipline earnestly occupy themselves, labor, make great exertion in emending the best authors, that the true reading of the same, corrupted by the undeserved injury of time, may finally regain its former light and be restored to wholeness, something which we have both done ourselves in the case of Livy, Cicero, Pliny, and many others and seen that others have done, I swear I cannot be sated with wondering why in the case of Sallust — an author so ancient, so profitable, of such good repute finally among all the classics that Quintilian did not hesitate to compare him to Thucydides [*Inst.* 10.1.10] — no one today has attempted anything worth reading, so far as I know, to heal a man stabbed with so many wounds by barbarism of long standing, so mutilated, so lacerated that, if today he [Sallust] were to rise from the dead, he would indeed by likely to recognize the fragments of his work but hardly to look upon them without tears. ..."

[40] "I say the same regarding the Commentary on the Catilina, which certainly starts out in a splendidly rhetorical manner, and not at all foolishly, so that you almost think that it is the work of Valla or of some not unlearned man; but then in the later commentary you will think that it is by someone who is scarcely educated, so far removed is it from what can

Thereafter, in the annotations on single passages of the *Catilina* Glareanus described the 1491 commentary as "attributed by certain persons to Valla." In a note to *BC* 24.2, in which he repeated this judgment, he also drew attention to a misreading of the text. Whereas Sallust had written [*Catilina*] ... *pecuniam sua aut amicorum fide sumptam mutuam Faesulas ad Manlium quendam portare, qui postea princeps fuit belli faciundi*, the author of the commentary had turned Manlius into *Faesulae princeps*.

Like Badius, Glareanus was well acquainted with Valla's work. In the dedicatory letter to his edition of the *Adnotationes* on Livy, which appeared in 1540, two years after his commentary on Sallust, he described Valla's emendations of Livy, Books XXI–XXVI, as *argutae, doctae, ac eo dignae*, and he cited Valla's readings and interpretations in his own notes on the same passages. Glareanus was interested not only in textual questions but also in the subject matter of history, and his notes on Sallust's monographs contain a number of digressions on laws and institutions, geography, and ethnography, especially when the text offered an occasion to expatiate on his native Helvetia.

Conclusions

Whether Badius and Glareanus were right in rejecting Valla's authorship and the Italians wrong in accepting it, or vice versa, we cannot say — at least on the basis of the present evidence. Recent scholarship has demonstrated that Valla's work was far more complex and contradictory (at least on the surface) than often represented. Marianne Pade has pointed out differences of style, as well as errors and inconsistencies, in his Latin rendering of Thucydides and noted that the translation provoked varying judgments, favorable and unfavorable, among later Renaissance editors.[41] Other scholars, too, have observed that his annotations on any given text, or passage, are not always consistent; that we find different "registers" in style and tone both within and among his

---

seem to be of Valla." On Valla's use of *tantum non* and *tantum abest*, see Marianne Pade, "La fortuna della traduzione di Tucidide di Lorenzo Valla con una edizione delle postille al testo," in Niccolò V nel sesto centenario della nascita. Atti del Convegno Internazionale di Studi, Sarzana, 8–10 ottobre 1998, eds. Franco Bonatti and Antonio Manfredi (Città del Vaticano, 2000), 255–93, at 276.

[41] Pade, "Valla's Thucydides," (see n. 5 above), 294–301; "La fortuna della traduzione di Tucidide," 257–59; and "Thucydides," in CTC 8.103–81, at 120–21, in which she mentions that, according to Pierre Daniel Huet in his *De claris interpretibus*, "Valla's Latin was not up to the standard Valla himself had promulgated in the *Elegantiae*." On the other hand, Pade points out that Valla, in explaining lexical and stylistic choices in his glosses on the translation, regularly returns to themes discussed in the *Elegantiae*, and in this sense does show consistency of method and interest.

various writings;[42] that the noble and ambitious principles enunciated in his prefaces are not necessarily translated into practice (as is said, for example, of his *Gesta Ferdinandi regis Aragonum*);[43] and that, while calling for a new, empirical study of grammar based on exemplary usage, his own *Elegantiae* was, in the final analysis, essentially prescriptive.[44] As mentioned at the outset, however, it has been the purpose of this paper not to resolve the question of authorship but rather to look at the assumptions underlying the issue of authenticity, investigate what contemporaries would deem the qualifying marks of a Valla commentary, and hence — considering Valla's representative role in the program of cultural renewal and the recovery of an elegant, refined Latinity — identify some of the features of a Renaissance commentary.

In the case of the Italian humanists, we have to draw our arguments, it is true, from silence, that is, from the lack of any protest, and from circumstantial evidence, that is, what we know of humanist schools, teaching traditions, and scholarship, especially in Venice. But it would appear that shared social values and cultural ideals, and an approach to the study of classical texts that (at least) aimed at imitating noble comportment as well as noble speech — what James Hankins has called "imitative reading"[45] — not to mention the consid-

---

[42] For other examples of changes or inconsistencies in Valla's work, see the remarks of Lucia Cesarini Martinelli and Alessandro Perosa in the "Prefazione" to their edition of Lorenzo Valla, Le postille all' "Institutio oratoria" di Quintiliano (Padua, 1996), XLVI–LXVI, especially XLIX, and of Paola Casciano in the "Introduzione" to her edition of Lorenzo Valla, L'Arte della Grammatica (Fondazione Lorenzo Valla, 2nd. ed., 1995).

[43] See Franco Gaeta, Lorenzo Valla. Filologia e storia nell'Umanesimo italiano (Naples, 1955), 176–77 and ff., and Ottavio Besomi, ed., *Gesta Ferdinandi regis Aragonum*, "Introduzione", XXV–XXVI. In regard to humanist teaching in general, Anthony Grafton and Lisa Jardine point to a discontinuity between humanist declarations of lofty moral aims and the routine, often tedious, drilling in language that characterized classroom practice in From Humanism to the Humanities; similarly, Robert Black notes "the gulf between [the] moralizing programmes [of Florentine schoolbooks] and the philological character of the subsequent glosses and commentaries" in Humanism and Education, 316. For other views, see n. 45 below.

[44] Percival, "Lorenzo Valla and the Criterion of Exemplary Usage," 143, notes that Valla distinguished between "the higher level of elegant phraseology to which the consummate Latinist should finally aspire and the lower stratum of useful regulations which bring the beginner to the point of being able to approach the lofty heights of inspired composition."

[45] James Hankins "Introduction," Plato in the Renaissance, 2 vols., 2nd impression with addenda and corrigenda (Leiden, 1991), "Towards a Typology of Reading in the Fifteenth Century," 18–26, at 21–23. Hankins also calls attention, however, to the co–existence of various modes of reading in the fifteenth–century classroom, e.g., the older "doctrinal reading," the humanist "imitative reading," and "critical reading." Craig Kallendorf finds evidence of moralizing as well as philological approaches to the reading of ancient authors in his "In the Margins of Virgil: Venetian Renaissance Books in the Biblioteca Nazionale

erable economic interests at stake — probably inclined readers to accept Valla's authorship and to focus on evidence that supported this view, namely, the thematic correspondences between the proem and other, known writings by Valla, and that lofty sense of mission in restoring the Latin language and rescuing the *monumenta* of Roman literature. In 'Virgil and the Myth of Venice', Craig Kallendorf observes ways in which humanist studies accommodated the interests of Venetian culture and society, affirming, not challenging, the collective identity of the city, and containing, that is, attempting to limit or remove, potentially subversive responses to a text.[46] In the case of the Valla commentary, or, that is, the responses to the Valla commentary, we can see, I believe, a similar pattern: Venetian humanists predisposed to accept Valla's authorship, to adopt and adapt the work to pedagogical needs and an aristocratic republican ethic, and to contain possible objections by avoiding public debate.

In Northern Europe, on the other hand, new approaches to the emendation and explication of ancient authors, including Sallust, along with a more critical study of Valla's own philological work, and, not least, increasing rivalry between transalpine humanists and their Italian contemporaries or predecessors, seem to have stimulated a more careful reading of the 1491 commentary, a closer comparison with other references to Sallust in Valla's known writings, or with what was observed of Valla's critical method, and, as a result, the first questioning of the authorship.[47] By challenging the attribution of the Valla commentary, Badius and Glareanus were, in fact, advertising the fact that they knew Sallust's *Catilina* better than did the commentator of the 1491 edition, and that they knew Valla's philological work better than Valla's supposed pupils or followers, at least in Italy. They were ready to adopt Valla's own exam-

---

Marciana and Their Early Readers," Miscellanea Marciana, 7–9 (1992–94), 179–206. These questions are also discussed in the articles in this volume by Craig Kallendorf on "Marginalia and the Rise of Early Modern Subjectivity" and Marianne Pade (see n. 26 above).

[46] Craig Kallendorf, Virgil and the Myth of Venice. Books and Readers in the Italian Renaissance (Oxford, 1999), chapter 1, especially 11–23 (including references to the discussions of patrician ideology in Margaret King's 'Venetian Humanism' and Patricia Labalme's 'Bernardo Giustiniani') and chapter 2 on accommodation and containment. I am indebted to Kallendorf's analysis of reader–response criticism and his discussion of the Venetian interpretive community for my own interpretation of Renaissance responses to the Valla commentary.

[47] Jean Balsamo describes the early stages in the cultural rivalry between Italians and French in chapter 1 of his Les rencontres des muses: Italianisme et anti–italianisme dans les lettres françaises de la fin du XVIe siecle (Geneva, 1992): "Les Italiens . . . dénonçaient encore la barbarie des Français, les Français insistaient à l'inverse sur la décadence de l'Italie" (38). It is true that editors and commentators typically criticized their predecessors, but Glareanus issues a sweeping condemnation of all the earlier (and chiefly Italian) studies of Sallust.

ple and follow his own methods, scrutinizing his usage and exercising their critical acumen. In their eyes, the commentary did not measure up to their expectations of Valla; it did not meet the best standards of Renaissance scholarship.

One may, of course, perceive a thread of continuity, a common attitude linking northern humanists to their Italian contemporaries or predecessors, in the very notion of authenticity: an awareness of what was appropriate to an author, genre, or historical epoch — a characteristic element of what has been called the Renaissance sense of history. Northern and Italian humanists also shared an appreciation of rhetoric, the art of persuasion. When considering the authorship of the Valla commentary, therefore, they would probably have agreed that an authentic work by Valla would not only reflect his own pedagogical program but also further their own aims and interests, honoring those who edited, printed and published Valla's work and providing persuasive instruction in the classroom. Where the northern humanists parted company with the Italians was in selecting different criteria, and different features or parts of his commentary, by which to judge Valla's writing. Their questioning of his authorship was a consequence, in other words, of changing expectations and attitudes, of new views as to what was meaningful and relevant: views that were formed and elaborated in different social and cultural contexts. Whether or not the commentary on Sallust's *Bellum Catilinae* was *eligible* as a Renaissance commentary, as an expression of *renovatio litterarum*, ultimately depended on the understanding and uses of Valla's work that readers in particular humanist circles chose to cultivate and promote. As in Valla's own study of the Latin language and standards of good Latin style, the test of authenticity was based on *consuetudo* (usage) or, more precisely, *consensus eruditorum*, and the exercise of *iudicium* (critical judgment).

Patricia J. Osmond   Iowa State University/Rome, Italy

Appendix

LAURENTII VALLENSIS IN .C. CRISPI SALVSTII CATILINARIVM
COMMENTARII
(Edition of Venice 1491)*

OMNIS HOMINES: [BC 1.1]. Patritia gente Crispus Salustius Romae natus, post rem publicam ciuili discordia concussam, quum nulla illius administrandae ratio bonis superesset amplius, se ad scribendi ocium contulit. In quo genere, Quintiliani iudicio, qui eum Thucydidi in historia eminentissimo opposuit [*Inst.* 10.1.101], praecipuam inter eos qui res romanas litterarum monumentis tradidere est laudem adeptus. Et enim quo Thucydides est Herodoto maior, cui secundae tribuuntur partes, eo certe hic noster Livio praestantior, quem Herodoto ille comparat. Accedit & Martialis urbanissimi poetae carmen: Hic erit, ut perhibent doctorum corda uirorum // Primus romana Crispus in historia [14.191], quo haud dubie apparet doctorum hominum iudicio Crispum caeteris romanarum rerum scriptoribus praelatum. Quod si tantorum uirorum testimonio primum in historia locum obtinet, summa nos ope niti decet [*cf.* BC 1.1] ut praeclara eius monumenta, si qua adhuc restant, non tantum ipsi studio condiscamus sed, si fieri etiam possit, quam plurimis nostra industria omni sint ex parte conspicua; atque id ipsum hoc enixius praestandum, quod post tantam nostratium litterarum iacturam, quantam gotthicis temporibus factam fuisse constat, paucissima quaedam uestigia, ne fragmenta dicam, ac illa ipsa pene euanescentia ex locupletissima Crispi ornatissimaque historia ad haec tempora peruenere & quod iniquius ferat aliquis fuerunt haec progymnasmata quaedam, ut graeco utar uerbo, castissimae illius Mineruae, quae nobis reliqua cum temporis tamen [tum *ed.* 1500] hominum fecit iniuria. Nam quod plenissimam Crispus scripserit historiam, quae non res romanas solum sed externarum etiam gentium sit complexa, abunde constat, uerum a Catilinae coniuratione, quasi ingenii experientiam daturus, eam uideri potest auspicatus, quod & ipsum operis proemium haud dubie demonstrat, cui ad stili consummationem credibile est Iugurthae bellum subiecisse. Sed quanti illa momenti fuerint, quae prorsus interiere, ex iis quae hodie extant facilis est coniectura, quippe cum nulla possit uirtus in historia elucere, quum non in hac

---

* The title given here is that preceding the proem and commentary. In the list of contents of the Venice 1491 edition, the title reads: *.C. Crispii* [sic] *Sallustii bellum catilinarium cum commento Laurentii uallensis*. In transcribing the proem I have retained the spelling but capitalized proper nouns and regularized the punctuation. The proem has been previously published by Patricia J. Osmond and Robert W. Ulery, Jr. in "Sallustius Crispus, Gaius," *Catalogus translationum et commentariorum: Mediaeval and Renaissance Latin Translations and Commentaries* (=CTC), vol. 8, Editor in Chief, Virginia Brown; Associate Editors, James Hankins and Robert A. Kaster (Washington, D.C., 2003), 183–326, at 237–38.

uel illa meditatione facile recognoscas, sed quo eius sunt uirtutes altiores minusque uulgo proxime, eo maiore nobis studio, ut dixi, est nitendum, ne illae nostra uel inertia uel negligentia diutius in obscuro sint. Et enim quam cognitu sint difficiles, uel ex eo potest intelligi, quod non pauci, ut uideo in proemii fronte, allucinati dant illi uicio quod nepharium Catilinae scelus scripturus inde potissimum sit exorsus, ut dixerit animum corpori et ingenium uiribus praestare, uelut nihil magis ab eo quod dicturus erat alienum dici potuisset, sed accurate omnia ac magis erudite quam uerbis explicari possit. Redditurus nanque sui consilii rationem quod a re publica digressus se ad historiam scribendam contulisset, nulla potuit honestior causa demonstrari quam eo se consilio id fecisse ostenderet, ut ea parte corporis uteretur quae potissima in homine esset, nec ita multo post non magis se ratione quam necessitate, ut id consilii caperet, adduci oportuisse demonstrat, quoniam ambitione malisque artibus ciuitate corrupta nullus uideretur innocentiae locus huic qui ad eam capiendam accederet relictus; uerum qua [quia *ed. 1500*] praeclara ingenia aut domi consulendo suorumque facta illustrando aut foris rem publicam administrando patriae uideri possunt utilia, sublata optimatium administratione omnique recte uiuendi ratione mutata, merito unum hoc scribendi officium quod reliquum erat, quia & potuit & debuit, non minori ingenio quam pietate patriae ciuibusque suis, optime de ea bene meritis, praestitit Crispus.

Niccolò Perotti's *Cornu Copiae*: Commentary on Martial and Encyclopedia*

MARIANNE PADE

The Roman poet Martial (c. 30–104) was read throughout the Middle Ages, but his influence was relatively small and it can be shown that he was known mostly through *florilegia*. He was never a school author — for good reasons some would say — and he does not appear to have been the subject of ancient or medieval commentary. Boccaccio must be considered the man who really discovered Martial after the end of Antiquity. He found a complete copy of the epigrams in Southern Italy, probably in Casino; it was only after Boccaccio that manuscripts of Martial started to proliferate and his poems became an object of continued interest and study among Italian humanists. The epigrams were often imitated, for instance by Antonio Panormita in his scandalous *Hermaphroditus*, and Martial's popularity is witnessed by the more than 110 fifteenth-century manuscripts of his work still extant, many of them heavily annotated.[1] In spite of the obvious interest, and need, as one would think, no commentary in the proper sense seems to have been published before the 1470s, at a period when we find a vivid interest in Silver Latin authors in the circle of humanists who gathered around Pomponio Leto, the leading figure of the Roman Academy.[2] The editions of Martial's epigrams as well as the commentaries on them produced in these years were the subject of violent philological quarrels. The protagonists were, amongst others, Pomponio Leto, the Veronese humanist Domizio Calderini,[3] and Niccolò Perotti from the town of Sassoferrato in the Marche.

---

* I am grateful to Dr. John Blundell, Munich, who read through this article and suggested a number of linguistic improvements.
[1] For the textual tradition of Martial, see M.D. Reeve's article in Texts and Transmission. A Survey of the Latin Classics, ed. by L.D. Reynolds (Oxford, 1983), 239–44; for his *fortuna* in the Middle Ages and the Renaissance, see F.-R. Hausmann, "Martialis," *Catalogus Translationum et Commentariorum* IV (Washington, 1980), 249–96: 250–51.
[2] Cp. V. Zabughin, Giulio Pomponio Leto. Saggio critico I–II (Rome and Grottaferrata 1909–12), I passim; A. Perosa, "L'edizione veneta di Quintiliano coi commenti del Valla, di Pomponio Leto e di Sulpizio da Veroli," Miscellanea Augusto Campana, II, Medioevo e Umanesimo 45 (Padova, 1981), 575–618; Rosella Bianchi, "Due citazioni attribuite a Festo nel commento a Lucano di Pomponio Leto," Atti e memorie dell'Arcadia s. III, 7 (1980–81), 235–62.
[3] For Calderini see Donatella Coppini, "Il commento a Properzio di Domizio Calderini," ASNP 9 (1979), 1119–73; and J. Ramminger, "Brotheus e Timon: il vocabolario della polemica tra Domizio Calderini e Niccolò Perotti," Studi umanistici Piceni 21 (2001), 147-55.

Niccolò Perotti (1429/30–1480) had been the secretary and close collaborator of Cardinal Bessarion from c. 1447.[4] From then on he was in close contact with Roman humanist circles, notably with Lorenzo Valla and Giovanni Tortelli, and later he worked closely with Pomponio Leto. Supported by his patron the Sassoferratese humanist had a distinguished career as a papal administrator. He was elected Archbishop of Siponto in 1458 — whence he is often called *Sipontinus* — and was papal governor of Viterbo 1464–69, of Spoleto 1471–72/73 and of Perugia 1474–77. He retired to his native town in 1477. Perotti translated works of Plutarch, St. Basil, Epictetus, Polybius, ps.–Aristotle, Libanius, and Bessarion into Latin, and he was the author, amongst other works, of the extremely successful *Rudimenta grammatices*,[5] which also contained the *De componendis epistolis*, completed towards the end of 1468 (1st ed. 1473),[6] and commentaries on Martial and Statius' *Silvae*.[7] His most volumi-

---

[4] Cp. John Monfasani, "Il Perotti e la controversia tra platonici ed aristotelici," Res Publica Litterarum 4 (1981), 195-231; Id., "Bessarion Latinus", Rinascimento, ser. 2, 21 (1981), 165–209; Id., "Still More on Bessarion Latinus", Rinascimento, ser. 2, 23 (1983), 217–35; Id.,"Platina, Capranica, and Perotti: Bessarion's Latin eulogists and his date of birth," Bartolomeo Sacchi il Platina (Piadena 1421–Roma 1481): Atti del convegno internazionale di studi per il V centenario (Cremona 14–15 novembre 1981), a c. di P. Medioli Masotti (Padova, 1986), 97–136; all four articles are reprinted in Id., Byzantine Scholars in Renaissance Italy: Cardinal Bessarion and Other Emigrés (Aldershot, 1995); and Concetta Bianca, Da Bisanzio a Roma. Studi sul cardinale Bessarione, Roma nel Rinascimento, inedita, 15, saggi (Roma, 1999), passim.

[5] Cp. W. Keith Percival, "The Place of the *Rudimenta grammatices* in the History of Latin Grammar," Res Publica Litterarum 4 (1981), 233–264; *Id.*, "Early Editions of Niccolò Perotti's *Rudimenta grammatices*," Res Publica Litterarum 9 (1986), 219–229; and Id., "The Influence of Perotti's *Rudimenta* in the Cinquecento," Protrepticon: Studi di letteratura classica e umanistica in onore di Giovannangiola Secchi–Tarugi, ed. Sesto Prete (Milano, 1989), 91–100; all three articles are reprinted in Id., Studies In Renaissance Grammar, Variorum Collected Studies Series (Aldershot, 2003).

[6] *Rudimenta grammatices* (Roma: Conradus Sweynheym and Arnoldus Pannartz, 19 Mar. 1473 = HC 12643). The editio princeps was set from Perotti's manuscript, Vat. lat. 6737; cp. Percival, Early Editions, 219.

[7] For the life of Perotti G. Mercati, Per la cronologia della vita e degli scritti di Niccolò Perotti, arcivescovo di Siponto, Studi e Testi 44 (Roma, 1925, rist. anast.1973) remains fundamental though superseded on some points. For more recent works on Perotti's biography, see A. Greco, "Vecchi e nuovi elementi nella biografia di Niccolò Perotti," Res Publica Litterarum 4 (1981), 77–91; John Monfasani, Platina, Capranica, and Perotti; J.–L. Charlet, "État présent des études sur N. Perotti," Umanesimo fanese nel '400. Atti del convegno di Studi nel V Centenario della morte di Antonio Costanzi — Fano 21 giugno 1991, Quaderno di "Nuovi studi fanesi" (Fano, 1993), 69–110; and Id., "Niccolò Perotti," *Centuriae Latinae*. Cent une figures humanistes de la Renaissance aux Lumières offertes a Jacques Chomarat, réunies par Colette Nativel, Travaux d'Humanisme et Renaissance No CCCXIV (Genève, 1997), 601–605.

nous work, the *Cornu copiae seu linguae Latinae commentarii*,[8] was left unfinished at his death, but the postscript of the first version probably dates from 1479. It is written in the form of a commentary on Martial, but on account of the wealth of lexicographical material it contains, it was for generations used as an 'encyclopaedia' of the language and culture of Antiquity; after more than 36 editions it was replaced only in the sixteenth century by Robert Estienne's alphabetical Latin dictionary.[9]

Perotti's work on Martial

Perotti was able to spend much of the years 1469–71 in Rome, pursuing his philological projects, partly in collaboration with Pomponio Leto. By this time he had been interested in Martial for many years. We have a witness to that in a manuscript in the Vatican library, Vat. lat. 6848 which contains Perotti's autograph edition of the epigrams,[10] surrounded by his commentary. Internal evidence shows that Perotti worked on the commentary for more than twenty years, before he abandoned it for the more ambitious project which was to become the *Cornu copiae*. Most pages of the manuscript present a complex picture. Perotti would write short interlinear glosses to the text and in the margins he would explain the glosses and other words in notes of various length, which were distinguished from each other by being written in ink of various colours. Even this first commentary is copious; in fact there are several pages in the manuscript that consist only of commentary. The general impression,

---

[8] Modern edition in Niccolò Perotti, *Cornu copiae seu linguae Latinae commentarii*. Vol. 1–8 Sassoferrato, 1989–2001, vol. 1 ed. by J.–L. Charlet and M. Furno, vols. 2–3 ed. by J.–L. Charlet, vol. 4 ed. by M. Pade and J. Ramminger, vol. 5 ed. by J.–L. Charlet and P. Harsting, vol. 6 ed. by F. Stok, vol. 7 ed. by J.–L. Charlet, M. Pade, J. Ramminger and G. Abbamonte, vol. 8 ed. by J.–L. Charlet, M. Furno, M. Pade, J. Ramminger and F. Stok. Editio princeps ed. Ludovicus Odaxius (Venezia: Paganinus de Paganinis, 14 May 1489 = H 12697*).

[9] For the *fortuna* of the *Cornu copiae*, see J.–C. Margolin, "La fonction pragmatique et l'influence culturelle de la *Cornucopiae* de Niccolò Perotti," Res Publica Litterarum 4 (1981), 123–71; W. Milde, "Zur Druckhäufigkeit von Niccolò Perottis *Cornucopiae* und *Rudimenta grammatices* im 15. und 16. Jahrhundert, Res Publica Litterarum 5 (1982), 29–42; and J.–L. Charlet, "Observations sur certaines éditions du *Cornu copiae* de Niccolò Perotti (1489–1500)," Res Publica Litterarum, 11 (1988), 83–96; Fabio Stok, "Olao Magno e Plutarco," Classiconorroena 6 (luglio–novembre 1995), 12–14, and Id., "Perotti, Calepino, Forcellini e l'OLD," Studi sul *Cornu Copiae* de Niccolò Perotti, Testi e studi di cultura classica 2 (Firenze, 2002), 217–30.

[10] For Perotti's work on the text of Martial, see Francesco Della Corte, "Niccolò Perotti e gli Epigrammi di Marziale," Res Publica Litterarum 9 (1986), 97–107. For Perotti's first commentary on Martial, see Johann Ramminger, "Auf dem Weg zum *Cornu copiae*. Niccolò Perottis Martialkommentar im Vaticanus lat. 6848," Neulateinisches Jahrbuch 3 (2001), 125–144. There is a description of the Vat. lat. 6848 in M. Buonocuore, "Orazio in greco," Bolletino della Badia Greca di Sassoferrato n.s. 52 (199), Ὀπώρα. Studi in onore di mgr Paul Canart per il LXX compleanno, II, a c. di S. Lucà e L. Perria), 31–48.

however, is that the annotator always keeps the text in view, an impression reinforced by the lay-out of the manuscript. We also find part of the material collected for the commentary in this early form in the margins of a manuscript of Martial, written and annotated by Pomponio Leto. This manuscript is now MS King's 32 of the British Library. In the margins, besides the hand of Leto, we find that of Perotti.[11] We know that Perotti and Leto worked together on Martial in Rome during the winter of 1469/70. They also collaborated on another commentary on a text from the Silver Age, namely the *Silvae* of Statius. A very large fragment of this commentary has survived in another Vatican manuscript, the present Vat. lat. 6835, again written by Perotti with the same system of notes in different types of ink surrounding the text.

The last years of Perotti's life were dedicated to his *opus magnum*, the *Cornu copiae*. It has come down to us in a manuscript from the Urbino collection, now Urb. lat. 301 in the Vatican Library. This is a huge volume of about 671 folios, with numerous corrections and additions in the hand of Perotti himself.[12] The work was left incomplete at Perotti's death in 1480, in the sense that he never finished his very thorough revision of the text, in the course of which he also added substantially to the original material.[13] The *Cornu copiae* covers only one book of the epigrams, that is the *Spectaculorum liber* and the present book one, which at the time were normally copied as a unity.

The work has a letter of dedication and a postscript to Federigo da Montefeltro, the Duke of Urbino, whom Perotti hope would finance the printing. The letters to Montefeltro and the text of the original version are written by a scribe who purports to be Perotti's nephew, Pyrrhus, and who is also presented as the author of the dedication. This piece of fiction goes together with the pretence that Perotti did not wish to publish the work: some people might find it inappropriate that an archbishop, such as he was, should occupy himself with the overtly sexual poems of Martial. However that may be, Perotti had certainly not shied away from explaining any sexual vocabulary or explicit description in the epigrams in every salacious detail.[14] In the letter to Monte-

---

[11] Cp. M. Campanelli, "Alcuni aspetti dell'esegesi umanistica di 'Atlas cum compare gibbo' [Mart. VI 77 7–8]," Res Publica Litterarum 21 (1998), 169–180. For the relations between the manuscripts of the two humanists, see Ramminger, Auf dem Weg zum Cornu copiae; for their collaboration G. Abbamonte, "Niccolò Perotti, Pomponio Leto e il commento di *Seruius auctus* alle *Georgiche*," Studi umanistici Piceni 19 (1999), 25–37.

[12] Stornajolo, Codices Urbinates III, 269–70; and F. Stok in his introduction to vol. VI of the *Cornu copiae*, 3 (the entire MS is of paper, however).

[13] For this revision, see F. Stok, "La revisione del *Cornu copiae*," Studi Umanistici Piceni 22 (2002), 29–46, revised version in Id. Studi sul *Cornu Copiae*, 71–93.

[14] E.g. CC 75, 1: *CUM DICIS PROPERO. Ex persona sua notat eos, qui nimio coitu exhausti et impotentes facti exercere tamen libidinem non cessant. PROPERO FAC SI FACIS. Verba sunt He-*

feltro we hear that Pyrrhus was aware of his uncle's reluctance to publish the work. Regretting that this masterpiece of scholarship should not be made generally known, he had stealthily removed the original manuscript from Perotti's library, transcribed it, and now presented it to the Duke. In the postscript, however, the pretence is abandoned, and it is unequivocally Perotti, the author of the work, who addresses Federigo.

Perotti on the *CC*

The preface and the postscript both contain valuable information bearing on the question of whether the *Cornu copiae* is indeed a commentary, and if so, of what sort. Perotti, in the guise of nephew Pyrrhus, relates how, more than five years earlier, Pomponio Leto and other scholars had asked him to correct the text of Martial, which had been thoroughly corrupted by the mistakes and errors of the scribes who had copied it over the centuries. To his edition of the text, published in 1473,[15] he added a *corollarium*, that is the *Cornu copiae*.[16] The task was arduous, he worked endless nights and read through innumerable Greek and Latin authors within all fields of learning (that this is not an empty boast is proved by the *index fontium* in volume eight of the modern edition, which is more than 100 pages long). Perotti's long studies had been necessary for various reasons. One was the variety of subjects treated by the poet, and the recondite nature of many of them. A second reason was the corrupt state of the text. A third, and the most important one, was that Perotti had not followed the usual method of commentators: he had expounded the poet so that not even a single word had been left untouched, and he had thereby given the impression that he intended to make a commentary not on one poet but on the entire Latin language:

> CC, prohemium, 2: *Nam qum iam supra quintum annum Pomponius Fortunatus, uir saeculo nostro doctissimus et Romanae Academiae princeps, ac plerique alii studiosi uiri Nicolaum Perottum Siponti Pontificem, patruum meum, hortati essent ut M. Valerium Martialem, optimum quidem poetam, sed uitio librariorum infinitis pene erroribus plenum, pro communi studiosorum utilitate emendandum susciperet, aggressus est ille hanc prouintiam libens et corollarium addidit: et enim lepidissimum Poetam non modo emendauit, sed etiam interpretatus est. In qua re haud facile dictu esset quos sustinuerit labores, quot noctes insomnes duxerit, quot graecorum simul ac latinorum in omni disciplinarum genere uolumina euoluerit, tum propter multarum rerum ac reconditarum in hoc poeta uarietatem, quarum etiam uocabula uix aut nullo*

---

dyli, dum cum eo coit Martialis. Et est sensum: 'Qum dicis mihi coeunti tecum haec uerba, ego propero, hoc est, mihi propere abeundum est, fac si facis, hoc est, exple opus, si potes explere'.

[15] Marcus Valerius Martialis, *Epigrammata* (Roma: Conradus Sweynheym and Arnoldus Pannartz, 30 Apr. 1473 = H 10811).

[16] For the meaning of *corollarium*, see the contribution of J. Rammiger in this volume.

> *modo intelligi poterant, tum propter magnitudinem errorum quos emendare fere supra uires hominis fuit, tum uero in primis, quod non est in eo opere communem interpretum morem secutus. Sed ita hunc Poetam exposuit ut ne uerbum quidem reliquerit intactum uisus que plane fuerit non unum Poetam, sed uniuersam Latinam linguam uelle interpretari.*

Again Pyrrhus' assertions are borne out by the text itself: the index of the words commented upon by Perotti, printed in two columns, is more than 250 pages long. In spite of the vastness of the material, every difficulty was overcome by hard work, and Martial, having been incomprehensible for more than 800 years could now be read even by young people and non–specialists:

> Ibid.: *Omnem tamen difficultatem superauit studium et diligentia hominis qui que omnia uincit improbus labor; talem que post tot epotas lucubrationum fuligines hunc Poetam reddidit, ut qui supra octingentos annos a nemine fuerat intellectus, iam ab adolescentibus quoque uel mediocriter eruditis possit intelligi.*

Apart from his misgivings about people's reactions we hear in the next chapter that Perotti had another reason for not wanting to publish the work: he had in fact never planned to do so. It was meant for his own use, so that he would have easy access to the results of all his long, laborious studies. Because he had produced the work for that purpose, the margins of his manuscript were full and he had compiled separate lengthy and copious entries on many subjects, instead of small and neatly divided ones, as commentators usually did; and he often had literal quotations from his Greek and Latin sources. If the work were to be published, it would swell into an immoderately large volume and might be seen as a commentary not on just one poet but on the entire Latin language:

> Ibid., 3: ... *Ad haec non eo animo scriptos a se commentarios ut proferrentur in lucem, sed sua causa dumtaxat, ut quae tanto studio, labore, uigiliis inuestigauerat, quotiens opus esset, haberet in promptu. Idcirco non modo hinc atque hinc plenos esse totius sui codicis margines, sed multa quoque a se seorsum, non breuiter et carptim ut interpretum mos est, uerum longe diffuse que conscripta, saepe etiam ex libris autorum qui graece latine que scripserunt fere ad uerbum sumpta, quae si aedi oporteret, in grande nimis uolumen opus excresceret, nec tam unius Poetae quam totius linguae latinae interpretatio uideri posset.*

But 'Pyrrhus', as we know, was undeterred by this reasoning. When he managed to lay hands on the book, he read it secretly and was overwhelmed by the wealth of subjects treated in it. If we look more closely at the list of what he noticed we see that the lexicographical and stylistic aspects are emphasised — "quae interpretationes uocabulorum, quae explicatio elegantiae ac proprietatis latinae linguae" — as is also the mythological and historical material. The work was not a mere book but a repository, a treasure–chamber of the most valuable and recondite knowledge within all fields of learning — and as such useful and even necessary for men of almost any profession. If they read the book they would recognise that one could fairly claim that it was not a commentary on one poet but on all Latin authors:

> Ibid., 6: *Vix possem exprimere quo statim ardore flagrauerim id opus aedendi. Subreptis itaque mox ex bibliotheca patrui commentariis, coepi clam legere quae notauerat: ubi quantum, dii boni, rerum, quantum uerborum, quantum uetustatis, quae interpretationes uocabulorum, quae explicatio elegantiae ac proprietatis latinae linguae, quae fabularum monumenta, quae numina historiarum, quae dignitas exemplorum atque maiestas! Certe non liber mihi, sed thesaurus quidam uisus est optimarum in omni genere rerum, ac reconditarum. Hinc grammatici, hinc rhetores, hinc Poetae, hinc Dialectici, ... hinc fabri omnes atque opifices multa et pene infinita haurire possunt eorum studiis necessaria ...; si haec legent ... hoc opus non unius Poetae, sed omnium latinorum autorum commentarios iure optimo dici posse intelligent.*

So Pyrrhus began to arrange the material in some sort of order; he did not add anything of his own, except in the cases where his uncle, with an episcopal sense of propriety, had touched only briefly on some obscene words. These Pyrrhus would explain more thoroughly because nothing "is so foul that it is not most disgraceful to be ignorant of it" ("nihil tam foedum esse existimans quod non turpissimum sit ignorare," ibid., 7). Then he arranged the text so that readers interested only in the commentary on Martial would not be deterred by the sheer size of the volume. At the beginning of each epigram there would be a short explanation of its meaning. Then there would be rubrics written in capitals where one could look up the information most necessary for the understanding of the passage. This would suffice for the reader interested only in Martial. Of the rest, everybody could use what they liked; there would in any case be an alphabetical index at the end of the work:

> Ibid., 7: *Ita praeterea opus digessi, ut si quis sola huius poetae interpretatione contentus esse uelit, deterreri libri magnitudine non possit. Habent enim singula quaeque epigrammata sententiam suam in principio summatim expressam. Deinde ubi rubrae sunt ac grandiusculae litterae, uis uocabuli siue fabula siue historia ad cognitionem autoris necessaria succincte ostenditur, quibus ii qui praeter intellectum poetae nihil optabunt poterunt esse contenti. De caeteris uero tantum sumere cuique fas erit quantum uolet, cum in fine operis quid singulis libris contineatur seruato litterarum ordine ueluti quibusdam tabellis mirifice sit expressum.*

This description only partially fits the book as we have it today. It is true that the *incipits* of the poems are followed by short summaries, and that it is fairly easy to identify the words or phrases from Martial because they are indeed in red capitals, and followed by a synonym or explanation. One may, however, have to look through many pages to find them, because by far the greater part of the text seemingly expounds matters not directly relevant to an understanding of Martial's poems, which apparently provided no more than the point of departure. The ordering principles are manifold, for instance derivation or association, and one regularly gets the impression that Perotti was completely unable to resist information arranged in alphabetical order. When quoting an entry in a dictionary relevant to the subject he is discussing, he will often quote the nearby entries too, just for good measure.[17] At the end of the work, however, the lexicographical material decreases and in some cases the commentary on an epigram contains little more than the short summary of the poem.[18]

We do not, however, find the index that Pyrrhus promised. As it is now, the retrieval of material is facilitated only by the index notes that Perotti himself wrote in the margins of the manuscript. The mention of the index is one of several indications that Perotti changed his plans for the book after he had finished the original version. As Fabio Stok has shown in a recent article, the physical evidence of the manuscript makes it probable that it was once intended as the presentation copy, but that Perotti changed his mind during the revision and started instead to use it as a working manuscript in order to prepare a second version.[19]

Apart from this, the postscript addressed to Federigo seems to refer only to the original version of the work, which would mean that Perotti could not take account of the ample lexicographical material that he added during his revision. Nevertheless, he claims even there to have finished his commentary on about half of the Latin language. There is no mention at all of Martial. At the end of the letter Perotti says he is confident that Federigo will not cease to encourage him to go on with the work. As the pope's condottiere the duke was leading the campaign against the Florentines after the Pazzi conspiracy. Referring to this campaign, Perotti promises that he will indeed continue the work, so that it will be known to all that not only was the power of the Ro-

---

[17] Cp. *CC* 99,14: **Claros** *uero insula est una ex Cycladibus, de qua diximus; et* **Clarium** *oppidum Colophoniorum, in quo Apollo colebatur, ob id* **Clarius** *dictus.* **Clanius** *uero fluuius est Campaniae prope Neapolim*, from G. Tortelli, Orthographia (Roma: Ulrich Han (Udalricus Gallus) and Simon Nicolai Chardella, [after 10 Aug.] 1471 = HC(+ Add) 15563), the entries *Claros, Clarium, Clarius* (?), and *Clanius*.
[18] E.g. *epigr.* 127 (= 1,98 of modern editions) *AD FLACCUM: LITIGAT ET PODAGRA. Lepidus iocus in Diodori auaritiam, qui nihil patrono suo porrigebat. Hic podagra uexabatur. Martialis per iocum chiragram hanc esse dicit, quod nil patrono porrigat. Quid podagra, quid chiragra sit, et quae horum uocabulorum ratio, superius diximus.*
[19] Cp. F. Stok, La revisione, in Studi sul *Cornu Copiae*, 78–80.

man church enlarged by Federigo's might, but that the Roman language too had been explained — or made famous — and enriched under his rule:

> *CC*, epilogus: *Habes, Federice princeps, interpretationem primi libri, quod est uniuersi operis et totius fere Latinae linguae dimidium. Tot enim ac tanta et tam uaria hoc uno libro explicata sunt, ut aliquanto minus sit id omne quod superest. In quo animaduertere facile erit quot et quanti essent, in quibus antehac uersabamur, errores, quam multa forent a clarissimis etiam Latinae linguae autoribus per ignorantiam rerum ac uocabulorum falso exposita, quam multa ob nimiam difficultatem praeterita ac prorsus ommissa. (2) Nos enim famae omnium parcimus, nec aliter ea iudicamus* (sic = *indicamus* ?). *Diligentis lectoris officium erit aliorum scripta cum nostris conferre; quod, siquando a nobis alicubi quicquam praeteritum uidebitur, quod dici eo loco commode potuisset, nolim desperet lector id alio loco se non minus apte commode que lecturum. Si uero aliqua bis tertio que non nunquam a nobis repetita uidebuntur, id quoque quisquis diligenter animaduertat, non sine causa a nobis factum intelliget, nec inculcatum quicquid, sed necessario aliquando replicatum iudicabit. (3) Verum tu quidem, Federice princeps, quamuis in praesentia Thuscos domas et rebellantes Romanae ecclesiae populos iugum ferre compellis, non desinis tamen nos subinde hortari, ut reliqua prosequamur, quod certe libenter facimus, ut omnes non modo tuis armis ac uiribus sacrosanctae Romanae ecclesiae imperium auctum, sed sacram etiam Romanam linguam te imperatore, te duce illustratam locupletatam que cognoscant. VALE.*

What is the *CC*

I have related these remarks at length because I think they show how Perotti felt that some sort of explanation was called for. He is definitely aware that he has not produced a traditional commentary, and that the reader might need an introduction to the work. But must we therefore conclude that the *Cornu copiae* is simply a commentary gone astray, a text that got out of hand? I think not.

I believe that Perotti's *Cornu copiae* is an expression of one important way in which humanists read classical texts. In the Introduction to his book 'Plato in the Italian Renaissance', James Hankins includes a section entitled "Towards a Typology of Reading in the Fifteenth century," in which he tries to distinguish the main purposes readers had in reading texts. In humanist secondary schools the pupils would be taught to read classical texts not only to acquire learning, but also to be able to imitate systematically the discourse of the best ancient writers. Hankins called the process imitative reading, and it is attested by numerous humanist treatises on education. As Leonardo Bruni put it in his *De studiis et litteris*, the reader should acquire not only *rerum scientia* but also *litterarum peritia*, or eloquence. The imitation was not only stylistic; it was taken for granted that the *ethos* of a text was transmitted to the reader, that the imitation of noble behaviour was inseparable from imitation of noble speech: in short that good letters make good men. In essence this is a revival of the educational ideas of Isocrates, Cicero and Quintilian, but in fifteenth-century humanism it is linked to the conscious effort to 're-conquer' or 'reacquire' classical Latinity. Once the student had acquired the linguistic proficiency, he was expected to compile commonplace books with the best *sententiae* of the authors, arranged under various headings so that they could be introduced more readily into his own compositions.[20] Guarino Veronese instructed Leonello d'Este to gather excerpts from his reading into compendia which would serve as a sort of depository, in order to have the material 'ready' for his own compositions. The expression he uses is that the compendia would be at hand, *praesto*.[21] As we remember, one of Perotti's reasons for not wishing to publish the work, or perhaps part with his working copy, was that he wanted to have easy access to the results of all his long studies, to have them ready at hand, *ut ... haberet in promptu* (*CC*, *prohemium* 3). The phrase *in promptu* is almost a synonym of *praesto*, used by Guarino.

We still possess a considerable number of Perotti's books, and here marginal notes and various types of exclamation marks show him in the process of 'imitative reading'.[22] His notes in a way reduce the text to a lexicon of syno-

---

[20] J. Hankins, Plato in the Italian Renaissance 1–2, Columbia studies in the Classical Tradition 17, 1–2 (Leiden–New York, 1990, repr., 1991), vol. 1, 18–26. For a more technical description of the teaching methods used to approach this ideal, see A. Grafton and Lisa Jardine, From Humanism to the Humanities (London, 1986), Ch. 1 The School of Guarini: Ideals and Practice, 1–28. In his contribution to the present volume Craig Kallendorf discusses marginalia in printed books that are testimonies of the same reading technique.

[21] *Has ad res salubre probatumque praestatur consilium, ut quotiens lectitandum est paratum teneas codicillum tanquam fidelem tibi depositarium ... praesto codicillus erit qui sicuti minister strenuus et assiduus petita subiciat*, Guarino Veronese, Epistolario 1–3, ed. Remigio Sabbadini, Miscellanea di storia veneta 8, 11, 14 (Venezia, 1915–1916–1919), vol. 2, 270; for a discussion of this passage, see Grafton & Jardine, From Humanism, 14–15. The reading strategies taught by Guarino are described in the treatise A Program of Teaching and Learning, compiled by his son and successor, Battista Guarino. It recently appeared with an English translation in Humanist Educational Treatises, ed. and translated by Craig W. Kallendorf, ITRL 5 (Cambridge, Mass. 2002), 260–309. The relevant passage is §§ 30–31. For further discussions of the mechanisms of 'imitative reading,' see Ann Moss, Printed Commonplace-Books and the Structuring of Renaissance Thought (Oxford, 1996), and Anthony Grafton, Commerce with the Classics: Ancient Books and Renaissance Readers (Ann Arbor, 1997).

[22] Cp. Olga Marinelli Marcacci, "Di alcuni codici appartenuti a Niccolò Perotti (un inventario del 1481)," Chiesa e società dal secolo IV ai nostri giorni: Studi storici in onore del P. Ilarino da Milano I–II, Italia sacra 30–31 (Roma, 1979), 361–81; Adriana Marucchi, "Codici di Niccolò Perotti nella Biblioteca Vaticana," Humanistica Lovaniensia 34A (1985), 99–125; J. Fohlen, "Un nouveau manuscrit autographe de Niccolò Perotti (Ottob. lat. 643)," Miscellanea Bibliothecae Apostolicae Vaticanae VII, Studi e Testi 396 (Città del Vaticano

nyms, syntax, orthography, prosody etc. and we find the results of his studies reproduced in his own works, for instance in the *Cornu copiae*, his own large depository of knowledge of all sorts.

We can often follow the process by which Perotti appropriates a word or expression found in a classical author, as it occurs first in a marginal gloss and eventually becomes an active part of his own language and manner of writing.[23] We have an example of this in his spelling of the word *aedo*. The oldest known book of his, written and heavily annotated when he was only 17 years old, contains a number of Latin grammatical texts. One of the passages which Perotti marks is from ps.–Apuleius' *De diphthongis*. The grammarian discusses the use of 'ae' before the letter 'd', for instance in 'aedo' meaning to put forth, to publish. In modern texts the word is spelled with an 'e' only, but in his own writings Perotti almost consistently distinguishes between *aedo* 'to publish', and *edo* 'to eat', as we have also seen in Chh. 3 and 6 of the proem of the *CC*, and he also has a lemma in the *CC* about *aedo*, to publish, with the first syllable long. The passage in Ps. Apuleius may well be the source of this custom:

BAV, Urb. lat. 1180, Ps–Apuleius, *De diphthongis* f. 113^v–14^r: *Ante .b. quoque et .c. ae diphthongo non utimur. Ante .d. reperitur in aedes, quod ab aedendo secundum Varronem derivatum est, et .a. quam in diphthongo habet á principali traxit. Sed melius uidetur dicere quod á principali traxit .e. quum edo breuietur in prima syllaba;* cp. *CC* 2,686: *Item aedo, qum primam syllabam producit, quod est emitto, quasi extra do.*

Perotti himself describes the process of appropriating the style and vocabulary of a classical author in his treatment of letter writing in the *Rudimenta grammatices*,[24] though he there confines his attention to that genre. He singles out Cicero as the unique paradigm for teachers and pupils alike; Ciceronian vocabulary and even entire phrases should not only be imitated but even purloined by pupils, who should be wholly nurtured, so to speak, on his milk:

2000), 193–98; M. Pade, "Valla e Perotti," Studi umanistici Piceni 20 (2000), 72–85; and Ead. "I manoscritti del Perotti (1429/30–80) e il materiale utilizzato per il *Cornu copiae*," Les lexiques et glossaires de la Renaissance, Textes et études du moyen âge (Louvain la Neuve, 2003).

[23] For similar examples of this, see Craig Kallendorf's article in the present volume, where he discusses, among other annotations, those of Guillaume Budé's annotations in his copy of Homer and the marginal notes by the Spanish poet Francisco de Quevedo in the 1502 Aldine copy of Statius, now in the Princeton University Library.

[24] For Perotti's treatise on letterwriting, see Gian Carlo Alessio, "Il *De componendis epistolis* di Niccolò Perotti e l'epistolografia umanistica," Res Publica Litterarum 11 (1988), 9–18; and Maria Elena Curbelo Tavío, "Teoría y prática epistolar de Niccolò Perotti," Humanistica Lovaniensia 49 (2000), 1–29.

Perotti, *De componendis epistolis: Quis maxime preponendus est quem studeant adolescentes imitari? Marcus Cicero. Hic in omni dicendi genere omnium optimus fuit. Hunc solum preceptores legant. Hunc discipuli imitentur, nec modo verba eius hauriant sed etiam clausulas, quinetiam partes ipsas epistolarum interdum furentur et suis inserant. Ita enim fiet ut, succo Ciceronis quasi lacte nutriti, veri illius imitatores evadant.*[25]

We have yet another indication that Perotti intended the *Cornu copiae* to convey linguistic instruction. Apart from innumerable classical authors, Perotti quotes a number of more or less contemporary writers, but the only one he mentions by name is Lorenzo Valla, the author, amongst other works, of the *Elegantiae linguae latinae*, the *Dialecticae disputationes*, the *Antidota in Poggium* and the annotations on Quintilian. As a young man Perotti admired Valla inordinately, and he quotes the works I have mentioned here at length, especially the *Elegantiae*. Valla for his part considered Perotti his heir. It is therefore at first surprising, as both Jean–Louis Charlet and Fabio Stok have recently pointed out, that every time Perotti mentions Valla's name it is to criticise him, although he regularly honours him with epithets such as "vir nostrae aetatis doctissimus". The implicit message is, of course, that Perotti in the *Cornu copiae* surpasses the author of the *Elegantiae*, one of the most highly regarded books on the Latin language.[26] The arguments of Charlet and Stok are convincing, but I think that one might add to their observations, since this is not the only way in which Perotti signals his rivalry with Valla. In chapter 6 of the preface, as we remember, Pyrrhus explains that he was overwhelmed by the "explicatio elegantiae .. latinae linguae", surely a reference to Valla's masterpiece. The postscript, too, I believe, refers to the *Elegantiae*. In his famous preface, Valla had compared the Roman language to the Roman empire, and its present state to the sorry state of Rome after the invasion of the Gauls; like the city itself, so too its language was oppressed by barbarians and only a great

---

[25] From Perotti's *Rudimenta grammatices* (Parisiis : Udalricus Gering, 1479, = C 4682), sign. k.i.ᵛ. Cp. Robert Black's discussion of the passage in Humanism and Education in Medieval and Renaissance Italy. Tradition and Innovation in Latin Schools From the Twelfth to the Fifteenth Century (Cambridge, 2001), 355 and n. 130. I have profited from Black's English summary of Perotti's text.

[26] Cp. Jean–Louis Charlet, "Tortelli, Perotti et les *Élégances* de L. Valla," Res Publica Litterarum 23, ns. 4 (2001), 94–105: especially 96 and 104–5; and the paper of Fabio Stok, "Perotti critico del Valla," Studi umanistici piceni XXIV, 2004 11–20. On Valla and Perotti see also M.C. Davies, "Niccolò Perotti and Lorenzo Valla: four new letters," Rinascimento 24 (1984), 125– 47; B. Marx, "Zu einem Briefwechsel zwischen Lorenzo Valla und Niccolò Perotti," *Commemoratio*. Studi di filologia in ricordo di Riccardo Ribuoli (Sassoferrato, 1986), 81–103; M. Furno, "'Qu'il lui fasse tout passer par l'étamine' (Montaigne, Essais, 1, 26): ou de l'appropriation par Perotti d'un passage des *Elegantiae* de Lorenzo Valla," Res Publica Litterarum 11 (1988), 141–153; and M. Pade, Valla e Perotti.

general would be able to deliver it. Valla himself would endeavour to imitate Camillus, as far as his strength allowed, and lead an army towards the enemy. He did not think that he could achieve great things alone, but he hoped to be able to encourage others to continue his work. Obviously they did, above all Perotti, who confidently asserts that with Federigo as *dux* and *imperator* the Roman language will be explained and enriched.[27] In other words, if Perotti finishes the *Cornu copiae* he will have achieved what Valla only began.

As Vincenzo Fera has pointed out, military imagery pervades the philological writings of fifteenth–century Italy.[28] Nonetheless I am convinced that the verbal similarities are too many and the comparison between the Empire and the language too poignant for the similarities between the preface of the *Elegantiae* and Perotti's letters to Federigo to be due merely to a general tendency.

The comparison between the Roman Empire and the Roman language, the intellectual heritage that had lasted longer and brought more blessings than the political structure, is the central theme of Valla's preface;[29] in Perotti's let-

---

[27] The two letters to Montefeltro have been discussed in J.–L. Charlet, "Le lexicographe et le prince: Federico d'Urbino dans le *Cornu copiae* de Niccolò Perotti," Cultura e potere nel Rinascimento (Cianciano–Pienza 21–24 luglio 1997) a c. di L. Secchi Tarugi (Firenze, 1999), 87–99; and F. Stok, "Il proemio del *Cornu copiae*," Studi Umanistici Piceni 21 (2001), 37–54, revised version in Id. Studi sul *Cornu Copiae*, 43–70.

[28] V. Fera, "Poliziano, Ermolao Barbaro e Plinio," Una famiglia veneziana nella storia. I Barbaro. Atti del convegno di studi in occasione del quinto centenario della morta dell'umanista Ermolao. Venezia, 4–6 novembre 1993 (Venezia, 1996), 193–234: 195 and n. 11 about the 'gladiator' metaphor.

[29] (2) *quosdam* (i.e. Persians, Medes, etc.) *etiam, ut aliquanto inferius quam Romanorum fuit, ita multo diuturnius imperium tenuisse constat*; (3) *nullos tamen ita linguam suam ampliasse ut nostri fecerunt, ...* (5) *opus nimirum multo preclarius multoque speciosius quam ipsum imperium propagasse.* (6) *Qui enim imperium augent, magno illi quidem honore affici solent atque Imperatores nominantur; qui autem beneficia aliqua in homines contulerunt, ii non humana, sed divina potius laude celebrantur ...* (7) *Itaque nostri maiores rebus bellicis pluribusque laudibus ceteros homines superarunt, lingue vero sue ampliatione seipsis superiores fuerunt, tanquam relicto in terris imperio, consortium deorum in celo consecuti ...* (11) *Illos enim regios homines, hos vero divinos iustissime dixeris, a quibus non, quemadmodum ab hominibus sit, aucta res publica est maiestasque populi romani solum, sed, quemadmodum a diis, salus quoque orbis terrarum.* (12) *Eo quidem magis quod qui imperium nostrum accipiebant, suum amittere et, quod acerbius est, libertate spoliari se existimabant, nec fortasse iniuria*; (13) *ex sermone autem latino non suum imminui, sed condiri quodammodo intelligebant ...* (19) *Ac, ne pluribus agam de comparatione imperii sermonisque romani, hoc satis est dixisse.* (20) *Illud iam pridem, tanquam ingratum onus, gentes nationesque abiecerunt; hunc omni nectare suaviorem, omni serico splendidiorem, omni auro gemmaque pretiosiorem putaverunt, et quasi deum quemdam e celo demissum, apud se retinuerunt ...* (23) *ibi namque romanum imperium est, ubicunque romana lingua dominatur ...* (30) *Siquidem multis iam seculis non modo latine nemo locutus est, sed ne latina quidem legens intellexit ...* (31) *quasi, amisso Romano imperio, non deceat romane nec loqui, nec sapere; fulgorem illum Latinitatis situ ac rubigine passi obsolescere*, ed. Mariangela Regoliosi, Nel cantiere del Valla. Elaborazione e montaggio delle "Elegantie", Humanistica

ters to Federigo it is not of the same importance, but its poignant use in the very last sentence of the entire work emphasises the message. Perotti ends the *Cornu copiae* by juxtaposing Federigo's military services towards the States of the Roman Church, the *Romanae ecclesiae imperium*, and towards the Latin language:

> *CC*, postscript 2: *ut omnes non modo tuis armis ac uiribus sacrosanctae Romanae ecclesiae imperium auctum, sed sacram etiam Romanam linguam te imperatore, te duce illustratam locupletatam que cognoscant.*

Valla had complained that for centuries nobody had spoken Latin or even been able to understand the Latin they read: students of philosophy had been unable to comprehend the philosophers, orators the rhetorical texts and lawyers the juridical writers, just as other readers had not, and still did not, thoroughly understand what the ancients wrote.[30] He had also pointed out the strange coincidence that the revival of letters and knowledge of Latin, which had taken place during his lifetime, coincided with a revival of the very crafts that were closest to the liberal arts: painting, sculpture, statue–making, and architecture.[31] Perotti makes the same connection between the study of the Latin language and the flowering of the sciences, liberal arts and higher crafts when he, or Pyrrhus, maintains that students of these matters and members of all these professions would profit from the study of the *Cornu copiae*:

> *CC*, prohemium 6: *Hinc grammatici, hinc rhetores, hinc Poetae, hinc Dialectici, hinc earum artium quas liberales uocant studiosi, hinc medici, hinc philosophi, hinc ciuilis ac pontificii iuris antistites, hinc rei militaris periti, hinc agricolae, hinc pictores, hinc architecti, hinc fabri omnes atque opifices multa et pene infinita haurire possunt eorum studiis necessaria, et ita necessaria ut affirmare ausim plurima eos, nisi haec legerint, ad ipsorum disciplinas artes que maxime pertinentia ignoraturos, ne dicam in multis ut nunc faciunt permansuros erroribus, quos si haec legent aliquando recognoscent, et hoc opus non unius Poetae, sed omnium latinorum autorum commentarios iure optimo dici posse intelligent.*

---

13 (Roma, 1993), Appendice 119–25. Regoliosi's edition is definitely superior to the text published in L. Valla, Opera omnia 1, a c. di Eugenio Garin (Torino, 1962), reprint of the Basle edition of 1540, 3–5.

[30] (30) *Siquidem multis iam seculis non modo latine nemo locutus est, sed ne latina quidem legens intellexit: non philosophie studiosi philosophos, non causidici oratores, non legulei iurisconsultos, non ceteri lectores veterum libros perceptos habuerunt aut habent,* ibid.

[31] (32) *non magis quam cur ille artes, que proxime ad liberales accedunt, pingendi, sculpendi, fingendi, architectandi, aut tamdiu, tantoque opere degeneraverint, ac pene cum litteris ipsis demortue fuerint, aut hoc tempore excitentur ac reviviscant, tantusque tum bonorum opificum, tum bene litteratorum proventus efflorescat,* ibid.

But does all this mean that the *Cornu copiae* is not a commentary ? Or, to rephrase the question in accordance to the common theme of these six articles: is the *Cornu copiae* a Renaissance commentary ? I believe that for Perotti and for many other Renaissance humanists the purpose of reading and understanding a classical text was to acquire an active mastery over its linguistic and doctrinal universe, and therefore the purpose of a commentary was to help the reader do that. In the letter to Federigo da Montefeltro, Perotti praised the vast variety of subjects treated by Martial. Indeed, he maintained that Martial surpassed all other Latin writers in this respect. To explain all this properly, Perotti had of course drawn on the results of a lifetime of reading from all fields of learning, as he himself says in the preface. Thus by their very nature Martial's epigrams had led to a work dealing with almost the whole of classical Latinity. Perotti shared the conviction of his contemporaries that the educational programme consisting of the literary interpretation of the poets provided the individual with a secure foundation for a full and active life in the community. He could therefore claim that his commentary on a text as rich and varied as Martial's epigrams was almost equivalent to a commentary on the whole of Latin literature and was thus useful to students of practically any subject and to members of many professions.

I admit that this may be stretching Perotti's words a little, but I am convinced that, as I have tried to show, the form of the *Cornu copiae* is the result, if a somewhat extreme one, of humanist ideas about the purpose of reading a classical text.[32]

Marianne Pade   Aarhus University

---

[32] For other discussions of the form of the *Cornu copiae*, see F. D'Episcopo, "L'estetica del poeta–teologo e l'enciclopedismo di Niccolò Perotti," Res Publica Litterarum 4 (1981), 43–66; M. Furno, "Du *De orthographia* de G. Tortelli au *Cornu copiae* de N. Perotti: points communs et divergences," Res Publica Litterarum 12 (1989), 59–68.

A Commentary? Ermolao Barbaro's Supplement to Dioscorides

JOHANN RAMMINGER

The Venetian humanist Hermolaus Barbarus belonged to the patrician family of the Barbaro. Born in 1453 or 1454 as grandson of the famous Francesco Barbaro (1390–1454), he attended university at Padova, where he took doctoral degrees in the arts (1474) and *utriusque iuris* (1477). From 1474 he taught Aristotle (Ethics, Politics and Rhetoric) at the university for several years.[1] Already very early Barbaro expressed the conviction that in the study of Aristotle it was not enough to rely on the medieval translations and commentaries used at the university; to achieve a deeper understanding it was necessary to go back to the Greek sources, so as to recover the original text of the Stagirite as well as the ancient interpretive tradition. Consequently, his first published work was a Latin translation of the paraphrases of Aristotle written by the hellenistic Greek philosopher Themistius, printed in 1481. The recovery of Aristotle was not to be confined to the works of the university syllabus; not much later, in the introduction to a lecture series on Aristotle held in Venice in 1484 he announced that his course was to include "all of Aristotle", also works that were passed over in the university curriculum.[2]

This attention to all the works of Aristotle may have been the starting point for Barbaro's interest in Pliny and Dioscorides and the herbal science of antiquity in general, because the *Corpus Aristotelicum* also contained two works on

---

[1] Cp. L. Panizza, "Learning the syllogisms: Byzantine visual aids in Renaissance Italy — Ermolao Barbaro (1454–93) and others," in: Philosophy in the Sixteenth and Seventeenth Centuries. Conversations with Aristotle, ed. C. Blackwell and S. Kusukawa (Aldershot etc., 1999), 22–47: 22–33; and V. Cox, "Rhetoric and Humanism in Quattrocento Venice," Renaissance Quaterly 56 (2003), 652–94. Fundamental for the study of Barbaro is V. Branca, "L'umanesimo veneziano alla fine del Quattrocento. Ermolao Barbaro e il suo circolo," in: Storia della cultura veneta 3: Dal primo quattrocento al concilio di Trento, a cura di G. Arnaldi e M. Pastore Stocchi (Vizenca, 1980), 1, 123–75, repr. with additions as "Ermolao Barbaro e il suo circolo tra azione civile, fede religiosa, entusiasmo filologico, presperimentalismo scientifico," in: Id., La sapienza civile. Studi sull'Umanesimo a Venezia (Firenze, 1998), 59–127; see also C. Griffante, "L'umanesimo a Venezia. Note critiche per un aggiornamento bibliografico del capitolo 'Ermolao Barbaro e il suo circolo'," in: ibid., 197–216.

[2] If not indicated otherwise, I will quote Barbaro's works from the following editions: Ermolao Barbaro, *Epistolae, Orationes et Carmina*, ed. crit. a cura di V. Branca, 2 vols., Nuova collezione di testi umanistici inediti o rari V. VI (Firenze, 1943); *Hermolai Barbari Castigationes Plinianae et in Pomponium Melam*, ed. G. Pozzi et al., 4 vols., Thesaurus mundi 11, 14, 18, 19 (Patavii, 1973–1979). *Hermolai Barbari patricii Veneti et Patriarcae Aquileiensis Corollarium libris quinque absolutum* (Venetiis: Fratres Gregorii, 1517). The introductory lecture was edited as *oratio III* in Barbaro, *Epistolae*, II, 107–109 (the quotation is on p. 108; for the transmission of the lecture see vol. I p. XXXIII f.).

herbal science. One was a shortish tract *De plantis* (falsely) attributed to Aristotle, widely used in the Middle Ages[3] and first printed in the Latin edition of Aristotle's *opera de naturali philosophia* in 1482.[4] The other were the ten books of the *Enquiry into plants* by Aristotle's successor Theophrast. The Greek text of Theophrast was only printed in 1497 by Aldus in the fourth volume of Aristotle's *Opera*, whereas the Latin translation made by Theodore Gaza in the 1450s was already printed in 1482.[5] A further major Greek text on herbs was Dioscorides' work Περὶ ὕλης ἰατρικῆς, commonly cited under its Latin title *De materia medica*.[6] The book treated the medical simples, i. e. the basic substances of pharmacology, mainly plants, but also animals, liquids and minerals. The Greek text was translated into Latin in late antiquity and into Arabic in the ninth and tenth centuries. When the great Arabic medical authors, who quoted Dioscorides copiously (notably the *Liber aggregatus de simplicibus* of Serapion iunior), were translated into Latin, the Arabic Dioscorides entered

---

[3] Nicolaus Damascenus, *De plantis*. Five translations, ed. H.J. Drossaart Lolofs and E.L.J. Poortman. Aristoteles semitico–latinus. Verhandlingen der Koninklijke Nederlandse Akademie van Wetenschappen, afd. Letterkunde nieuwe reeks, deel 139 (Amsterdam, Oxford, New York, 1989), 465–561, Latin text: 515–61.

[4] Venetiis: Philippus Venetus, 1482, H 1682. The next print only appeared in 1496. See M. Flodr, Incunabula classicorum. Wiegendrucke der griechischen und römische Literatur (Amsterdam, 1973), 19f., 'Aristoteles' no. 4 and 9. Barbaro himself doubted the attribution to Aristotle (*Coroll.* 28: *si modo liber eius est qui de plantis ad autorem Aristotelem refertur*); as his (Latin) quotations show, his knowledge of the work is based on the medieval translation of the Latin text into Greek.

[5] See C. B. Schmitt, "Theophrastus," CTC II (Washington, 1971), 242–322: 266–68. Barbaro was familiar with both the original and Gaza's translation; and later came to use the latter as a commentary on the former. It should perhaps be added that Barbaro was not aware of Theodore Gaza's subsequent corrections, which are contained in a manuscript now in the Fondo Chigi of the Biblioteca Apostolica Vaticana (BAV, Chigi F.VIII 193); the text he quotes always follows the print.

[6] From the few indications available, modern scholarship has concluded that the work was probably finished between 65 and 75 AD (cp. Pedanios Dioskurides, in: Der Neue Pauly IX 462–65 [Alain Touwaide]), i. e., shortly before Pliny's Natural history, the preface of which is dated to 77. This coincides more or less with Barbaro's own view, that Dioscorides was a contemporary of Pliny or even slightly younger (Castig. primae 29,29 III p.988 *Dioscoridem, cuius nos volumina in latinum vertimus, Plinio aut contemporaneum aut non multo posteriorem fuisse*; cp. also 26,1 III p.923); — this was important from Barbaro's point of view, since Pliny thus could not have cited the Greek writer. Nicolò Leoniceno, on the other hand, in the *De Plinii in medicina erroribus*, expressed the belief that Dioscorides was one of the sources of Pliny (ed. L. Premuda, Milano, 1958, p. 151, quoted with corrections from the incunable, Ferrara: Laurentius de Rubeis, de Valentia, with Andreas de Grassis, de Castronovo, 18 Dec. 1492, sig. a2v, HC 10021*): *Nam et Plinius ipse non hunc minus quam Theophrastum in hac parte secutus uidetur, ut, qui utramque linguam et graecam et latinam nouerit, sententias integras Dioscoridis quasi uerbum ex uerbo a Plinio translatas agnoscat.*

occidental medical literature. In the eleventh century, the old Latin translation from the Greek was reworked into an alphabetical treatise of simples and their virtues, in which there remained only little of the Greek author. It was printed in 1478 in Tuscany,[7] and — even though we have so far no evidence that Barbaro was even aware of this print — certainly exemplified the desperate state of Dioscorides–scholarship at the time when Barbaro began to work on this author. The old Latin version did not completely fall into disuse either; we find it cited intermittently throughout the later Middle Ages, until its importance was reasserted by Marcello Virgilio.[8]

Barbaro began to translate Dioscorides into Latin very early in the 1480s.[9] This translation was in itself a daring project, since a Dioscorides–text translated directly from the Greek could hardly avoid showing that the Latin Dioscorides–excerpts translated from the Arabic, on which specialists relied, were woefully inadequate. It must have been in connection with the research necessary for the translation that Barbaro conceived an even more ambitious plan: to provide a *corollarium* to Dioscorides, which would altogether present an overview over pharmacological knowledge based directly on the classical Greek and Latin sources, completely bypassing accepted medieval scholarship. Barbaro worked on this project with interruptions till his death of the plague in the summer of 1493.

Modern scholarship has often seen the work as a commentary on Dioscorides; as such it has found its place in the fourth volume of the *Catalogus Translationum et Commentariorum*.[10] It is the purpose of this article to question

---

[7] Johannes de Medemblick, Colle (HC *6258).

[8] It is used by Simon Januensis in the *Synonyma medicinae* (finished ca. 1290) and Matthaeus Silvaticus († 1342) in his *Opus pandectarum medicinae*; see J. Ramminger, "Ne Dioscuride ne Plinio: Su alcuni testi medicinali del medioevo e il *Cornu copiae* di Niccolò Perotti," SUP 19 (1999), 104–14: 114, nn. 26 and 27, and id., "Zur Entstehungsgeschichte des *Dioskurides* von Ermolao Barbaro (1453–1493)," Neulateinisches Jahrbuch 1 (1999), 189–204: 189 n. 2. For Marcello Virgilio cp. Riddle (see n. 10), pp. 35 and 37.

[9] The first witness to the translation are several chapters published in Paolo Marsi's commentary on Ovid's *Fasti*, printed in 1482 (Venetiis: Baptista de Tortis, HC 12238; the colophon has the date "ANNO SALVTIS MCCCCLXXXII ... IX. CAL. IANVAR." (= 24 December 1482, according to the Venetian calendar); see G. Pozzi, "Appunti sul 'Corollarium' del Barbaro," in: Tra Latino e Volgare per Carlo Dionisotti, a c. di G. Bernardoni Trezzini et al., Medioevo e umanesimo 17–18 (Padova, 1974), 619–40: 625.

[10] J. Riddle, Dioscorides, CTC 4 (Washington, 1980), 1–143, on Barbaro's 'commentary': 46–48. Cp. E. Bigi, "Barbaro, Ermolao," in Dizionario biografico degl Italiani 6 (Roma, 1964), 97: "intraprende nel 1481–82 [!] il commento a Dioscoride," Pozzi, Appunti, p. 619: "Il volume (i.e. the translation) è accompagnato da un largo commento dello stesso Barbaro."

that characterization; it is hoped that a closer analysis of some of the work's features will lead to a more nuanced appreciation of the *Corollarium*.

The original manuscript of Barbaro's *Dioscorides* has perished. In the print of 1517 we first have the translation, divided into five books, but with continous numbering of the chapters; then, seperately, Barbaro's own book on the *materia medica*, with the same chapter headings as the translation. Barbaro himself sometimes calls his book on medical simples *commentatio*.[11] This and related terms like *commentarius, commentum* and the verb *commentari* from antiquity onwards had been used for 'commentary' in the modern sense as well as other kinds of scholarly discourse (see Appendix). Barbaro himself uses these terms for the whole or parts of such different works as his Themistius–translation (*commentarii, commentatio, –tiones*), Francesco Barbaro's *De re uxoria* (*–arii*), a tract in Plutarch's *Moralia* (*–arius*), the *Castigationes Plinianae* (*commentum, –arius*), Aristotle's *Metaphysics* (*–arii*), unspecified modern scholarship (*commentatio*) and the pseudo–Aristotelian *De plantis* (*commentatio*). Obviously *commentatio* describes only in very generic terms, how Barbaro viewed his work. Certainly structurally it is a commentary insofar as it strictly follows the structure of the text it accompanies. Further than that, the similarities with what we would expect of a commentary are not many. The most noticeable difference is the absence of lemmata, otherwise a standard feature of commentaries from antiquity onwards. For Barbaro the framework supplied by Dioscorides just serves as a point of departure for an overview over all information to be gleaned from botanical, medical and other sources. In this overview Dioscorides has a privileged place only insofar as Barbaro occasionally relates information found in Dioscorides to what other writers have to say. In all, the name of Dioscorides is mentioned about 350 times in the over thousand chapters of Barbaro's book; in many chapters there are neither explicit nor implicit references to his work. In comparison, the name of Pliny occurs over 700 times, that is twice as many, and Theophrast is named nearly as often as Dioscorides.

Barbaro regularly called his book *corollarium* to Dioscorides.[12] This is a term of medieval logic, where it denotes a supplementary conclusion derived from a syllogism, or a summary. At the same time *corollarium* more generally can be an

---

[11] Coroll. 134 *in commentatione post hypocisthidem proxima*.

[12] For the term *corollarium* in Barbaro's writing cp. J. Ramminger, "*Rem latinam iuuare*: Zur Funktion nichtfachlicher Zitate im *Corollarium* des Ermolao Barbaro," SUP 18 (1998), 139–55: 139 n. 2. The letter from 1489, where Barbaro first calls his book *Corollarium*, has been edited by id., "Die 'Irrtümer Perottis' von Ermolao Barbaro d. J. Ausgabe und Kommentar von Brief 135," in: WS 114 (2001), 677–700.

additamentum, a supplement.[13] Thus, when Barbaro announces the imminent publication of the "Dioscorides cum corollario nostro",[14] he defines his work as a supplement to Dioscorides and a summary of related pharmacological knowledge.

How this terminology related to the work itself can be seen in an analysis of one of Barbaro's *commentationes*. As an example I have chosen the entry on *cardamomum*, not least because it is relatively short (*Coroll.* 5, interpunction and orthography modernized):

¹ *Cardamomum Theophrastus refert alios e Media putare, alios ex India cum amomo atque nardo et plurimis id genus aduehi.* ² *Simile amomo frutice toto praedicant, semine oblongo. Quatuor eius genera. Viridissimum et pingue acutis angulis, fricanti pertinax, quod et maxime laudatur. Proximum e ruffo candicans. Tertium minutius atque nigrius. Peius uarium et friari facile odorisque parui. Id, quod uerius est, uicinius esse costo debet. Precium optimi ait Plinius in libras denarii II.*
³ *Recentiores Mauritani hoc non cardamomum, sed cordumeni et syluestre caros uocant.* ⁴ *Cardamomi uero nomine genus aliud intelligunt in geminas diuisum species, alterum lentis amplitudine, alterum ciceris obnigri, in quo granum album sit, gustu mordaci. Vtrunque odoratum.* ⁵ *Quid quod officinae cardamomo utuntur alio, quam quod a Mauris et a Dioscoride perscribitur, duplicis fastigii, minus et maius appellantes?* ⁶ *Cui simile id semen sit, quod uulgo melligeta dicitur, praelatum uiribus.*

¹ According to Theophrast there are some who believe that cardamom is imported from Media, others who believe that it comes from India together with Nepaul cardamom and spikenard and many similiar species. ² It is said to be similar to Nepaul cardamom in the overall appearance of its fruit, with longish seed. It has four varieties. One is very green and fat, with sharp points, it resists rubbing it down; it is the best liked of the four. The next one is reddish–white. The third one is smaller and darker. The worst kind is mottled, easily crumbled and with little smell. The purer it is, the nearer it is to the *costum*. The price for the best according to Pliny is two *denarii* per pound.
³ The younger Mauritanians call this not cardamom, but *cordumeni* and wild cumin. ⁴ By the name of cardamom they understand another sort, consisting of two species, one with the size of a lentil, the other a darkish

---

[13] See Mittellateinisches Wörterbuch, vol. 2 (München, 1997), s. v., col. 1901–1902 (Leithe–Jasper); Dictionary of Medieval Latin From British Sources, fasc. 2 (London, 1981), 494 (Latham). Cp. the definition by Perotti, *Cornu copiae* 27,3 vol. 6 p. 86 *corollarium dictum, quod significat id, quod additur praeter illud, quod est debitum.* For Perotti's own use see M. Pade, "Niccolò Perotti's *Cornu copiae*: Commentary on Martial and Encyclopedia," in this volume, p. 53.
[14] Preface to the Castigationes in Melam Pomponium (III, p. 1307).

chickpea, containing a white seed, with pungent taste. Both kinds are fragrant. ⁵ But what about the apothecaries, who use a kind of cardamom different from that of the Mauritanians and Dioscorides, with two kinds, called greater and lesser? ⁶ Similar to this is the seed which is commonly called 'grains of paradise'. It is preferred because of its potency.[15]

Barbaro does not arrange his authorities according to the amount of material they have; such an order would have put Pliny in the first place, since everything under number 2 in the first paragraph comes from the *Naturalis historia*. Instead Barbaro chooses what is clearly a descending hierarchy of authority: First Theophrast, then Pliny, who as a source was less valuable because his information might sometimes be copied from Theophrast,[16] then the Mauritanians (the Arabic authors), finally the contemporary apothecaries whose information was furthest removed from the authorities of antiquity.

Parts of the information attributed to the *Mauritani* can be found in many medical manuals. It goes back to Avicenna, who treated the simples in the second book of his *Canon* (Avicenna, *Canon* 2, 159, Patavii: Johannes Herbort, de Seligenstadt, 1476; Hain 2201, sig. l₃r; underlining indicates text not used by Barbaro):

> *Cardamomum quid est. aliud est magnum sicut cicer nigrum. quod qum frangitur interius habet granum album mordicans linguam sicut cubebe in quo est aromaticitas. et aliud est parvum sicut lens aromaticum etiam. Natura. Calidum est et siccum in tertio. Operationes et proprietates. In ipso cum calefactione est stipticitas et proprie in illo quod habet caput et proprie in capite ipso. Membra. Nutrimenti. Confert vomitui et nausee cum aqua masticis et utriusque granati.*

As in the other cases, Barbaro takes over the information accurately; it had, however, to be reformulated entirely, since the technical language of medieval medicine was not suited to his own work.

---

[15] This translation relies (with the necessary modifications) on the English translations of Barbaro's sources, Theophrastus, Enquiry into Plants and Minor Works on Odours and Weather Signs, with an english translation by A. Hort, vol. 2, Loeb Classical Library 79 (Cambridge Mass./London, 1980), 249; Pliny, Natural History, with an english translation by H. Rackham, vol. 4, Loeb Classical Library 370 (London/Cambridge Mass., 1968), 37. The distinction between the greater and the lesser cardamom is common in later herbals. I have taken the phrase from Culpeper's (1616–1654) *Herbal.*

[16] Cp. *Cast. primae* 14,31 II p.739 *in Theophrasto, unde Plinius et Athenaeus mutuati sunt*; ibid. 16,23 p.765 *Theophrastus auctor duobus locis, unde Plinius haec ad verbum sumpsit*, ibid. 18,18 II p.795 *Theophrastus, unde accepit haec Plinius. Coroll.* 4 *ut inquit Theophrastus, unde sumpsit Plinius.* ibid. 12 *Dissentit a Dioscoride Plinius Theophrastum, ut arbitror, secutus*, ibid. 98 *Plinius haec de pinu a Theophrasto dicta transtulit ad laricem.*

So far I have not been able to identify a specific source for what Barbaro has to say about the *officinae*, the apothecaries. But in the course of my research I came across a shortish tract, which seemed rather typical for the kind of manual Barbaro would have had to deal with. It is the *onomasticon de simplicibus eorumque virtutibus medicis* by Galeatius de Santa Sofia (BAV, Pal. lat. 1279), which says about the *cardamomum* (fol. 32v): *Cardamo(m) est genus quoddam cuius due sunt speties est enim maius et minus*. The de Santa Sofia are a famous dynasty of professors of medicine in Padua. Galeazzo had died in Padova in 1427. His works continued to circulate: The copy of his *Simplicia* which I used was written in 1468, forty years after his death. We know that Barbaro was in contact with a later descendant of the family, Felice di Santa Sofia, to whose garden he occasionally refers.[17] The last piece of botanical lore, concerning the *melligeta*, I have not yet been able to trace in a contemporary source, but undoubtedly it is well founded; we find a similar, if somewhat longer note in Caspar Bauhinus' *Pinax theatri botanici*, from 1623.[18]

Thus, Barbaro not only gives an overview over Greek and Roman pharmacological knowledge, he also crosschecks contemporary usages against it — and usually finds the contemporaries deficient. All this contributes only incidentally to an understanding of Dioscorides. It is definitely not a commentary to the Greek author. There is a further limitation: Barbaro ignores those parts of Dioscorides' work, which dealt with the effects and uses of the various drugs. These are mentioned by Barbaro occasionally when they help to distinguish between various homonymous plants, but hardly ever otherwise. In the case of the *cardamomum*, more than half of Dioscorides' chapter is thus skipped over. As marked in the quotation from Avicenna above, Barbaro also bypasses the corresponding information from other authors. Partially this restriction may reflect a personal preference on the part of Barbaro, since it is clear from his letters that he had an enthusiastic interest in the *realia*, the reconstruction of the natural science of antiquity. In addition, it can hardly be a

---

[17] *Coroll.* 1, 461, 543.
[18] ΠΙΝΑΞ *theatri botanici Caspari Bauhini, ... sive Index Theophrasti Dioscoridis Plinii et botanicorum qui a seculo scripserunt opera*, Basileae, typis Ludouici Regis, 1623, in the chapter *grana paradisi et cardamomum* (p. 413): *Hoc Cardamomi minoris loco aliqui utuntur et Melegeta dicitur, propter similitudinem quam cum Melicae semine habet*. The similarity to the seed of *melica* (a kind of millet) is already emphasized earlier, cf. Simon Januensis, *Clavis sanationis*, s.v. *cobzbagne: Cobzbagne sic scribitur in secundo canonis Auicennae, sed in arabico chobezbaca. dixit mihi arabs quod est nunc xarch, que uulgo dicitur melegeta, eo quod gramina eius similantur milice granis, et si hoc est, falsum est quod ibi scribitur quod portatur de sclauonia*. (I quote from the edition Mediolani: Antonius Zarotus, 3 August 1473, HCR 14747). I found the reference to *cobzbagne* in the edition of the *Clavis*, Venetiis: Guilelmus de Tridino, 13 november 1486 (HC 14749*) s.v. *melegete*. So far it has not been established which print(s) or manuscript(s) of the *Clavis* Barbaro used.

coincidence that the parts of Dioscorides Barbaro does treat, concerning the description of plants, their provenience etc., are the same as those, which had been quoted from Dioscorides in Arabic and late medieval compilations of herbal medicine.

Even though Barbaro treated a medical subject–matter, at least in part using medical literature, the work in itself was not an encyclopedia of medicines, but a work of humanist philology in the field of medicine. Thus Barbaro in general has little interest in updating the knowledge he has collected. As we have seen, when he gives prices, the prices are not contemporary ones, but taken from Pliny, expressed in *denarii*. Moreover, Barbaro pays close attention to textual problems in his sources and proposes emendations not only in Dioscorides, but also in Pliny, Aristotle, Columella, and others.[19] Barbaro further emphasizes the philological nature of his work by interspersing his discourse with the discussion of textual or interpretational problems taken from Latin non–technical literature.[20] In all I have counted about 150 references or quotations, half of them from Plautus or Vergil. This was not, or not only, an overflow of the discussion into unrelated matters, a lapse of concentration, as it were, but should be related to Barbaro's insistence on the validity of philological methods in a field which had so far been reserved for specialists hardly concerned with the historical authenticity of their texts. It connected the *materia medica* with other types of texts, where the authority of the humanists had long been established.[21] Barbaro was aware of the fact that to the reader these discussions at first might seem extraneous.[22] I quote from chapter 240, *pulmones animalium* ('animals' lungs'): *Pulmones agnini, suilli et ursini caeterorumque animantium ex Dioscoridis instituto referendi erant. In his quando nihil erat scitu admodum dignum, ad diuerticula multae lectionis uenimus, quae nec inutilia nec iniucunda futura sint lectoribus* ("The lungs of sheep, swine and bear had to be mentioned because they are in Disocorides. Since, however, in these there was nothing worth knowing, we have added something from our extensive reading, which the

---

[19] Variant readings or corruptions in Dioscorides are discussed in *Coroll.* 9, 206 (*ex Columella*), 256, 385, 414, 425, 567 (*exemplaria depravata*), 625 (*graeci codices ambusti*), 628, 616, 695, 740. Emendations in Aristotle are proposed in *Coroll.* 195, 303, 543, in Columella in *Coroll.* 124, 173, 312, 314, 322, 469, 472, 562, 904.
[20] G. Pozzi, the main editor of the *Castigationes Plinianae*, characterized the style of discourse of the *Corollarium*: "... che l'excursus è qui la normalità". Pozzi, ed., *Castigationes*, I, p. XLIII.
[21] There is a slight irony in the fact that Barbaro himself firmly rejected as unsuitable the incursion of a doctor into the field of philology. In a letter to Michele Alberto da Carrara from 1490 he critizises a work of the latter, because, although he was a *medicus*, he had treated matters belonging to grammar or literary studies (*quamobrem aliena medico multa sis complexus et quae ad grammaticum potius et poetarum interpretem pertineant, ep.* 132, II p. 50).
[22] For a discussion of the function of such digressions in another context see J. Gaisser, "Filippo Beroaldo on Apuleius: Bringing Antiquity to Life," in this volume, p. 90ff.

readers may find useful and entertaining"). Similarly Barbaro in the chapter on the *squama aeris*, the red cuprous oxide, adduces what little information he has found in Palladius and Celsus. The mention of copper, however, gives him a chance to discuss the etymology of the word *rantium* or *arantium*, the orange. In conclusion Barbaro says: *Sed uereor ne quis me alias inuidiae obnoxium etiam nimio iuuandi rem latinam studio lapsum praedicet* ("I am afraid that some with their usually envy will say that I have digressed too far in an excessive zeal for the *res latina*, the Latin culture").

The emphasis on the support of Latin culture/literature (*res Latina, res literaria, lingua Latina, lectio Latina, studia humanitatis* are overlapping expressions) is rather a commonplace amongst Barbaro's contemporaries. Giorgio Merula had formulated similar aims already at the beginning of the 1470s (in the epilogue of his edition of Martial) — for himself as well as for his readers:[23] Not only would he like to be of use to the community of letters (*dum rei literariae prodesse cuperem*); the studious reader, too, could contribute to the *res Latina* by explaining passages of Martial's text, which were still obscure (*si varia et assidua lectione, ut fieri per studiosos solet, quid illa significent deprehenderint, juvent et ipsi rem Latinam*). Similarly, Merula's younger contemporary Marcantonio Sabellico defined the community of humanists as those, *qui recentissimis temporibus latinam linguam iuvere* ("who in our time have helped the Latin language").[24] Poliziano formulated the same aim for himself (*si rem iuuare Latinam studemus, Misc. prima* 4,3) as well as for Lorenzo de Medici (*perge a situ recipere rem Latinam*, praef. 91).[25]

Barbaro himself proposed already in 1481, in his first letter to Politian, to join forces with the Florentine humanist in his endeavour to rescue the *litterae et bonae artes* from their ruinous state.[26] He expressed a similar sentiment in a let-

---

[23] Marcus Valerius Martialis, Epigrammmatum Libri XV ex recensione Georgii Merulae Alexandrini ... [Venice]: Vindelinus de Spira, [about 1472], H 10809*. The *postfatio* ed. by B. Botfield, Praefationes et epistolae editionibus principibus auctorum veterum praepositae (Cantabrigiae, 1861), 151–53; the quotations are on pp. 151 and 152.

[24] Marcantonio Sabellico, De latinae linguae reparatione, a cura di G. Bottari, Percorsi dei classici 2 (Messina, 1999), 87. The catalogue of humanists, which follows in Sabellicus' work, shows that *lingua Latina* in this case includes the study of Latin literature and (written) culture. This seems to be an unusual expansion of the meaning, which otherwise relates to proficiency in Latin; cp. Tortelli *profuturus sane pro mea virili studiosis linguae latinae*, preface of *De orthographia*, ed. Rizzo, see n. 43, p. 119; Valla, *eleg.* 6 praef.: *quo prodessem aliquid linguam Latinam discere volentibus*.

[25] I cite the *Miscellanea prima* from the Aldina of 1498 (HC 13218*), the numbering follows H. Katayama, ed. (Tokyo, 1981/82).

[26] Barbaro, *ep.* 56 (I p. 74) *litteris ... et bonis artibus, quibus ... succurrendum est ruinosis et nutantibus brevique casuris.* The letter is dated *Venetiis, idibus septembribus* MCCCCLXXXXI, quoted by V.

ter, written in February 1489, to the same: "Then I will be able to stop loving you, when you desert the study of Latin" (*Tunc amare potero desinere quom tu rem latinam deserere, ep.* 125 II p. 41). Similarly, Barbaro critizised errors contained in Perotti's *Cornu copiae, ut rei litterariae proficerem* (*ep.* 135,36).[27] Contrariwise, on account of a Plautus–supplement composed by himself Barbaro is afraid that people will think it ridiculous that he presumed "to help Latinity with some substituted baby like an extra" (*rem latinam supposititio quodam partu velut auctario iuvare, ep.* n. d. 5, II p. 89).[28] One of the highest ranking Latin authors was Pliny, *sine quo vix potest latina res consistere*, "without whom there would hardly be any Latin culture" (preface of the *Castigationes*);[29] likewise, without Pliny every hope *latinae rei constituendae* would be in vain: *alii rem latinam iuverunt, ille ipse nobis est Latium* (*ep.* n. d. 8, II p. 92).[30]

From very early on Barbaro's definition of his field of study had included natural philosophy.[31] Thus he formulated the aim of his future studies as follows: *ut ... naturalis philosophia cum studiis humanitatis in gratiam redeat* (letter to Gerolamo Donato, 1480, *ep.* 12, I p. 17). In 1483 he praised Nicoletto Vernia

---

Fera, "Poliziano, Ermolao Barbaro e Plinio," in: Una famiglia Veneziana nella storia: I Barbaro, ed. M. Marangoni e M. Pastore Stocchi (Venezia, 1996), 193–234: 193.

[27] Ed. Ramminger, see n. 12, p. 690.

[28] Barbaro skilfully underscores his mastery of Plautinian style by expressing his anxiety in terms of Plautinian comedy: the vocabulary alludes to Plautus, *supposititius* occurs in *Pseudolus* 1167, *auctarium* in *Mercator* 490; both are otherwise rare in classical literature (Barbaro uses *auctarium* in the same sense in *ep.* 108, II p. 29). The picture of baby–swapping at birth alludes to a standard ploy of comedy. The word *auctarium* seems to have been rare also in the Latin of the Middle Ages; the Dictionary of Medieval Latin From British Sources, fasc. 1 (London, 1975), 157 (Latham) has two examples, both from wordbooks; the Mittellateinisches Wörterbuch, vol. 1 (München, 1967), and J. F. Niermeyer, Mediae Latinitatis Lexicon Minus, vol. 1 (Brill, ²2002) do not have an entry. The (numerous) examples in the Patrologia Latina Database nearly all occur in modern additions.

[29] Ed. Pozzi, Castigationes, I p.3, earlier ed. as *ep.* 156, II p.80.

[30] Other examples in the *Castigationes* are: *Castig. primae* 9,10 (II p.604): *si pictoribus, cur non et rem latinam iuvantibus in parerga licet excurrere?* (an allusion to Vitruvius 9,8,5); ibid. 26,13 III p.926: *Theodorus 'herbam pirum' interpretatus est immodico ne dicam parum necessario augendi rem latinam studio;* ibid. postfatio ad lectores III p.1209: *malui tamen ingenuum illud propositum mecum tueri iuvandae lectionis latinae.* The expression *res latina* for 'Latin knowledge/culture' is a creation of the humanists. I have only been able to find two classical examples of the phrase (Ov. met. 14, 610 and Liv. 1,3,1); in both cases it denotes a political entity (i. e. Latium). Barbaro's second quotation shows, that he was aware of (and playing with) the potential ambiguity of the phrase. I would like to thank Prof. Stroh, who alerted me to the stylistic problem.

[31] Already in *De coelibatu* (1473) he defended his discussion of the medical complications of immoderate eating thus (3,5,79): *Plura dicerem nisi vererer ne suum sibi munus superstitiosa quorundam medicorum impudentia reddi vellet ... non timide ea omnia usurpabo quae ad rem facere videbuntur;* (80): *haec, tametsi medicorum erant, non tamen ut medicus sum persequutus.*

for his efforts in teaching Aristotle "with regard for the splendor of the peripatetic name as well as the general profit of the studies" (*quoad splendori peripathetici nominis cum ... communi studiorum utilitate consultum erit*, ep. 31, I p. 47). That Barbaro in the eyes of his contemporaries reached his objective, becomes clear from a passage in Politian's first *Miscellanea*: "Ermolao Barbaro, the harshest enemy of barbary, who either polishes with a fine ear or forms newly on his anvil the weapons and linguistic equipment of Latin philosophy, so that in this *genre* we live on the same level as the Greeks".[32] Politian may principally have thought of Barbaro's Aristotelian studies and especially his translations; the expression *latina philosophia* would, however, not exclude Barbaro's work on Dioscorides, of which the Florentine humanist was well aware. The restoration of the language of (Latin) philosophy would include the medical lexicon; since the Middle Ages medical theory had been part of the realm of philosophy,[33] its theoreticians were commonly denoted as *philosophi et medici*.[34]

---

[32] *Hermolaus Barbarus, barbariae hostis acerrimus, qui latinae philosophiae velut arma instrumentumque uerborum sic aut aure diligentissima terget aut incude noua fabricatur, ut ... in isto quidem genere ... uiuamus ex pari cum Graecis* (90,4). Fera, Poliziano, p. 194 n. 4, emends the *diligentissima* of the first print to *diligentissime*. This emendation may not be necessary, since Politian alludes to Martial, 6,1,3, *quem* (sc. *libellum*) *si terseris aure diligenti*, cp. *Thes. Ling. Lat.* I 1515,41–1518,30 *de auribus instrumento quodam iudicii ac vocum mensura* (Ihm); see also F. Grewing, Martial, Buch VI. Ein Kommentar, Hypomnemata 115 (Göttingen, 1997), 74–5 ad l. The ear as instrument of literary criticism appears also elsewhere in the *Miscellanea*, e.g. 1,13: (Cicero) *Et ut homo erat omnium — ut tum quidem uidebatur — acerrimus in disputando atque aurem, quod ait Persius* (5,86)*, mordaci lotus aceto*, and 1,59: *qui tamen libri iudicio doctarum aurium sunt improbati*.

[33] See W. A. Wallace, "Traditional natural philosophy," Cambridge History of Renaissance Philosophy, ed. Ch. B. Schmitt et al. (Cambridge, 1988), 201–35: 205.

[34] Without claiming to be exhaustive or even representative, I have noted the following examples. Ermolao Barbaro himself addresses a letter to Antonio Piropilo "ἰατρῷ καὶ φιλοσόφῳ" (*ep.* n. d. 10, II p. 93); in another letter he recommends somebody well versed in philosophy, dialectics and medicine (27, I p. 42). It is hardly a coincidence, that the 1532-edition of Leoniceno's *De Plinii erroribus* has the title *Nicolai Leoniceni Vicentini, philosophi et medici clarissimi, opuscula*. Conversely, Leoniceno drew the ire of his fellow humanists by categorizing Pliny *in numero grammaticorum uel oratorum, non autem philosophorum aut medicorum* (ed. Premuda, p. 152). Similarly, according to Leoniceno, the Arabs had given up *omne philosophiae ac medicinae studium* on religious grounds (p. 180). Pietro de Abano's *Conciliator*, a standard text of medieval medicine, was commonly printed with the title *Conciliator differentiarum philosophorum et praecipue medicorum* (first ed. Venetiis: Gabriele di Pietro, for Thomas de Tarvisio, [after 5 Mar.] 1476; H 2); Petrarca, *Contra medicum quendam* 3, 10 *quid te vetat ... ut philosophum et medicum, sic oratorem esse* (ed. in Opere latine, a cura di A. Bufano, vol. 2, Torino, 1975, 934). Francesco Barbaro writes letters to Pietro Tomasi *illustri philosopho et medico* (Francesco Barbaro, Epistolario, vol. 2: La raccolta canonica delle Epistole, a cura di C. Griggio (Firenze, 1999), no. 278 (from 1448), and *claro philosopho et medico* (no. 344, 1449), and in a letter to Gerolamo Leonardi mentions his friendship *cum prestantissimo philosopho et medico Nicolao patre tuo* (no. 293, 1447). Giorgio Valla publishes in 1488 a translation of *Ale-*

Barbaro took this categorization for granted, as we see in the discussion of a linguistic problem common to the lexica of medicine and philosophy in the *Castigationes Plinianae*: *Operatio et operari pro eo quod est rem divinam facere aut agrum colere compertum omnibus; recentiores philosophi et medici pro eo quod Graeci energian vocant usurpavere, melius facturi si functiones et opera dixissent* ("*operatio* and *operare* for the performance of a religious rite are commonly in use. Recent philosophers and doctors have used them for what the Greeks call *energia*; it would have been better, if they had used the expressions *functio* and *opus*").[35]

Within the reconstruction of that part of "philosophy and medicine", which was the *res latina*, i.e. the knowledge of antiquity in Latin, Barbaro successfully focused on those aspects of the *materia medica* where the methods of humanist scholarship were most applicable und could yield the best results. After his premature death in 1493 the results of his research, as far as they were not contained in the *Castigationes Plinianae*, remained inaccessible. The situation only changed after the publication of the Dioscorides–translation by Jean Ruel in Paris in 1516. The next year Barbaro's *Dioscorides* was printed with the declared intent to vindicate the priority of Dioscorides–studies for the Italians.[36] And, even though the *Supplement to Dioscorides* may neither have been intended as a commentary to Dioscorides nor as a work of practical pharmacology, in the end Barbaro contributed to both fields. The *Corollarium* was instantly received into subsequent commentaries on Dioscorides and the many works on herbal medicine deriving from them. The period of intensive scholarly activity which now began culminated in the *Dioscorides* of Pier Andrea Mattioli, consisting of translation and commentary, which first appeared in Italian in 1544. Its Latin version (1554) became the probably most–read scientific book of the sixteenth century.[37] Now Barbaro was appreciated as the first of those *viri doc-*

---

xandri Aphrodisei philosophi ac medici praestantissimi Problemata (quoted by E. Cranz, "Alexander Aphrodisiensis," CTC I, Washington, 1960, 131).

[35] The quotation is taken from the *Glossemata*, an alphabetical explanation of difficult words of Pliny's Natural history, O 14, from: Hermolaus Barbarus, Castigationes Plinianae et Pomponii Melae, Rome: Eucharius Silber, 24 Nov. 1492, 13 Feb. 1493; HC 2421*; vol. II, sig. c7v; the text is edited with a slight difference in ed. Pozzi, III, p. 1417.

[36] The print is dated *Kal. Februariis .MCCCCC.XVI*. This led Riddle (see n. 10), p. 27–29, to the mistaken assumption that Barbaro's print predated Ruel's (*octauo Calendas Maias. Anno domini* MDXVI.). There can, however, be no doubt that Barbaro's book is dated according to the Venetian calendar which began the year on the first of march, and thus printed nine months after Ruel's; Ruel's translation is discussed in some detail in the brief commentary added to Barbaro's translation by the editor, Battista Egnazio. Cp. Pozzi, Appunti, p. 620.

[37] *Pedacii Dioscoridis Anazarbei de materi medica libri sex, innumeris locis ab Andrea Matthiolo emendati ac restituti*. Lugduni, apud Antonium Vicentinum, 1554; cp. P. Findlen, "The Formation of a Scientific Community: Natural History in Sixteenth–Century Italy," in: Natural Particulars. Nature and the Disciplines in Renaissance Europe, edited by A. Grafton and N. Siraisi

tissimi who, in the words of Pier Andrea Mattioli, "had pulled the *materia medica* out of the darkness, and restored it to the light of day."[38]

APPENDIX: *Commentarius, commentatio, commentum, commentari* in the late Quattrocento.[39]

With the following discussion of these words commonly used in the Quattrocento to designate scholarly literature of various kinds, I hope to supply the semantic basis for a closer understanding of Barbaro's own usage of these words. My discussion is based on a limited corpus of texts available to me in printed or electronic form, and therefore necessarily incomplete.

Commentarius

According to the 'Thesaurus linguae Latinae'[40] the original meaning seems to have been *collectio comminiscendi causa facta*; this definition encompasses a variety of journals and note-books, mainly produced by the public administration, to a lesser extent by private individuals. Thence the word is used for *doctrinae vel artis expositio*, with two sub-groups which comprise firstly *artis cuiuslibet doctrina* generally, including *rerum gestarum memoria litteris mandata* (Caesar's *commentarii* appear in this group), secondly specifically *interpretatio scriptorum*, the modern 'commentary'. The word is used frequently from the earliest inscriptions on; in literature it gains currency with Cicero (40 instances). As far as can be ascertained, the word is mainly used in the masculine; the neuter occurs from Cicero (*Brutus* 164) onwards, but rarely. In Medieval Latin the word is used mainly for 'commentary', 'summary, abridgment', and 'register'.[41]

(Cambridge, Mass., 1999), 369–400: 390. A useful overview over botany in the sixteenth century can be found in F. N. Egerton, "A History of the Ecological Sciences, Part 10: Botany during the Italian Renaissance and Beginnings of the Scientific Revolution," Bulletin of the Ecological Society of America, 84-3, July 2003, 130–37 (the article contains, however, some errors in the dating of earlier works).

[38] *Petri Andreae Matthioli Commentarii* (Lugduni 1562, sig. [*4] r) *complures aetatis nostrae clarissimi viri et rei medicae diligentissimi indagatores, Latini et Graeci sermonis peritissimi, Hermolaus Barbarus, Nicolaus Leonicenus, ... et alii strenuam nauarunt operam, vt discussa superioris seculi caligine, medicam materiam è tenebris eriperent, et suae luci restituerent.*

[39] I would like to thank F. Konstanciak, Munich, who commented upon an earlier draft of the appendix.

[40] Thesaurus linguae Latinae III (Leipzig, 1906–1912), ss. vv. *commentarius (–um)* p. 1856,3–61,41; *commentatio* p. 1861,49–62,24; *commentum* p. 1865,48–68,48; *commentor* p. 1863,64–65,40 (all by Bannier). Here and in the following I have shortened the Latin definitions given in the TLL.

[41] Mittellateinisches Wörterbuch II (München, 1974), 954 (MLW); Dictionary of Medieval Latin from British Sources II (London, 1981), 393 (DictBrit). See M. Teeuwen, The Vo-

In the Latin of the later Quattrocento the previous usage has undergone some modifications, which can best be discerned in Valla's codification of classical usage in *Elegantiae* 4,21, *Commentaria quid sint*. He distinguishes two meanings, either 'short treatment of a topic, libellus' (as opposed to *liber*), or *expositio et interpretatio auctorum*. In the first case singular and plural have neuter and masculine forms respectively, in the second both genders occur indistinctly. Valla also observes that the singular neuter form is rare in classical Latin. Examples for the first meaning discussed by Valla are numerous, although the restriction to shorter works was in practice not observed. Valla himself designates his *Elegantiae* as *commentarii* (preface to the second book): *meos hos commentarios*, the same does Angelo Decembrio regarding his *Politia litteraria* (1,1,1):[42] *Politiae litterariae commentarios* and 1,2,4 *praesentibus commentariis*. Tortelli, in the preface to *De orthographia*, prefers the plural, neuter form: *coeperam olim ... commentaria quaedam grammatica condere quibus omnem litterariam antiquitatem et orthographiae rationem cum oportunis historiis pro poetarum declaratione connectere conabar*.[43] The *De orthographia* also contains a lengthy discussion of *commentarius*, which surpasses Valla's in the breadth of the material collected, but is arranged in a less systematic way.[44] Perotti, *Cornu copiae* 44,9–10,[45] adopts Valla's doctrine with some simplifications. Whether or not Politian saw a difference in meaning between the masculine and neuter form, is difficult to ascertain. In the *Miscellanea prima* there are only six unambigous masculine or neuter examples (all in the plural); of these two are quotations from Censorinus (58,27 and 58,35, both masc., from Cens. 17,10–11). Of the others, two are masc. (praef. 13, the *Miscellanea*, and 9,11 *grammatici commentarii*, Calderini's commentaries on Martial and Juvenal), two neuter forms (praef. 13, the Στρωματεῖς of Clemens, and 54,2 *Graeca ... Latinaque commentaria*, philological works in general). Barbaro's *Castigationes* are called *commentarii* by Sabellicus.[46] Pico uses plural and (more

---

cabulary of Intellectual Life in the Middle Ages, CIVICIMA Études sur le vocabulaire intellectuel du Moyen Age X (Turnhout, 2003), 235–26 *commentari, commentarius (–ium), commentum, commentator*, also for these terms.

[42] Ed. N. Witten, Beiträge zur Altertumskunde 169 (München–Leipzig, 2002).

[43] Ed. S. Rizzo, "Per una tipologia delle tradizioni manoscritte di classici latini in età umanistica," in: Formative Stages of Classical Traditions: Latin Texts from Antiquity to the Renaissance. Proceedings of a conference held at Erice, 16–22 October 1993, as the 6th Course of [sic!] International School for the Study of Written Records. ed. by Oronzo Pecere and Michael D. Reeve (Spoleto, 1995), 371–407, Appendix 402–407: 402.

[44] In the chapter *De syllabis desinentibus in M*; see J.–L. Charlet, Index des lemmes du De orthographia de Giovanni Tortelli, avec la collaboration de M. Furno (Aix, 1994).

[45] Vol. 6, ed. F. Stok (Sassoferrato, 1997), 247.

[46] In a letter dating probably from 1493, quoted by G. Mercati, "Attorno a Marco Antonio Sabellico," in Ultimi contributi alla storia degli umanisti, vol. II, Studi e Testi 91 (Città del Vaticano, 1939), 1–23: 7 n. 1.

rarely) singular forms for various philosophical works (e.g., *in commentariis eius* [*Trapezuntii*] *in Centiloquium Ptolemaei, Adv. astrologiam divinatricem* 8,5 p. 452; *Nicolaus Oresmius ... astrologicam superstitionem peculiari commentario ... insectatur,* ibid. 1 p.24). The singular form is also rare otherwise, Poliziano quotes *Varro in Latinae linguae commentario* (*Misc. prima,* 58,49; the form obviuously can be both masc. and neutr.); his booklet about the Pazzi–conspiracy has the title *coniurationis commentarium.*[47] Ficino's book is called *Commentarium in Convivium Platonis de amore.*[48] Concurrently, *commentarius* is used for 'commentary'. To designate the whole book the humanists normally use the plural; examples are Calderini's *commentarii in Martialem* (1474),[49] and Paolo Marso's commentary to Ovid's *Fasti* (*in commentariis nostris*), where the first excerpts from Barbaro's forthcoming Dioscorides–translation are published (1482).[50] An example of the neuter is in a letter written by Pico to Barbaro in 1484 (*commentaria quae petebas in Aristotelem*).[51] It should at least be noted, that besides *commentarii* most authors use a variety of terms for 'commentary', such as *annotationes, enarrationes,* and verbs such as *explanare, interpretari, enarrare, exponere,* etc.[52]

Barbaro shows a marked preference for the meaning 'study', disregarding Valla's restriction to shorter works and applying *commentarius* to all kinds of humanist literature (I have not found any unambiguous *–um*). In the singular he uses *commentarius,* amongst others, for a tract in Plutarch's *Moralia* (*Plutarchus in eo commentario* Πῶς ἄν τις ὑπ' ἐχθρῶν ὠφελοῖτο, *Castig. primae* 7,15, II p. 540), an analysis of Thucydides' style (*Dionysius rhetor de phrasi Thucydidis commentarium secundum edidit, quoniam in priori ieiunior et contractior fuisse videbatur, Castig. secundae,* preface, III p. 1213), and once for 'explanation' without reference to a specific work (*sed haec, quae carptim cursimque velut semina materiae difficillimae libavimus, dilato in aliud tempus pleniore commentario, sufficiant, Castig. Glossemata* T 6,

---

[47] Cf. A. Poliziano, Della congiura dei Pazzi, ed. A. Perosa, Miscellanea erudita III (Padova, 1958), VI and 3.
[48] Cf. Marsil Ficin, Commentaire sur Le banquet de Platon, De l'amour, ed. P. Laurens (Paris, 2002), 5.
[49] Examples of Calderini's usage can be found in the parts of the prefaces published in F.-R. Hausmann, "Martialis, Marcus Valerius," in: Corpus Translationum et Commentariorum IV (Washington, 1980), 262–63.
[50] *Sunt tamen ... loci quidam in commentariis nostris paululum immutati, ne dixerim deprauati,* Venetiis: Baptista de Tortis, 24 Dec. 1482, HC 12238, all quotations are from sig. (R/ iv) recto.
[51] *Ep.* 22, Basileae: ex officina Henricpetrina, 1572, 368, anast. repr. in: Joannes Picus Mirandulanus, Opera omnia, con una premessa di Eugenio Garin. Tomus primus: Scripta in editione Basilensi anno MDLXXII collecta (Torino, 1971).
[52] A comprehensive example is Merula's letter of dedication accompanying his Juvenal-commentary to Federigo da Montefeltro, Venetiis : per Gabrielem Petri, 1478, sig. A ii r–v (HC 11090), partially printed in E. Sanford, "Juvenalis, Decimus Junius," in: CTC I (Washington, 1960), 221–22.

on *talentum*, III p. 1464). With the plural *commentarii* he designates Francesco Barbaro's *De re uxoria* (*paterni commentarii*, 1472)[53] and a work on birds (*Boethus ... qui Ornithogonia, id est de avitii natura commentarios reliquit, Castig. primae* 10,2,2, II p. 629).[54] There is a group of examples where Barbaro applies *commentarii* to philosophical works, such as Aristotle's metaphysics (*corruptos commentarios Aristotelis, Castig. primae* 5,202, II p. 433), a manuscript with works (the Aristotle–commentaries?) of Alexander of Aphrodisias (*commentarios Alexandri tuos, ep.* 123, II p. 39),[55] his own Themistius–translation (*in nostris commentariis, Castig. primae* 8,23, II p. 583), and the *commentarii quos in Posteriores Analyticos iam perfecimus* (*ep.* 115 II p. 33).[56] Comparable is Barbaro's use of *commentariolus* for his *compendium Ethicorum* (*ep.* 2 I p. 5).

Commentatio

In classical Latin the word means *actio cogitandi, deliberandi*, only from Pliny onwards it can be used for *scriptum, liber*, even rarer is the meaning *interpretatio librorum*, which was cultivated by Boethius. In general the word is popular with Cicero (15 instances), but used only infrequently by other authors (40 examples in all). The word seems to be practically nonexistent in Medieval Latin.[57]

The humanists, too, seem to use *commentatio* infrequently, for 'commentary' as well as for 'study'. Theodore Gaza thus designates Theophrast's *De plantis*: *commentationem plantarum attingere nemo ausus est*.[58] Calderini announces his

---

[53] *De coelibatu*, praef. 3, ed. V. Branca (Firenze, 1969), 55.
[54] The information comes from Athenaeus, *deipn.* 9,49.
[55] Addressed to Baldassare Meliavacca (1488).
[56] The work is contained in Bologna, Bibl. Univ. 124 under the title *Hermolai Barbari in primum Posteriorum enarratio*, see Branca, see n. 1, p. 129 n.8 = (repr.) p.68 n. 10. Its methodology is discussed by Panizza, see n. 1.
[57] MLW has one example (*opinio*), ibid., c. 954; DictBrit has none. This is confirmed by the Patrologia Latina Database, which among the Medieval authors furnishes only thirteen examples of *commentatio* (with a wide range of meanings): vol. 86 c. 1221D (*falsa c.*); 90 c. 1082B (*philosophorum vita c. mortis est*); 121 c. 519C (*fraudulosa c.*); 126 c. 460C (*praevaricatorem canonum, eisdem c.num tuarum vinculis astrictum*); 139 c. 1147B (*sapientium vita c. debeat esse mortis*, = 139 c. 1166C); 142 c. 41C (*diapsalma c.nem metri dixerunt esse*); 149 c. 101B (*verisimili c.ne*), 149 c. 0118B (*falsas c.nes*); 150 c. 1231D (*legantur ... libri Job, Tobias ... cum c.nibus*); 155 c. 1513C (*qui sacram Scripturam non putant aliud esse nisi hominum inventionem et c.nem*); 159 c. 397D (*statim omnis c. implacitandi Anselmum compressa omissa est*); 188 c. 631A (*inauditorum c.ne suppliciorum in torquendis miseris ... tripudiabat*). The Manuscripta Mediaevalia Datenbank (www.manuscripta–mediaevalia.de) yields only 19 examples (in more than 60000 manuscripts).
[58] In the preface to his translation of *De plantis* (1553/54), see C. B. Schmitt, "Theophrastus," CTC II (Washington, 1971), 267.

planned *commentationes in epistulas ad Atticum*.[59] Poliziano calls his own *Miscellanea commentationes* (*nostris commentationibus, Misc.* praef. 63 and 7,12). The word is consistently used by Pico; there, however, I have not found any example for 'commentary'. He applies it to unspecified philosophical writings in his famous letter to Barbaro from 1485: *etsi non egeant per se philosophiae commentationes amoenitate*,[60] and twice in the *Oratio de hominis dignitate* (1486): *Fuit enim cum ab antiquis omnibus hoc obseruatum, ut omne scriptorum genus euoluentes, nullas quas possent commentationes illectas preterirent* (30) and *me in primis annis, in tenera etate, per quam uix licuit ... aliorum legere commentationes, nouam afferre uelle philosophiam* (35).[61] Later, it is applied to Plato's and Aristotle's works, in *Adversus astrologiam divinatricem* (1492): *toto decursu suorum commentationum*.[62] Ficino once uses *commentatio* for the *actio* itself of explaining something (*Tommas autem Bencius Socratis diligens imitator ad socraticorum verborum commentationem libenti animo ... se contulit*).[63]

Barbaro's use coincides closely with Pico's; I have only found examples for *commentatio* as 'analysis', 'treatment of a topic', *Castig. primae, monitum*, (I p. 4): *si ulla commentatione cavendi sunt errores*, ibid. 1,7 (I p.17; explanation of the word *encyclopaedia* in Plin. nat. 1,14): *Aristoteles in Ethicis commentationes encyclias intelligit*, ibid. 4,74 (I p.214): *Recentiores qui hunc locum ex Plinio in commentationes suas transtulere, in eundem prolapsi sunt errorem*, *Coroll*. 28 (regarding an information from the pseudo–Aristotelian *De plantis*): *Haec commentatio Graecis perierat*, *ep*. 18 (I p. 26) and 19 (I p. 29; both Themistius). *Commentatio* as opposed to *annotatio*, *ep*. 115 (II p. 33): *inibo* (sc. *Aristotelis opera*) *naturalia et divina, item rhetorica et poetica, partim commentationibus, partim annotationibus ... instruens*.[64]

Commentum

Originally a participle of *comminisci*, in classical Latin the word means *id quod cogitamus*, mainly *cum nota figmenti, mendacii*, although there are a few instances where it means *scriptum, liber* (Martianus Capella) or *enthymema* (Quintilian). The

---

[59] In the *Epilogus* of his Statius–commentary, Brixiae: Henricus de Colonia, 1476, sig. (d7)v (HR 4244).
[60] *Ep*. 21,70, ed. in Ermolao Barbaro — Giovanni Pico della Mirandola, Filosofia o Eloquenza? A cura di F. Bausi, Sileni 2 (Napoli, 1998), 50.
[61] Giovanni Pico della Mirandola, Oratio de hominis dignitate. Rede über die Würde des Menschen. Auf der Textgrundlage der Editio princeps hg. und übers. von Gerd von der Gönna (Stuttgart, 1997), 56 and 48–50.
[62] Ed. E. Garin, 2 vols. (Firenze, 1946–1952), I p. 48.
[63] Commentarium in Convivium Platonis 6,1, ed. see n. 48.
[64] *Commentatio* here may mean a more ample treatment of a topic suggested by the text commented upon, whereas *annotatio* probably is to be understood as a commentary which accompanies the text closely. In the two other examples from Barbaro known to me, *annotatio* designates the *Castigationes Plinianae* (*Coroll*. 221 *ut in annotationibus libri undecimi docuimus*, 410 *Nos id in annotationes Plinianas distulimus*).

secondary meaning *interpretatio scriptorum* appears only late and remains rare; it is however used by Priscian to designate Donatus' Vergil–commentary and is contained in the title of Porphyrio's *commentum in Horatium Flaccum*. The word has a substantial medieval *fortuna*, which largely fits into the classical framework; the meanings 'book' and 'commentary' are well established.[65]

Renaissance readers must have been familiar with *commentum* as 'commentary, explanation' from the countless *commenta* transmitted in medieval manuscripts.[66] This meaning was noted by Valla, *Elegantiae* 4,21 (taken over by Perotti, *Cornu copiae* 44,9) and Tortelli.[67] Naturally the word could not be avoided, when titles of medieval works were quoted; an example is furnished by Pico in the *Conclusiones nonaginta*: *quod ratio Avenrois in commento ultimo primi Physicorum contra Auicennam concludat*.[68] Otherwise it seems relatively rare in our period (probably because of its medieval flavour). Often *commentum* is used for 'fiction, lie', the meaning codified by Perotti.[69]

In Barbaro *commentum* refers to the parts of the *Castigationes*, in the preface to the *Glossemata*: *In hoc quarto lucubrationis nostrae commento, pontifex maxime, continentur delectu quodam glossemata et expositiones* (III p.1353), in two other instances the

---

[65] MLW, ibid., c.955–56; J. F. Niermeyer and C. van de Kieft, Mediae Latinitatis Lexicon minus, revised by J.W.J. Burgers, I (Leiden, 2nd ed. 2002), 284; DictBrit does not have the entry. The difficulty of any kind of generalization about Medieval Latin is illustrated by the material cited in the Lexicon mediae et infimae latinitatis Polonorum II (Wroclaw, 1959–1967), 657–58, which nearly exclusively belongs to the groups *consilium, propositum (in malam partem)* or *mendacium*. The meaning 'commentary' is only documented with examples from the late 15th and 16th centuries.

[66] The on-line catalogue of the Hill Monastic Manuscript Library (URL: www.hmml.org) contains over a hundred entries with *Commentum* ... , the Manuscripta Mediaevalia Datenbank (www.manuscripta-mediaevalia.de) has several hundred corresponding items (including modern titles).

[67] *ponitur etiam ab auctoribus commentarius in singulari et masculino ac neutro in plurali in alia significatione hoc est pro expositione et interpretatione auctorum ... Quidam etiam talia huiusmodi opera commentum uocauerunt ut Nigidius: Donatus: Priscianus: Aliique nonnulli*, De orthographia, chapter *De syllabis desinentibus in M*, Romae: Ulrich Han (Udalricus Gallus) and Simon Nicolai Chardella, 1471, HC(+ Add) 15563.

[68] *Conclusiones sec. opinionem propriam* 2,43, ed. S. A. Farmer, Syncretism in the West: Pico's 900 Theses (1486). The Evolution of Traditional Religious and Philosophical Systems, MRTS 167 (Tempe, 1998).

[69] *Cornu copiae* 44,9–10, vol. 6 p. 247. Examples are Calderini in the Statius–commentary *Praxitelen exclamasse: '...' atque ita Phrynen eo commento deprehendisse hoc (i. statua Cupidinis) pulcherrimum esse*, commentary on Silv. 2, 7, 16, Romae: A. Pannartz, 1475 (HC 14983). and Beroaldo in the *Annotationes centum* (62,1): *sicut Lacedemonii ueteres facere consueuerunt, qui, occultare uolentes litteras publice ad imperatores suos missas ne ab hostibus exceptae consilia sua reuelarent, epistolas mirando commento scriptas mittebant*, ed. in: Filippo Beroaldo the Elder, Annotationes centum, ed. L. A. Ciapponi, MRTS 131 (Binghamton, 1995).

word designates (insufficient) explanations: *Castig. primae* 11,32,5 (II p. 667): *alios nomen loci Calvum credere, alios praefecti custodiarum, vanissimo utrumque commento,* and *Glossemata* S 75 (III 1452) *deridicula quaedam commenta et plane sordida confinxerunt.*

Commentari

In classical Latin the verb is mainly used for *meditari, disserere (apud audientes),* only in Pliny (and rarely later) for *cogitata scripto explicare, scribere,* and even rarer, from Suetonius onward, for *scripta explicare.* Some Christian authors also used the word for *imaginari, fingere.* Within a wide range of meanings, Medieval Latin retains 'to treat in writing' as well as 'to write a commentary'.[70]

In the period in question the verb seems to have been used more sparingly than some of the nouns from the same family. The examples I have collected mainly illustrate the use for 'to discourse on a topic', so already Alberti in *De re aedificatoria* (4,1,453): *nobis, qui aedificia commentamur.*[71] Beroaldo the Elder uses it to designate his *Annotationes centum* (praef. 8): *nec ulli obesse uolumus detrahendo, sed pluribus prodesse cupimus commentando* (i.e. the composition of his *Annotationes*). In Bembo's *De Aetna* (ca. 1493) the verb is used for his own theorizing as opposed to what he had seen or heard from others: *si ea lege inceperis, ut nequod pulchrum praetereatur, siue uidisti aliquid, siue audiuisti, siue quid es ipse commentatus.*[72] A similar meaning ('compose') we find in Valla, *Gesta Ferdinandi* (3,10,8): *Aduersus hanc orationem, multis iam annis commentatam meditatamque ... hortabatur rex ut concordie ecclesie, ut saluti animarum, ut conscientie consuleret.*[73] Ficino uses *commentari* for the contents of his comparison of the sun and God (though some kind of explanation of the Greek texts he translates is clearly implicit): *Leges ergo feliciter, Phoebee princeps, quae de comparatione solis ad Deum partim Plato Dionysiusque Areopagita tractarunt partim ego interpretor atque commentor.*[74] A similar ambivalence may also be present in Perotti's *Cornu copiae* (41,33) *Ab hoc Pyrrhonii dicti sunt philosophi, qui a Graecis* Σκεπτικοί *..., hoc est commentantes et ueluti quaestores quidam ac consyderatores appellantur.*

Equally *commentari* is used for the critical study of other texts, normally written commentaries. I quote two examples. Valla, *eleg.* 2,15: *Sergius quoque commentans Donatum* (the *Explanationes* or *Comentaria in artem Donati,* the name *Sergius* is a

---

[70] *MLW,* ibid. c.955; DictBrit, ibid. p.393.
[71] L. B. Alberti, L'Architettura [*De re aedificatoria*], testo latino e trad. a cura di G. Orlandi, intr. e note di P. Portoghesi, 2 vols. (Milano, 1966), I, 271.
[72] Venetiis: Aldus Manutius Romanus, Feb. 1495/96, HC 2765*, sig. A6r.
[73] *Laurentii Valle Gesta Ferdinandis Regis Aragonum,* ed. O. Besomi, Thesaurus mundi 10 (Patavii, 1973), 170–71.
[74] Ficino, letter from 1493, ed. R. Hartkamp, no. 6, published at the URL: http://www.phil.uni-freiburg.de/SFB541/B5/Eberhard/Ficino.html, 14. 3. 2002.

corruption for *Servius*), Sabellicus, *Reparatio*: *Angeli Sabini turrensis ... maior in commentando auctoritas* (Sabellicus is referring to the *Paradoxa in Iuvenalem*, [Bottari: 154–55]). The word exceptionally designates an oral commentary in Perotti, *Cornu copiae* 31,18 (about the disciples of Pythagoras): *is autem, qui tacebat, quae dicebantur ab aliis audiebat neque percontari, si parum intellexerat, neque commentari, quae audierat, fas erat.*[75]

Barbaro uses *commentari* for a treatment of a specific topic, with reference to the *Corollarium*: *ego alias ... multa de saccharo commentatus sum* (*ep.* n.d. 7 II p. 91), about other discourses e.g. *Castig. primae* 1,54 (I p. 33): *Appion certe, ut Plinius testatur, de metallica medicina commentatus est*, *Coroll.* 83: *nos Plinium secuti sumus, quamquam de myrrha commentantem.* A parallel to the passage from Ficino quoted above is in *ep.* 17 (I p. 26, about the Themistius): *hoc genus commentandi vertendique.*

This overview could easily be enlarged through inclusion of more texts and other words.[76] Even the limited material presented suggests some conclusions about the Latin of the period in question and its relationship to previous phases of the same language; obviously their validity must remain confined to the words analysed here. Medieval Latin mainly seems to have had a negative impact; *commentum* for 'commentary' is popular in the Middle Ages, but rarely used by the humanists, even though they knew that the usage was attested in antiquity. For exclusively medieval usages such as *commentarius* for 'register' I have not found any examples in humanist literature. Obviously it was classical Latin which presented the norm our humanists aspired to conform to. Not in the least because the Latin of classical antiquity was not a static entity, attempts to reproduce it were bound to lead to wildly differing results. As we have seen, authors such as Priscian and Boethius — who in the eyes of the humanists hardly represented Latin in its purest form — coined usages that thrived in humanist Latin. Another decisive influence were the needs and preferences of the humanists themselves. As our discussion of *res latina* shows (see n. 30), the humanists themselves coined expressions, which through their appropriateness and frequent repetition became part of humanist Latin although they were not of classical origin. Even though Barbaro's Latin generally shows a certain independence, it may not be a conincidence that there are similarities with Pico. In all, his Latin exemplifies, what S. Rizzo recently has

---

[75] The unquestioned authority of Pythagoras' doctrines amongst his disciples is often mentioned in antiquity, e.g. Cic. nat. deor. 1,10, Val. Max. 8,15 ext.1, Quint. inst. 11,1,27; more material has been collected by E. F. Rice. jr., ed., The Prefatory Epistles of Jacques Lefèvre d'Etaples and Related Texts, New York & London 1972, 282.

[76] More material will be presented in my Neulateinische Wortliste, URL: http//www.lrz–muenchen.de/~ramminger/index.htm

called "the dialectical movement between tradition and innovation which is one of the most fascinating characteristics of humanism."[77]

Johann Ramminger   Thesaurus Linguae Latinae, Munich

---

[77] S. Rizzo, Ricerche sul latino umanistico, Storia e letteratura 213 (Roma, 2002), 149: " ... di quella dialettica fra tradizione e innovazione che è tra gli aspetti più affascinanti del periodo umanistico."

Filippo Beroaldo on Apuleius: Bringing Antiquity to Life[*]

JULIA HAIG GAISSER

Filippo Beroaldo (1453–1505) was one of the most prolific scholars of his time as well as one of the most famous teachers in Europe.[1] He taught his students at the University of Bologna all day long: in large lectures of two or three hundred in the morning and in smaller groups or individual tutorials in the afternoons.[2] Many of these students were foreign, for Beroaldo's reputation extended far beyond Italy. They came from Spain and France, but above all from Germany and eastern Europe; indeed, a contemporary chronicler tells us both that he had two hundred students "from the other side of the Alps" and that they all left Bologna after his death.[3] Beroaldo achieved his success not only through his learning but also through the charismatic personality that he presented in the classroom and projected all over Europe by means of his printed commentaries. Perhaps his most striking quality, however, was the almost necromantic ability to bring the world of the ancient author into that of fifteenth–century Bologna — not as a dead artifact but as a living entity reflecting both the everyday experience and the religious and moral aspirations of himself and his students. We do not have a transcription of any of Beroaldo's lectures.[4] But we can get an excellent idea of them from his commen-

---

[*] I want to thank the Afton Historical Society Press for permission to publish some of the material in this paper that appeared in an earlier version in my article, "Reading Apuleius with Filippo Beroaldo," in Philip Thibodeau and Harry Haskell, eds., Being There Together: Essays in Honor of Michael C. J. Putnam on the Occasion of His Seventieth Birthday (Afton, Minnesota, 2003), 24–42.

[1] For Beroaldo's life see especially Konrad Krautter, Philologische Methode und humanistische Existenz. Filippo Beroaldo und sein Kommentar zum Goldenen Esel des Apuleius (München, 1971). See also Anna Rose, Filippo Beroaldo der Ältere und sein Beitrag zur Properz–Überlieferung (München and Leipzig, 2001), 4–150.

[2] Beroaldo describes his teaching in a letter of 1499 to Pietro Váradi, dedicatee of his commentary on Apuleius: *Lectionibus publicis distringor, quarum quottidiani auditores sunt circiter tercenteni; occupatum quoque occupant privatae lectiones, quarum sitientes sunt complusculi principes scholasticorum*, Modena, Biblioteca Estense, Ms. Campori App. 324 (γ, S, 5, 25) fol. 23v ff., quoted from Eugenio Garin, "Note sull'insegnamento di Filippo Beroaldo il vecchio," in La cultura filosofica del Rinascimento italiano (Florence, 1961), 377.

[3] "Era in questa terra doxento scholari oltramontani per lui, che dopo la soa morte tutti se partino," Fileno dalla Tuata, in Bologna, Biblioteca Universitaria, ms. 1438, fol. 277v, quoted from Ludovico Frati, "I due Beroaldi," Studi e memorie per la storia dell'Università di Bologna 2 (1911), 212.

[4] But some tantalizing student lecture notes from his 1495 course on Statius' *Thebaid* have been preserved. See Italo Mariotti, "Lezioni di Beroaldo il vecchio sulla *Tebaide*," in Roberto Cardini et al., eds., Tradizione classica e letteratura umanistica. Per Alessandro Perosa (Rome, 1985), II, 577–93.

tary on the 'Golden Ass'.⁵ This work, which was written for his course on Apuleius, brings us into the lecture hall and almost lets us hear his voice.

In this paper I will look at some of the ways in which Beroaldo brought Apuleius to life for his students and readers. My discussion has as its starting point several observations made over thirty years ago by Konrad Krautter in his fundamental study of Beroaldo's commentary. Krautter treated the commentary both as an expression of Beroaldo's personality and character and as a work in which Beroaldo linked Apuleius' world with his own. He pointed out Beroaldo's affinity with Apuleius, categorized his contemporary allusions, and suggested that in the digressions for which he is so famous, Beroaldo was both imitating Apuleius' technique and attempting to make philological commentary into a literary genre in its own right.⁶ In what follows, I will explore and amplify Krautter's ideas, but from a somewhat different perspective. I am particularly interested in Beroaldo's public persona and in his use of personal and contemporary references for both pedagogical and literary effect. I will suggest that in his digressions Beroaldo made both Apuleius and himself more interesting to his audience, and that in some of them he presented himself as a worthy emulator of Apuleius, creating his own small but self–conscious works of literary art. I will close with an epilogue on the ways in which Beroaldo promoted himself and his work to achieve celebrity and wealth.

Like all Renaissance teachers (and medieval teachers before them), Beroaldo directed his lectures directly to the text, going through it line by line and word by word, explaining as he went. In a commentary, and hence in the lectures for which it was used, Beroaldo provided not merely a course on a particular author, but a whole education in Roman antiquity. As he explained the words and ideas of the ancient author, he explained usage and etymology, to be sure, but also custom, law, mythology, religion, and history. Each course (and commentary) was an encyclopedia of the past — diffuse, discursive, constantly straying from the work at hand into other texts and genres.

---

⁵ *Commentarii a Philippo Beroaldo conditi in Asinum aureum Lucii Apuleii* (Bologna, 1500). The fundamental study is Krautter's Philologische Methode und humanistische Existenz. See also Maria Teresa Casella, "Il metodo dei commentatori umanistici esemplato sul Beroaldo," Studi medievali 16 (1975), 627–701; Julia Haig Gaisser, "Teaching Classics in the Renaissance: Two Case Histories," Transactions of the American Philological Association 131 (2001), 1–21.
⁶ Krautter, Philologische Methode und humanistische Existenz, 40–52. And compare his comment (p. 50): "Denn offensichtlich betrachtet er den philologischen Kommentar nicht nur als gelehrtes Hilfsmittel, sondern geradezu als literarische Gattung mit durchaus künstlerischen Ansprüchen."

A single example will suffice. Beroaldo's commentary on Apuleius is a large folio volume of nearly 600 pages. The commentary dominates and literally surrounds the text. The first page contains little more than the first four lines of the novel:

> *At ego tibi sermone isto milesio varias fabulas conseram: auresque tuas benivolas: lepido susurro permulceam: modo si papyrum egyptiam: argutia* ... (*Met.* 1.1.1 in Beroaldo, *Commentarii in Asinum Aureum*, fol. 5r).

> Well now, I am going to thread together different tales for you in the Milesian style you like and caress your ears into approval with a beguiling whisper — provided that [you don't mind looking at] an Egyptian papyrus ...[7]

Beroaldo's comments on these lines range from the assertion that Apuleius has written his preface in verse, to a note on the force of the opening word, *at*, to a long discussion of Milesian tales (with a quick correction of a passage in Jerome), and to another of papyrus and the ancient papyrus business. Perhaps most interesting from a literary point of view is his speculation that Apuleius may have used the phrase *lepido susurro* (beguiling whisper) to show that his words were "not to be disclosed or openly made known to the uninitiated, but revealed in secret in the presence of reverent ears."[8] Like many modern readers, it seems, Beroaldo is already looking ahead to the end of the novel and Lucius' initiations into the mysteries of Isis and Osiris. On a single page he has touched on Latin usage, text criticism, literary history, the technical details of ancient book production, and something that we could call literary criticism.

At this point, however, we might be inclined to wonder what made Beroaldo's lectures so exciting that students flocked to him from all over Europe. The first page of his commentary, although diverse and informative, is hardly riveting. Yet his students were obviously enthralled. Why? Partly, of course, because of Beroaldo's tremendous erudition and their own thirst for knowledge. But that cannot have been all. Successful teaching on the scale achieved by Beroaldo demands more than erudition and interested students. On the one hand, it requires showmanship, personality, and self-promotion. On the other, it requires something to promote. In the case of the 'Golden Ass' that was Beroaldo's deep engagement with Apuleius, his understanding of the ways in which the life and experience of his students could be used to illuminate the

---

[7] Unless otherwise noted, all translations are my own.
[8] *Potest et ob hoc videri usus hac dictione susurro, ut ostendat haec non esse invulganda neque prophanis palam nuntianda sed clam apud aures religiosas promenda* ..., Beroaldo, *Commentarii in Asinum Aureum*, fol. 5r.

ancient text, and his ambition to emulate Apuleius as a literary artist. I will begin with this aspect of Beroaldo's teaching, and come back to his flair for self-promotion at the end.

In order to link the world of everyday experience in the 'Golden Ass' to the life and customs of his own time Beroaldo constantly interjects lively digressions into his line–by–line discussion of the text.[9]

Sometimes his juxtaposition of past and present takes the form of a simple comparison. In Book 9 of the novel the fuller's wife hides her lover under the wicker cage on which clothes were bleached with sulphur fumes.[10] Beroaldo comments:

> *Foeminae nostrates hoc hodie quoque usurpant, ut scilicet sub cavea viminea circumdent velamenta, eaque fumo sulphuris suppositi impune candificent inalbentque,* (*Commentarii in Asinum Aureum*, fol. 207r).

Our women make use of this today too, so that they put their clothes all around under a wicker cage and safely bleach and whiten them with the fumes of the sulphur below.

At *Met.* 8.29.2 the charlatan priests of the Syrian goddess use a false prophecy to cheat a farmer out of his fattest ram, and Beroaldo exclaims:

> *Dii boni, quam saepe hoc videri contingit in territorio nostro, ut quaedam hominum mendicabula sub religionis praetextu tamquam ministratores sint antistitesque divi Pauli et Antonii, circumeant castella pagos villas et quibusdam affaniis vaticinationem mentientes prospera denunciantes divos quos palam iactitant propicios futuros spondentes ab rustico hoc bruto et credulo poscant et accipiant arietem, ab illo gallinas, ova, caseum, ab alio porcellum, ab alio supersticioso et attonito tritici sestarium,* (*Commentarii in Asinum Aureum*, fol. 188r).[11]

Good gods! How often we see this going on in our own territory, that certain mendicants, posing on the pretext of religion as servants and priests of Saint Paul and Saint Anthony, wander the towns and countryside and farms; and making up a prophecy with some hocus pocus, announcing good fortune, promising that the saints they boast of will be well disposed, from one foolish and credulous rustic they demand and

---

[9] See Krautter, Philologische Methode und humanistische Existenz, 40–52. For a useful but incomplete list of Beroaldo's digressions, see Casella, "Il metodo," 685–701.

[10] [E]*undem illum subiectum contegit viminea cavea, quae fustium flexu tereti in rectum aggerata cumulum lacinias circumdatas suffusa candido fumo sulpuris inalbabat*, Apuleius, *Met.* 9.24.2.

[11] Beroaldo's use of Apuleian vocabulary in this passage is worth noting. *affaniae (afannae)* is attested only in Apuleius (cf. *afannas Met.* 9.8.4, *Met.* 10.10.2). *mendicabulum* (used in Plautus) appears three times in Apuleius in singular or plural (*Met.* 9.4.3; *Apol.* 22.9; *Fl.* 9.9), but not again before the fourth century (TLL VIII. 705).

receive a ram, from a second hens, eggs, cheese, from one a suckling pig, from another superstitious and astonished soul a measure of grain.

In other cases Beroaldo conflates his world and Apuleius', eliding their differences. He so admires Lucius' hymn to the moon at *Met.* 11.25.1–6 that he considers it worthy of the Virgin Mary herself:

Hac rogata dea nostra non minus placaretur fieretque propitia, quam omnibus sanctorum orationibus, (*Commentarii in Asinum Aureum,* fol. 275v)

If our goddess were called upon by this prayer, she would be no less won over and propitiated than by all the prayers of the saints.

Digressions like these are liberally sprinkled throughout the commentary — and not by accident. They are a part of the design of Beroaldo's work, as he says in the preface:

Interdum ex instituto prope peculiari, flosculos ex doctrinarum prato decerptos decenter intexui, et more pictorum parerga frequenter adieci, quibus lassescens lector reficeretur, (*Commentarii in Asinum Aureum,* fol. 2v).

Sometimes in accordance with my particular custom I have neatly woven in little flowers plucked from the meadow of learning, and I have frequently added extra details [*parerga*] as painters do, so that the flagging reader might be refreshed.

Beroaldo's digressions undoubtedly did provide variety and refreshment to his readers — and to the three hundred students in his lecture hall. By opening a window — many windows, in fact — from Apuleius' world into that of contemporary Bologna, the digressions brought the ancient novel to life — or we could say that they brought modern life into the ancient novel. But that is not their only function. Beroaldo's digressions correspond to the embedded tales in the 'Golden Ass', and he uses them in imitation of Apuleius' technique.[12] He even describes them in similar language. Like Beroaldo's digressions, Apuleius' embedded tales refresh the flagging reader and provide variety with artfully disposed "little flowers."[13] Apuleius' digressions refresh the commentator as well, as Beroaldo points out in his elaborate introduction to the first adultery tale in Book 9 (*Met.* 9.5–7):

---

[12] Krautter, Philologische Methode und humanistische Existenz, 40–52. See also Casella, "Il metodo," 660–9.

[13] E.g., on the story of the adulterous slave and his terrible punishment related at *Met.* 8.22: *Hac narrationis varietate quibusdam quasi flosculis exornat venustat Lucius noster suum hoc opus, ne lectores morosa continuatae narrationis aequalitate lassescant,* Beroaldo, *Commentarii in Asinum Aureum,* fol. 180r. Also see Krautter, Philologische Methode und humanistische Existenz, 50.

> *Nos quoque mythopoion, hoc est opificem fabellae, Lucium nostrum latialiter personantem et graphice lepidissimeque explicantem inaudiamus legamus pensitemus auribus oculis animis lubentibus, cum talibus egressionum amoenitatibus non solum lectores verum etiam commentatores reficiantur,* (*Commentarii in Asinum Aureum,* fol. 193v).

With willing ears, eyes, and minds let us also hear and read and ponder our Lucius as a *mythopoios* [that is, "story maker"] giving utterance in Latin and explaining vividly and with great charm, since by such delightful digressions not only readers but commentators, too, are refreshed.

Introducing Apuleius' tale of the crimes of the condemned murderess (*Met.* 10.23–28), Beroaldo claims for him the painter's license to embellish his work with extra details (*parerga*). Both the word and the comparison echo Beroaldo's description of his own additions in the preface.[14]

Most of Beroaldo's digressions are used in a general imitation of Apuleius — breaking up the steady stream of his line–by–line exposition as Apuleius breaks up the forward march of his narration, and often highlighted with Apuleian diction and vocabulary.[15] But in several cases he achieves a more elaborate effect. In a digression in Book 2 Beroaldo's contemporary and literary interests completely overshadow an essential moment in the novel. The hero Lucius has been invited to the house of his mother's old friend Byrrhena, where he sees a sculpture of Diana and Actaeon, which he describes in a detailed ecphrasis (*Met.* 2.4.3–10). Lucius admires the sculpture, but he fails to understand its obvious warning of the dangers of curiosity. Apuleius' imaginary statue depicts Diana standing in a grotto with her dogs on either side. The image of the voyeur Actaeon appears twice — once in stone, and again, reflected in the pool beneath the goddess's feet — "already animal–like, on the point of becoming a stag."[16] Modern readers shiver with ominous anticipation a line or so later when the kindly Byrrhena tells Lucius, "Everything you see belongs to you."[17] But this is not what concerns Beroaldo. He is fasci-

---

[14] *Inseritur tempestiviter haec fabula ... quae narratione lepida et speciosa demulceat aures animosque lectorum, et sicut pictoribus datum est excurrere in parerga, idem quoque ius plausibiliter conceditur luculentis auctoribus, ut in parecbases in egressiones favorabiliter exspacientur. Qua in re prope eximius est Lucius noster, qui fabellis intextis et id genus parergis reficit lectorem nauseamque discutiens omne tedium levat,* Beroaldo, *Commentarii in Asinum Aureum,* fol. 239r. Compare the phrase *more pictorum parerga* on fol. 2v quoted above.

[15] Casella argues that Beroaldo's excurses imitate the style of whatever author he is commenting on ("Il metodo," 667). See also note 12 above.

[16] *iam in cervum ferinus, Met.* 2.4.10. The translation is by P. G. Walsh, The Golden Ass (Oxford, 1994), 20.

[17] *'Tua sunt' ait Byrrhena 'cuncta quae vides,' Met.* 2.5.1.

nated by Apuleius' insistence on the naturalistic quality of the statue, and a single phrase in the description — *ars aemula naturae* (art rivalling nature) — prompts him to launch into a digression on a contemporary example of artistic realism — a recently completed religious painting. Beroaldo comments:

> *Me ista condente artem emulam naturae esse evidenter ostendit municeps meus Francia,* (*Commentarii in Asinum Aureum,* fol. 34v).

> While I was writing this commentary, my fellow townsman Francia clearly demonstrated that art rivals nature.[18]

Beroaldo has a definite painting in mind — an Adoration of Christ that Francesco Francia painted for a church in Bologna around 1499.[19] The religious message conveyed by Francia's tender picture of the infant Christ is antithetical to that of Apuleius' imaginary statue of the vengeful goddess. But, again, this is not what concerns Beroaldo. His interest is in an exciting contemporary event in Bologna, the dedication of Francia's painting and its occasion, the return of Antongaleazzo Bentivoglio, a member of Bologna's reigning family, from a pilgrimage to Jerusalem. Beroaldo's digression pays an obvious compliment both to his friend Francia and to the ruling Bentivogli, but it was also designed to make a vivid impression in the lecture hall. Antongaleazzo's return, the painting, and the ceremonies attending its dedication would all have been fresh in the minds of his students, and Beroaldo could have expected his allusion to the event to catch and hold their interest.

But he had a literary purpose as well. Beroaldo's discussion of Francia's painting is the centerpiece in an excursus on the topic *ars aemula naturae* in which he not only compliments Francia, but also suggests that he himself is an artist — with words. The digression is symmetrically structured, framing the account of Francia and his work with general comments on art and nature and illustrative quotations. Beroaldo begins with a striking gloss on the phrase *ars aemula naturae*: *Imitatrix studiosa effectrix* (imitator, devotee, creator). He continues: *Ars enim naturam imitatur eamque usquequaque effingere ac representare contendit* (Indeed,

---

[18] The passage is translated and discussed by Michael Baxendall and E. H. Gombrich "Beroaldus on Francia," Journal of the Warburg and Courtauld Institutes 25 (1962), 113–15. (But they wrongly render the phrase *me ista condente* as "in my opinion" [113].)

[19] As Beroaldo notes (*Commentarii in Asinum Aureum,* fol. 34v), the work was commissioned by Antongaleazzo Bentivoglio on his return from a pilgrimage to Jerusalem. The painting is to be dated between his return (23 October 1498) and the publication of Beroaldo's commentary. See Baxandall and Gombrich, "Beroaldus on Francia," 114 n. 7. It was placed over the altar of S. Maria della Misericordia, but is now in the Pinacoteca in Bologna. For an illustration see Baxendall and Gombrich, plate 18a. The painting shows Antongaleazzo Bentivoglio kneeling next to the virgin, and some art historians believe that the shepherd standing at the far right is another member of the Bentivoglio family.

art imitates nature and strives to portray and recall her in every possible respect). Three quotations follow: from *Ad Herennium*, the elder Pliny, and Plato. The quotations are different in kind, and each is directed to a different point: the quotation from *Ad Herennium* to the guiding power of nature, that from Pliny to the importance of following nature, not other artists, and that from Plato to the creative power of art. The quotations from *Ad Herennium* and Plato are taken out of context and rephrased, as Baxandall and Gombrich have noted.[20]

Now let us look more closely. First, Beroaldo's quotation from *Ad Herennium*:

Libro tertio rethoricorum ad herennium. Imitatur inquit ars naturam et quod ea desiderat inveniet si quod ostendit sequatur, (*Commentarii in Asinum Aureum*, fol. 34v).

In book three of the *Rhetorica ad Herennium* the author says, "Art imitates nature and will discover what nature requires if she follows her example".

The quotation is not exact. The sentence in *Ad Herennium* reads:

Imitetur ars igitur naturam, et, quod ea desiderat id inveniat, quod ostendit sequatur, (*Rhet. Her.* 3.22).

Therefore, let art imitate nature, let her discover what nature requires, and let her follow her example.

For the exhortation in *Ad Herennium* Beroaldo has substituted a general principle: for him it is not that art should imitate nature but that she does, and that she will succeed by following nature's example. He has obviously "misquoted," but he has not done so carelessly.[21] Rather, he has tailored the "quotation" to suit his own context, and to bolster his opening assertion, *Ars enim naturam imitatur eamque usquequaque effingere ac representare contendit*. It is tempting, however, to suspect that Beroaldo has not completely ignored the context in *Ad Herennium*. He has taken his quotation from a passage on the role of nature and art in memory: by nature, the ancient author tells us, unusual events are

---

[20] Baxandall and Gombrich, "Beroaldus on Francia," 114–15.
[21] *Pace* Baxandall and Gombrich ("Beroaldus on Francia," 114): "the interest of the piece [Beroaldo's digression] lies ... in the clarity with which it brings into view some aspects of the relationship between humanist criticism and its sources in ancient literature: the dependence on memory in quotation, the degree of misacception, and the curious standards of relevance." Humanist reading practices are more complicated than this comment suggests. For a useful summary, see James Hankins, Plato in the Italian Renaissance (Leiden, 1991), I, 18–26.

more memorable than ordinary ones.[22] The idea provides an appropriate background for Beroaldo's digression on Francia's painting, concerned as it is to evoke a striking and out-of-the way occasion that was, as we might say, naturally memorable.

Beroaldo's quotation from Pliny is more straightforward. Quoting very closely, but not quite exactly, from *Naturalis historia* 34.61, he recalls the story of the painter Eupompus, who was asked which of his predecessors he followed. Pointing to a great crowd of people, he replied: "naturam ipsam imitandam esse non artificem" (nature herself is what one should imitate — not an artist).[23]

Beroaldo's quotation from Plato is a partial and selective citation, not of Plato himself, but of Ficino's Latin translation:

Plato volumine decimo de legibus tradit omnia natura et arte fieri, artemque ipsam simulacra veritatis genuisse, (Commentarii in Asinum Aureum, fol. 34v).

In the tenth book of his 'Laws' Plato teaches that all things are made by nature and art, and that art herself has created images of reality.

Compare Ficino:

Res omnes nonnulli aiunt, quae fiunt, quae futurae, quaeque factae sunt, vel natura, vel fortuna, vel arte fieri .... Ex quibus artem postea mortalem a mortalibus factam, posteriores quasdam res genuisse, non penitus veritatis participes, sed simulacra quaedam sibi ipsi cognata, qualia pictura, musica, caeteraque artes his similes generant.[24]

Some say that all things that are made, will be made, or have been made, are made by nature, by chance, or by art. ... From these, art, a mortal entity made afterwards by mortals, created secondary things not fully partaking of reality, but images of it related to herself — the sort of things that painting, music, and other similar arts create.

We can easily convict Beroaldo of quoting out of context, for he wrongly attributes to Plato himself views that Plato cites as those of the materialists with whom he disagrees.[25] He is also guilty of misrepresenting his source: in Plato there are three creative forces (nature, chance, and art) not only nature and art,

---

[22] In the sentence just before our passage, for example: *Docet ergo se natura vulgari et usitata re non exsuscitari, novitate et insigni quodam negotio commoveri, Rhet. Her.* 3.22.

[23] *Celebratum est Eupompi pictoris responsum qui interrogatus quem sequeretur antecedentium, dixisse fertur, demonstrata hominum multitudine naturam ipsam imitandam esse, non artificem,* Beroaldo, *Commentarii in Asinum Aureum,* fol. 34v.

[24] *Omnia divini Platonis opera tralatione Marsilii Ficini, emendatione, et ad graecum codicem collatione Simonis Grynaei* (Lugduni, 1548), 590–1. Cf. Plato, "Laws" 888–9.

[25] Baxandall and Gombrich, "Beroaldus on Francia," 114.

as Beroaldo asserts. Again, Beroaldo's changes are deliberate. He has tailored his "quotation" for his own rhetorical purposes: to emphasize the link between nature and art, to demonstrate art's creative power, and to characterize its productions as "images of reality."

It is at this point — after his preamble and three quotations — that Beroaldo introduces Francia and his painting as a modern and vivid demonstration of the proposition *ars aemula naturae*. In the Francia section, too, he artfully employs quotations, this time to compliment Francia and Antongaleazzo. Echoing Statius' characterization of his wealthy patron and friend Atedius Melior, he describes Antongaleazzo as *in omni vitae colore tersissimus* (most cultivated in every aspect of life).[26] Quoting Pliny's comment on Phidias, he begins his concluding sentence on Francia: *haec obiter dicta sint de artifice nunquam satis laudato* (let these things be said in passing about an artist who can never be praised enough).[27]

Beroaldo ends his digression with a final quotation, this time from his favorite model, Apuleius himself (the source is *De mundo* 20):

> *Artes autem ipsae naturam imitantes ex imparibus paria faciunt. Pictura vero peculiariter ex discordibus pigmentorum coloribus confusione modica temperatis imagines his quae imitatur similes facit*, (*Commentarii in Asinum Aureum*, fol. 34v).[28]

> Indeed, the arts themselves in imitation of nature make like things from unlike. But painting, in a particular way — from clashing colors of paint mixed in the right proportions — makes images like the things it imitates.

This conclusion achieves both a complimentary and a literary purpose. Its complimentary purpose is obvious: the reference to painting indirectly praises Francia and his imitative and creative powers. The literary purpose is more subtle, and it is achieved through both the source and the content of the quotation. By quoting Apuleius, and specifically in the context of a digression (or we might better say, of a digression on a digression, since Beroaldo has been commenting on Apuleius' ecphrastic excursus on Byrrhena's statue group), Beroaldo alludes to his imitation of Apuleius' technique. Indeed, his whole digression embodies and exemplifies what he has said of both his own and Apuleius' digressions. I give only one example, the programmatic announcement from his preface quoted above:

---

[26] Cf. *vir optime nec minus in iudicio litterarum quam in omni vitae colore tersissime*, Stat. *Silv.* 2, *praef.*
[27] The translation is that of Baxendall and Gombrich, "Beroaldus on Francia," 114. Cf. *Haec sint obiter dicta de artifice numquam satis laudato*, Plin., *Nat. Hist.* XXXVI. 19.
[28] Beroaldo has slightly abridged Apuleius, omitting his words *atris atque albis, luteis et puniceis* after *coloribus*.

Interdum ex instituto prope peculiari, flosculos ex doctrinarum prato decerptos decenter intexui, et more pictorum parerga frequenter adieci, quibus lassescens lector reficeretur, (*Commentarii in Asinum Aureum*, fol. 2v).

In the digresssion on the theme *ars aemula naturae* Beroaldo has indeed "woven in little flowers plucked from the meadow of learning" and "added extra details as painters do," but his technique has also been like the one Apuleius attributed to painting in the passage from *De mundo*. He has painted a picture with words, using a palette of different, if not clashing, sources: *Ad Herennium*, Pliny, Ficino's Plato, Statius, and Apuleius. Like Francia, he too is an artist.

Beroaldo creates even more elaborate effects in his discussion of the longest and most important embedded tale in the 'Golden Ass', the story of Cupid and Psyche at the heart of the novel. Using three long digressions of his own, he makes his commentary on the tale the centerpiece of his *Apuleius*. The digressions are strategically placed. Beroaldo opens his "Cupid and Psyche" with an elaborate discussion of Fulgentius and allegory (*Met.* 4.28.1), punctuates it near the middle with a description of the villa of his friend Mino de' Rossi at the beginning of *Met.* 5, and closes it with an autobiographical account of his own marriage (*Met.* 6.24.4). The digressions are different in kind. The first is an essay on hermeneutics, the second an ecphrasis, and the third an autobiographical idyll that functions as a sphragis or seal. All are metaliterary and self–referential — commenting, we could say, on Beroaldo commenting on Apuleius.

In the first digression (on hermeneutics) Beroaldo presents a programmatic statement in three parts: a discussion of the word *fabula*, a quotation of Fulgentius, and a declaration of his own method.[29]

Beroaldo's long discussion of *fabula* is ostensibly motivated both by the words of the old woman telling the story (she characterizes her narrative as "old wives' tales," *anilibus fabulis*) and by her fairy–tale opening: *Erant in quadam civitate rex et regina* (*Met.* 4.28.1). But Beroaldo also has something else in mind, for *fabula* was a hermeneutically loaded word, as both he and his audience were well aware. Discussion of the *fabula* had a rich and convoluted history, and its legitimacy and correct interpretation had been argued by not only late–antique authorities like Macrobius, Martianus Capella, and Fulgentius but also their mediaeval and Renaissance counterparts.[30] Beroaldo completely side–steps this debate, both by treating *fabula* as a lexical item to be defined instead of a

---

[29] Beroaldo, *Commentarii in Asinum Aureum*, fol. 95r–v.
[30] See Peter Dronke, Fabula: Explorations into the Uses of Myth in Medieval Platonism (Leiden and Cologne, 1974), 14–78; Paule Demats, Fabula. Trois Études de mythographie antique et médiévale (Geneva, 1973), 5–60.

genre to be discussed, and by systematically omitting any definition that would necessitate interpreting it philosophically or metaphysically. Macrobius and his successors had categorized, valued, and argued about the various types of fables.[31] Beroaldo, however, although ostensibly giving a systematic account of the meaning and use of *fabula* and its synonyms, in fact does nothing of the sort. Although he gives a large number of definitions, in fact he recognizes only three categories of fable: the practical story with its concluding moral, the obvious untruth, and the plausible plot of a play.[32] This treatment of *fabula* deliberately undercuts the next section of his digression, the allegorical account of "Cupid and Psyche" by Fulgentius the Mythographer, for the type of tale assumed by Fulgentius' reading — a "decent and dignified conception of holy truths, with respectable events and characters ... presented beneath a modest veil of allegory," as Macrobius terms it[33] — is conspicuously absent from Beroaldo's lexicon. Beroaldo goes on to quote Fulgentius' entire allegory without comment (the city of the girl's birth is the world; her parents are god and matter; the girl is soul, her sisters flesh and free will, etc.).[34]

In the last part of the digression Beroaldo contrasts the allegorical method with his own approach. Using the familiar example of Jerusalem, he explains the mediaeval four-fold system of allegory employed by interpreters of scripture: on the historical level Jerusalem is the city of Judaea, on the allegorical or tropological level the church, on the moral level the soul, on the spiritual level "the heavenly city to which the prayers of all aspire and desire to be made its inhabitants."[35] For him, however, the historical level is quite sufficient:

Sed nos non tam allegorias in explicatione huiusce fabulae sectabimur, quam historicum sensum, et rerum reconditarum verborumque interpretationem explicabimus,

---

[31] Macrobius' taxonomy, for example, divided *fabulae* into the merely amusing and those encouraging the listener to virtue, and the latter class into Aesopic fables and a higher type labeled *narratio fabulosa*, which could be further subdivided using the criteria of seemliness and suitability for allegory (*Somn. Scip.* 1.2.7–11). See the schema in Dronke, *Fabula*, 26 n. 1.
[32] Beroaldo, *Commentarii in Asinum Aureum*, fol. 95r.
[33] *sacrarum rerum notio sub pio figmentorum velamine honestis et tecta rebus et vestita nominibus*, Macr. *Somn. Scip.* 1.2.11. The translation is that of William Harris Stahl, Macrobius. Commentary on the Dream of Scipio (New York, 1952), 85.
[34] Fulg. *Myth.* 3.6. Beroaldo, *Commentarii in Asinum Aureum*, fol. 95r–v. For a detailed discussion of Fulgentius, see Julia Haig Gaisser, "Allegorizing Apuleius: Fulgentius, Boccaccio, Beroaldo, and the Chain of Receptions," Acta Conventus Neo–Latini Cantabrigiensis (Tempe, Arizona, 2003), 23–41.
[35] ... *hierusalem historice significat civitatem Iudaeae metropolim. allegorice ecclesiam, moraliter animam. spiritaliter celestem civitatem, ad quam cunctorum vota suspirant, et illius coloni effici concupiscunt*, Beroaldo, *Commentarii in Asinum Aureum*, fol. 95v.

ne philosophaster magis videar quam commentator, (*Commentarii in Asinum Aureum*, fol. 95v).

But I will not pursue allegories in the explanation of this story so much as the historical sense, and I will explain the meaning of words and obscure matters, lest I appear a bad philosopher instead of a commentator.

Beroaldo has accomplished both pedagogical and programmatic purposes in this long preamble to "Cupid and Psyche." On the pedagogical level, he has both reviewed the four–fold system of allegoresis (a staple of medieval and Renaissance education) and reminded his students of Fulgentius' allegory (first printed in 1498 by a former student, Giambattista Pio).[36] He endorses neither Fulgentius nor the allegorical system, but — good teacher that he is — explains them fully before putting them aside. On the programmatic level, he has firmly taken his familiar pragmatic stance, preferring as usual to explain the things of this world rather than to speculate about those of the next.[37] He has also intentionally insulted Pio, a proponent of Fulgentius and someone easily recognizable as a *philosophaster*.[38] Most important, however, he has presented a complex statement of his own hermeneutical method. In his (admittedly slanted) discussion of *fabula* he has treated the word like a lexicographer rather than a theorist, defining it from its use in ancient authors. His emphasis on the practical and moral fable at the expense of more metaphysical types not only invalidates Fulgentius' allegory in advance but implicitly identifies "Cupid and Psyche" as a moral rather than a philosophical tale. His final statement is the capstone: not as a "bad philosopher" but as a "commentator," he will undertake to explain "the historical sense" and "the meaning of words and obscure matters." His approach, in other words, is that of a philologist. Of course, this is his approach throughout his *Apuleius* (and in all his commentaries). But he states it at this particular point for programmatic reasons: both to contrast his method with the kind of speculation represented by

---

[36] Fabius Planciades Fulgentius, *Mitologiae* (Milan, 1498). For Pio see Rose, Filippo Beroaldo, 108–14.

[37] Or as he would put it: *divinis sepositis humana scrutari*. The phrase comes from one of Beroaldo's many similar pronouncements: *Socrates ille philosophorum fons ... dixisse fertur: quae supra nos, nihil ad nos. Ex hoc socratico documento commonemur, omissis rebus sublimioribus, circa humiliora versari et a coelestibus ad terrena descendere et divinis sepositis humana scrutari*, Beroaldo, *Oratio proverbiorum*, fol. a3r. See the important discussion of Eugenio Garin, "Note in margine all'opera di Filippo Beroaldo il Vecchio," in Gabriella Bernardoni Trezzini et al., eds., Tra latino e volgare: Per Carlo Dionisotti (Padua, 1974), II, 442–5.

[38] See Carlo Dionisotti, "Giovan Battista Pio e Mario Equicola," in Gli umanisti e il volgare fra Quattro e Cinquecento (Firenze, 1968), 78–130 especially p. 90. See also Ezio Raimondi, "Il primo commento umanistico a Lucrezio," in Politica e commedia. Dal Beroaldo al Machiavelli (Bologna, 1972), 101–40.

Fulgentius (and Pio), and to herald a reading of "Cupid and Psyche" based primarily on an understanding of its language and mythological and historical background.

True to his word, Beroaldo does explain the tale on "the historical level" of language, plot, and what he regards as universal human psychology. Reading the story in terms of human emotions and behavior, he points out the indulgence of mothers toward their sons, the universal hostility between mothers-in-law and daughters-in-law, and — in a very odd reading of Venus' response to Psyche's pregnancy — the desire for grandchildren and its softening effect on mothers-in-law.[39] Along the way, he indulges in more than a few misogynist stereotypes.[40] He situates the story in its Roman historical context with detailed explanations of essential points of Roman marriage law: paternal consent, marriage between persons of unequal status, legitimacy of offspring, and marriage by *manus*.[41] A philologist to the core, he is ever alert not only to unusual and difficult words but also to the nuances of common words in their contexts. He notes almost every occurrence of the word *anima* and points out its relation to Psyche. Thus, on Psyche's addressing Cupid as *tuae Psyches dulcis anima* (*Met.* 5.6.9), he comments: "The allusion is to the name of Psyche, which means soul, as if her husband was the soul of her soul."[42] He points out the word play in *Psyche ... in amoris incidit amorem* (*Met.* 5.23.3): "The one signifies the god Cupid, the other love."[43] When Cupid flees Psyche after the catastrophe and addresses her from the top of a cypress tree, Beroaldo (more acutely than the modern commentators, who fail to notice its significance)

---

[39] Indulgence (*Met.* 6.5.4): *Probabile videtur et satis credibile Cupidinem filium reperiri posse in materno domo, cum matres in filios sint longe quam patres indulgentiores*, Beroaldo, *Commentarii in Asinum Aureum*, fol. 120r. In-law hostility (*Met.* 6.9.2): *Inter socrus et nurus quoddam quasi genuinum et naturale dissidium est*, [fol. 122v]. Grandchildren (*Met.* 6.9.4): *Uterus foeminae turgidus et praegnatio conciliat favorem et quodam quasi lenocinio blandimenta conquirit; idque potissimum apud socrum quae futura est avia. Tales enim imprimis foeminae nepotulorum desiderio capiuntur*, [fol. 122v].

[40] I give only two examples. On *Met.* 5.10.6: *Mulierum est proprium invidere irasci furere ultionem parare; iuxta illud vindicta nemo magis gaudet quam foemina*, Beroaldo, *Commentarii in Asinum Aureum*, fol. 105v. On *Met.* 6.23.3: *... sed plerumque nova nupta ab alio praeflorata ad maritum venit. Tanta est morum corruptela ut virgines fiant mulieres in aedibus parentum exuantque pudiciciam, qua amissa omnis virtus in foemina ruit*, [fol. 132r].

[41] Beroaldo, *Commentarii ad Asinum Aureum*, fols. 123r, 132r–v, 134r.

[42] *Allusio est ad Psyches nomen, quo anima significatur, quasi anima animae maritus sit*, Beroaldo, *Commentarii in Asinum Aureum*, fol. 103v. Cf. E. J. Kenney, ed., Apuleius, *Cupid & Psyche* (Cambridge, 1990) ad loc.: "*anima* and ψυχή were common lovers' endearments, but ... [she is ignorant] of what *Psychae ... anima* implies — that only a complete and perfect union with Love can save her."

[43] *Alterum deum cupidinem, alterum dilectionem significat*, Beroaldo, *Commentarii in Asinum Aureum*, fol. 111r. He continues: *ex eadem elegantia est cupidine cupidinis flagrans, id est cupiditate dei amoris exestuans*.

sees why he lights in that particular tree. His note reads: "The cypress, clearly a tree associated with death and sacred to Dis, and for that reason placed before houses as a funereal sign."[44]

Beroaldo's second and third digressions in "Cupid and Psyche," like the commentary itself, are learned, highly personal, and characterized by close attention to words and word play. In each he uses significant words from Apuleius as the jumping off point for a little riff or arpeggio relating the tale to his own life in present–day Bologna. Common to both are *psyche* (soul) and *voluptas* (Pleasure — the child of Cupid and Psyche).

The second digression appears at the beginning of *Met.* 5. Psyche, awakening from her exhausted sleep, finds herself in the garden of a beautiful country house. An ecphrasis of the house follows, which Beroaldo imitates in an ecphrasis of the villa of his friend Mino de' Rossi. His description is explicitly intended to match Apuleius', as his introduction indicates:

Descriptio est graphica luculenti domicilii quo psyche divinitus accipitur. Caeterum cum egressiones tempestivae maiorem in modum reficiant recreentque lectores, tempestivum videtur et oportunum hoc potissimum loco Roscii mei Mini Ponticulanum summatim explicare, cuius topothesia haud sane multum distat ab hac cupidinei diversorii descriptione, (*Commentarii in Asinum Aureum*, fol. 100v).

This is an artistic description of the splendid dwelling in which Psyche [*psyche*] is received by divine agency [*divinitus*]. But since timely digressions rest and restore readers to a greater degree, it seems timely and opportune in this place in particular to give a summary account of the villa at Pontecchio of my dear friend Mino de' Rossi, the depiction of which is not far from this description of Cupid's retreat [*cupidinei diversorii*].

Beroaldo promises a restorative digression and a description, both emulating Apuleius. But he is also emulating Apuleius' word play. He uses both *psyche* and *cupidinei* in a double sense: we can understand the subject of *accipitur* in the first sentence above as either "Psyche" or "the soul" and translate the end of the last sentence as "Cupid's retreat," "the retreat of love," or even "the charming retreat" (if we take *cupidinei* as a simple adjective). Beroaldo's word play continues with *diversorium*, which I have translated as "retreat."[45] A *diversorium* is a temporary abode or stopping place — a place to which one turns aside (*diverto*) from one's journey or usual business. Beroaldo has taken the word from Apuleius' description (*Met.* 5.1.3) and uses it, as we will see, as a major theme for his digression.

---

[44] *Cypressum. Arborem scilicet feralem et diti sanctam, et ideo funebri signo ad domos positam*, ibid.
[45] I have borrowed the translation "retreat" from P. G. Walsh, Apuleius. The Golden Ass (Oxford, 1994), 80.

Beroaldo's description of Mino's villa has two primary intertexts: Apuleius and Pliny the younger (*Ep.* 2.17 and 5.6). He conspicuously evokes both authors early in his account. In the 'Golden Ass' Cupid's house obviously belongs to someone important: "You would know the moment you entered that you were seeing the splendid and delightful retreat of some god," says Apuleius.[46] Beroaldo echoes the comment:

> *statim ab ipso introitu haud dubie asseverabis principis id cuiuspiam et summatis viri luculentum esse diversorium*, (*Commentarii in Asinum Aureum*, fol. 100v).

> At once, from the very moment you enter, you will surely declare that it is the splendid retreat of some prince of the highest nobility.

Pliny's Laurentine villa (*Ep.* 2.17) is close to the city; so is Mino's retreat. One can travel the seventeen miles to Pliny's villa after a full day's work and arrive in time to spend the night, or ride the seven miles to Mino's after doing business in the morning and arrive for dinner.[47] In each case, there is more than one way to get there.[48]

These allusions to Pliny and Apuleius pay an elegant compliment to Mino. By referring to Pliny, Beroaldo implies that his friend's villa is on a par with that of the ancient Roman grandee.[49] By echoing Apuleius' reference to the villa's owner, he hints that Mino is worthy of comparison with Cupid himself. Beroaldo could count on his students and readers to appreciate the allusions. They had the text of Apuleius before them, and many would have seen the edition of Pliny's letters that Beroaldo had published in 1498 and again in 1500, just a few months before his lectures and commentary on Apuleius.[50] (The young dedicatee of his Pliny, Johannes von Wartenberg, was probably in Beroaldo's audience for the Apuleius lectures.[51]) Some readers might even have heard

---

[46] Met. 5.1.3: *iam scires ab introitu primo dei cuiuspiam luculentum et amoenum videre te diversorium*.

[47] Pliny, *Ep.* 2.17.2 : *Decem et septem milibus passuum ab urbe secessit, ut peractis, quae agenda fuerint, salvo iam et composito die possis ibi manere*. Beroaldo, *Commentarii in Asinum Aureum*, fol. 100v: *secessit ab urbe plus minus septem millibus passuum ... potesque peractis quae agenda in urbe fuerint matutinis negociis illuc transcurrere ad horam prandii*.

[48] Pliny, *Ep.* 2.17.2 : *Aditur non una via*. Beroaldo, *Commentarii in Asinum Aureum*, fol. 100v: *Aditur via non una*.

[49] It may even be better. Pliny's Laurentinum "lacks a running stream" (*deficitur aqua saliente*, *Ep.* 2.17.24). Mino's villa has them in profusion: ... *ex omnibus villae membris supernae infernaeque iuxta scaturiunt aquae salientes erumpuntque*, Beroaldo, *Commentarii in Asinum Aureum*, fol. 100v.

[50] For these editions, see Krautter, Philologische Methode und humanistische Existenz, 190; Rose, Filippo Beroaldo der Ältere, 73 n. 481. The second edition of Pliny's letters was printed in April 1500; Beroaldo's *Apuleius* appeared in August.

[51] Beroaldo lists him among his current noble foreign students in the dedication to Váradi (*Commentarii in Asinum Aureum*, fol. iv v): *Inter quos ad praesens est gemma scholasticorum et illiba-*

Beroaldo lecture on Pliny's letters on his villas, for a list of his explanations of "vocabula obscuriora" from *Ep.* 2.17 and 5.6 survives — perhaps from a student's notes.[52]

Beroaldo's principal subject, however, is not the architecture of Mino's villa, but the enjoyment it affords its owner and his guests. It offers boating, fishing, fowling, walking — even morning mass — each activity measured and watched over by the great clock near the roof that marks the hours with its bell.[53] But Beroaldo does not use *voluptas* for any of these enjoyments. He reserves that word for the account of his own annual visit to Mino at the end of the digression. The concluding passage is full of elaborate word play that looks back to the beginning, bringing Apuleius, Mino, himself, and the reader together in a grand finale:

> *Idem me quotannis prope solemniter in illum amoenissimum secessum, quo nihil amoenius novi, evocat post indictas ferias litterarias. Ubi et genialia colimus et voluptati meracissimae indulgemus tum corpus tum animum vicissatim refoventes, non tamen sine suavissimo librorum comitatu et pastu, sine quibus nulla est solida voluptas.*
>
> *libuit in hoc diversorium de industr<i>a divertere, ut tu qui libellos meos omnis studiose lectitas, ut per te caeteri lectores norint qui sit Roscius in meis voluminibus, cuius praetorium Ponticulanum non absurde domicilium voluptatis atque hospitium psyches videri potest.*
>
> *quod graphice et luculenter hoc in loco Asinus noster non asinali, sed philosophica curiositate perscribit. Sed nos institutas iam commentationes exequamur, cum non ab re sit in transcursu amicis satisfacere, varietatibus commentarios distinguere, et legentibus velut amoena diverticula quaerere,* (Commentarii in Asinum Aureum, fol. 101r–v).

Every year, almost as a solemn rite, after the university holidays have been proclaimed, he summons me into that most delightful refuge (I know of nothing more delightful). And there we practise good cheer and indulge in purest pleasure [*voluptati*], refreshing mind and body in turn — but not without the most agreeable companionship and sustenance of books, without which there is no true pleasure [*voluptas*].

It was agreeable to make a detour [*divertere*] deliberately into this retreat [*diversorium*], so that you who attentively read all my books (and through

---

tus eloquentiae candidatorum flos Johannes Vartimbergensis Boemus. Wartenberg (c. 1480–1508) was in Bologna from 1497 or 1498 to 1500; see Rose, *Filippo Beroaldo der Ältere,* 122–3.

[52] *Vocabula obscuriora in duabus epistolis Plinii existentia declarata ut infra per Philippum Beroaldum de anno 1484*; published by Ludovico Frati, "I due Beroaldi," 227–8. Several of these words (all architectural terms) appear in his description: e.g., *cavum aedium, andronites, gynecea, maceria*; Beroaldo, *Commentarii in Asinum Aureum,* fols. 100v–101r.

[53] Beroaldo, *Commentarii in Asinum Aureum,* fol. 101r.

you other readers) might know who the de' Rossi in my volumes is, whose castle at Pontecchio can appear — not inappropriately — as a dwelling of pleasure [*voluptatis*] and a lodging of Psyche [*psyches*].
Our Ass has given a detailed account of this artistically and excellently in this place — not with asinine but with philosophic curiosity. But now let us carry on with the commentary we have begun, since it is not out of place to give friends their due in passing, to embellish commentaries with varied elements, and to seek delightful by–ways [*diverticula*] (so to speak) for our readers.

This passage, like the digression as a whole, is both an affectionate tribute to Mino and a self–conscious assertion of Beroaldo's own literary achievement. The digression began with Cupid's retreat [*cupidinei diversorii*], the imaginary dwelling in which Psyche/soul was received, and where (as every reader knows) her child Pleasure (*voluptas*) was conceived. Mino's (real) villa — also called a *diversorium*[54] — is the metaphorical embodiment of Cupid's, for it is both "the lodging of Psyche/soul," and "the dwelling of pleasure" for Mino and his friends. But Beroaldo has also created his own *diversorium* — the digression itself. The idea is latent in the familiar language of rest and refreshment introducing the digression; it is brought to life by the word play on *diversorium* and its cognates *divertere* and *diverticula* at the end. In the last sentence Beroaldo calls his digressions *diverticula*, which I have translated "by–ways" (his usual word for "digressions" is *egressiones*).[55] He uses it, of course, to echo and suggest *diversorium*. But he comes even closer to *diversorium* in the preceding paragraph: "It was agreeable to make a detour [*divertere*] deliberately into this retreat [*diversorium*]." The word play nicely blurs the distinction between Mino's retreat and Beroaldo's digression — the one a physical refuge from the everyday world, the other (which describes the first) a literary respite from the task at hand, but both providing rest and enjoyment to others. Both the description and Beroaldo's claims for it result from Beroaldo's affinity with Apuleius and desire to imitate him. The digression is the emulative counterpart of Apuleius' ecphrasis, matching the creative power of the novelist with the literary skill of his commentator.

Beroaldo's third digression appears in Book 6, at the end of "Cupid and Psyche".[56] Again he plays on "soul" and "pleasure," but now he adds a major new

---

[54] Its temperate climate makes it an excellent "summer retreat" (*diversorium ... aestivum*). Beroaldo, *Commentarii in Asinum Aureum*, fol. 101r.
[55] Beroaldo has borrowed both the word and its surrounding language from Livy 9.17.1: *et legentibus uelut deuerticula amoena et requiem animo meo quaererem*.
[56] Beroaldo, *Commentarii in Asinum Aureum*, fols. 134r–v, 135r.

theme, marriage, taking his cue from Apuleius as before.[57] "Cupid and Psyche" ends:

> So Psyche was duly married to Cupid, and in the fullness of time a daughter was born to them, whom we call Pleasure [*Voluptatem*].[58]

Beroaldo notes:

> *Conducenter et scite voluptatem ex connubio cupidinis et psyches natam esse finxerunt, cum ex cupiditate animae et dilectione voluptas progignatur, qua summum bonum clarissimi philosophorum metiuntur,* (*Commentarii in Asinum Aureum*, fol. 134r).

> Both wisely and cleverly they say that Pleasure [*voluptatem*] was born of the marriage of Cupid [*cupidinis*] and Psyche [*psyches*], since pleasure [*voluptas*] — by which the most notable philosophers measure the highest good — comes into being from the desire [*cupiditate*] and love of the soul [*animae*].

He continues:

> *Condentibus haec nobis et has psyches ac cupidinis nuptias commentantibus siderali opinor decreto factum est, ut ego ... uxorem ducerem ... Dii faxint, ut hoc connubium sit nobis foelix faustum ac fortunatum, utque ex eo voluptas gignatur. ... gignaturque ex nobis soboles voluptifica, qualis ex psyche et cupidine progenerata est,* (*Commentarii in Asinum Aureum*, fols. 134r–v, 135).

> While I was writing these things and commenting on this marriage of Psyche and Cupid, it so happened ... that I took a wife — it was fated by the stars, I believe ... May the gods make this marriage fertile and happy and fortunate for us, so that from it pleasure [*voluptas*] may be born ... May the offspring born of us be pleasure–bringing [*voluptifica*], like that born of Psyche and Cupid.

A few lines later he proudly announces that his young wife is pregnant. The digression concludes:

> *spero et ominor filium anno hoc Iubilei memorando nasciturum, qui parentibus sit voluptati futurus et ornamento,* (*Commentarii in Asinum Aureum*, fol. 135r).

> I hope and predict that in this memorable jubilee year a son will be born, to be the pleasure [*voluptati*] and ornament of his parents.

In this digression Beroaldo's marriage both re–enacts the union of Cupid and Psyche and explains it — not in metaphysical terms, but in the language of

---

[57] See Gaisser, "Allegorizing Apuleius," 38–9.
[58] *Sic rite Psyche convenit in manum Cupidinis et nascitur illis maturo partu filia, quam Voluptatem nominamus, Met.* 6.24.4.

human experiences and feelings. His explanation is at once universal and intensely personal. It begins with what Beroaldo presents as a philosophic truth ("pleasure" is the "child" of "desire" and "soul") and continues with wishes appropriate to any marriage ("may the gods make this marriage fertile and happy and fortunate for us"). But the digression is also full of personal detail — biographical information about his wife and her family and musings on his own earlier reluctance to marry.[59] It is personal in another way as well, for if Beroaldo's marriage re-enacts Cupid and Psyche's, it also reflects those of several ancient authors, including Apuleius himself. His wife is not an impediment to his literary studies, Beroaldo says, but a comfort and a stimulus, making him believe the old story that:

> *Olim Martia Hortensio, Terentia Tullio, Calphurnia Plino, Pudentilla Apuleio, legentibus meditantibusque candelas et candelabra tenuerint,* (*Commentarii in Asinum Aureum*, fol 135r).[60]
>
> Long ago, Marcia held a candle and candlestick for Hortensius as he read and studied, as did Terentia for Tullius, Calphurnia for Pliny, and Pudentilla for Apuleius.

The authors are exemplary for Beroaldo (and we should remember that he had edited all of them except for Hortensius), but Beroaldo himself is exemplary for his students and readers:

> *Studentibus discendi per nuptias occasionem tribui, desidibus excusationem,* (*Commentarii in Asinum Aureum*, fol 135r).
>
> Through my marriage, to the studious I have afforded an opportunity for learning and to the lazy a justification.

---

[59] Beroaldo, *Commentarii in Asinum Aureum*, fols. 134v–135r.
[60] Beroaldo is quoting Sidonius Apollinaris, *Ep.* 2.10.5, but omits Sidonius' last pair, Rusticiana and Symmachus.

Epilogue

Beroaldo undoubtedly captured the interest of his students with his digressions on Francia and Cupid and Psyche, and with the other contemporary references that brought Apuleius to life in his classroom — to say nothing of his vast philological and historical knowledge. But he did not rely on the content of his lectures alone. He was a relentless and highly successful self promoter — and one of the few humanists I know of who actually made money by his profession.

Beroaldo gave rich former students the chance to bid on the dedications to his works, and the negotiations seem to have been accomplished with perfect good humor on both sides. The archbishop to whom the Apuleius commentary is dedicated supposedly couched his bid as follows: "If you send me that Ass of yours that you have kindly promised me, I will send it right back, laden with gold."[61]

He also made money on the sale of his books. In the case of Apuleius we are fortunate enough to have the contract he signed with his printer in the spring of 1499. Its provisions included: a print run of 1200 copies, equal division of the profits between Beroaldo and the printer, and the stipulation that Beroaldo was to lecture on this book and only this at the University of Bologna, and that he was to promote it as much as possible.[62] The 1200 copies stipulated in the contract is a very large number — two or three times as large as a typical press run for a commentary on a classical author in this period.[63] As we

---

[61] The story is told by Beroaldo's contemporary biographer, Jean de Pins, who presents it as hearsay. Thus: ... *in Apulejani asini commentariis nuper, quos dum se Thomae colocensi archiepiscopo, viro bonarum artium studioso, dicare velle scriveret, tale accepisse responsum dicitur: 'Asinum istum, quem tam benevole nobis es pollicitus, si ad nos propere miseris, denuo ipse ad te onustum auro remittam.'* (Philippi Beroaldi bononiensis vita, in J. G. Meuschen, ed., *Vitae summorum dignitate et eruditione virorum ex rarissimis monumentis literato orbi restitutae* (Coburg, 1735), I, 133–4.) As Krautter points out (Philologische Methode und humanistische Existenz, 24, n. 58), de Pins is confusing another Hungarian friend of Beroaldo's, Tamás Bakócz ("Thomae"), with the actual dedicatee, Peter Váradi. For other requests by Beroaldo for gifts, see Garin "Note sull' insegnamento di Filippo Beroaldi il Vecchio," 367–88, 371, 378.

[62] The contract between Beroaldo and his printer, Benedetto d'Ettore, was signed on 22 May 1499. For its terms, see Albano Sorbelli, Storia della Stampa in Bologna (Bologna, 1929), 61. See also Curt Bühler, The University and the Press in Fifteenth–Century Bologna (Notre Dame, Indiana, 1958), 39.

[63] We do not know enough about the size of editions in the fifteenth century. Bühler characterizes the press run of 1200 as "an unusually large one for those days" (The University and the Press in Fifteenth–Century Bologna, 39). Konrad Haebler mentions a Plato edition of 1025 copies in the mid –1490s (The Study of Incunabula, New York, 1933, 175); the other very large editions he cites are of religious and legal texts. Rudolf Hirsch (Printing, Selling and Reading 1450–1550, Wiesbaden, 1967, 66–7) cites figures from 200 to 400 cop-

might say today, the Apuleius commentary was expected to be a "blockbuster." Beroaldo planned to lecture from it in the fall of 1499, but publication was postponed by a paper shortage, and he had to lecture on Cicero instead.[64] He explained the matter to his students in the first lecture of the school year, using it as a demonstration of the Greek proverb, ἀνάγκῃ δ' οὐδὲ Θεοὶ μάχονται ("Not even the gods struggle against Necessity").[65] His purpose, however, was not only to explain, but to advertise. In the same lecture he promoted a book of his own orations, touted the usefulness of his Cicero lectures ("the only Cicero you'll ever need," he claims), and promised to lecture on Apuleius "in the memorable and auspicious Jubilee year."[66] His Apuleius finally appeared in August 1500, in time for the next school year, and sold well from the start.[67] It was reprinted ten times in the sixteenth century.[68]

---

ies for specific classical texts. The 1502 Aldine of Catullus, Tibullus, and Propertius was printed in an extraordinarily large edition of 3000 copies, but it was an octavo, not a folio edition, and contained the works of all three poets. (See Martin Lowry, The World of Aldus Manutius. Business and Scholarship in Renaissance Venice, Ithaca, 1979., 174 n. 96; Julia Haig Gaisser, Catullus and his Renaissance Readers, Oxford, 1993, 64–5, 309 notes 153–4.) The number of copies of Beroaldo's Apuleius may in fact have been much greater than the 1200 stipulated in the contract. In his dedication Beroaldo gives the number as around 2000: *Et sane impressor optimus operam dedit, ut volumina commentariorum circiter duo millia formis excussa divulgarentur*, Beroaldo *Commentarii in Asinum Aureum*, fol. a4v.

[64] See Krautter, Philologische Methode und humanistische Existenz, 38–9.

[65] Beroaldo, *Oratio Proverbiorum* (Bologna, 1499), fols. c4v–c7r. In the edition, the Greek lacks accents, spiritus, and the iota subscriptum, as is usually the case in incunables.

[66] Cicero lectures: *Erit autem haec procrastinatio scholasticis oppido quam conducibilis. Namque interea aliquot Ciceronis orationes explicabuntur a nobis, ea diligentia, eaque omnifaria eruditione, ut ianua laxissime reserata reliquis deinceps orationibus omnibus videri possit, ut qui vel paucissimas audierit, caeteras sine interprete citraque doctorem adire ipse et per se intelligere queat haud sane difficulter*, Beroaldo, *Oratio Proverbiorum*, fol. c7r. Orations (fol. c6v): *De quorum [Virgilii et Tullii] laudibus melius est ad praesens tacere quam pauca dicere, cum ad laudandum pro merito Virgilium et Tullium, Virgilio et Tullio laudatoribus opus fit. Praeterea in libro orationum mearum extant utriusque scriptoris luculenta praeconia*, Apuleius lectures (fol. c7r): *Anno autem a salute domini milesimo quingentesimo quem iubileum nominitant, perinde ac auspicatissimo et memorando anno Apuleium fauste ac feliciter initiabimus.*

[67] Krautter, Philologische Methode und humanistische Existenz, 39 infers as much from a comment in Beroaldo's opening lecture on Apuleius: *afficior gaudio non mediocri, cum video commentarios diutinis vigiliis absolutos per ora virorum et manus volitantes circumferri, cum labores nostros neque cassos neque penitendos fuisse conspicio*, Beroaldo, *Oratio habita in narratione Lucii Apuleii*, in *Orationes et poemata* fol. m8v. In the same oration Beroaldo boasts of the sales of all his works: *Quae omnia nisi mihi bibliopolae blandiuntur, expetuntur a studiosis, probantur a doctis, teruntur manibus scholasticorum tam provincialium quam Italicorum*, Beroaldo, *Oratio habita in narratione Lucii Apuleii*, fol. n1r.

[68] See the bibliography in Krautter, Philologische Methode und humanistische Existenz, 193–4. The last edition mentioned by Krautter was printed in 1823.

Beroaldo worked as hard for his fame as he did for his fortune. He basked in his renown and took pains to impress his image both on his current public and on posterity. His hero Apuleius wanted to be memorialized in statues.[69] But Beroaldo — a philologist to the core — pinned his hopes on the power of the written word. In the opening paragraph of his dedication he argues that monuments of the intellect are more durable than those of the body — books, the true and breathing likenesses of men — last longer than statues.[70] He has already hammered out several self–portraits of this kind, he claims.[71] Now his Apuleius — "this new image of my mind, thoroughly polished with versatile sculpting and careful elegance" — will be another.[72]

Beroaldo's commentary on the 'Golden Ass' did turn out to be his monument. It is a major landmark in the history of classical scholarship, and it does portray the mind of its author. Its success was instant and long–lasting. In fact, it is only now being fully superseded — by the multi–volume Groningen commentary, which has finally reached book 10.[73]

Julia Haig Gaisser   Bryn Mawr College

---

[69] See, for example, Apul. *Fl.* 16.

[70] *Siquidem statuae et imagines intereunt aut vi convulsae aut vetustatis situ decoloratae, volumina vero quae sunt vera spirantiaque hominum simulacra nulla vi convelluntur, nullo senio obliterantur. Fiuntque vetustate ipsa sanctiora durabilioraque*, Beroaldo, *Commentarii in Asinum Aureum*, fol. a2r. The theme is a favorite one of Beroaldo's. It appears in his account of the paper shortage that delayed the publication of his Apuleius: *Itaque haec civitas, quae alioque chartam finitimis populis affatim solet subministrare, inopiam chartae sensit, cuius usu constat immortalitas hominum*, *Oratio proverbiorum*, fol. c6r. He uses it again in his poem, *Quod veriores sunt imagines ex libris quam ex nomismatis* (*Orationes et poemata*, fols. q2v–q3r): *Est scriptis vivax facies: est forma perennis/ Magnorum Regum nobiliumque ducum./ Scriptis Caesarei proceres sanctique Catones/ Scriptus Pompeius noscitur atque Numa./ Haec verae effigies: haec sunt simulacra virorum./ Hi spirant vultus; haec monimenta vigent./ Id tibi scripta dabunt: quod nulla monumenta possunt./ Sic oculos poteris pascere: sic animum*, (vv. 7–14).

[71] *Ego iam pridem aliquot id genus effigies sub litteratoria incude procusas mihi ipsemet publice posui, quibus non minus opinor ingenii mei similitudo expressa conspicitur quam Olympionicarum simulacris perfecta corporum liniamenta spectabantur quae iconica auctores appellant*, Beroaldo, *Commentarii in Asinum Aureum*, fol. a2r.

[72] *Hoc vero novicium animi nostri simulacrum vario effigiatu cultuque laborioso perpolitum* ..., Beroaldo, *Commentarii in Asinum Aureum*, fol. a2r.

[73] M. Zimmerman, ed., Apuleius Madaurensis, *Metamorphoses*. Book X (Groningen, 2000).

Marginalia and the Rise of Early Modern Subjectivity

CRAIG KALLENDORF

In my own past work, I have generally not made much distinction between commentaries that were printed along with a text and those that were added by hand in early printed editions. I am not sure, however, that this is such a good idea. I would now, therefore, like to focus on handwritten commentaries (i.e., marginalia) and try to tease out what makes them distinctive. In doing so, I shall end up (perhaps surprisingly) concentrating not only on what these commentaries can tell us about the text, but also on what they can tell us about the people who wrote them. That commentary illuminates the text remains obvious; the question is, does it not also do more?

As is often the case, this study was born in two lines of argument that failed to converge as we might expect them to. The first begins from a premise that received its classic articulation by Burckhardt, that the period from the fifteenth through the seventeenth centuries was dominated by the charismatic, forceful individual. The medieval artist left his work unsigned and his brother the cleric toiled away anonymously in the vineyard of the Lord, but Benvenuto Cellini, Baldassare Castiglione, and Francesco Sforza strode vigorously onto center stage and stayed there for all to see and admire.[1] To be sure, Burckhardt has grown a bit dated, but his basic point lives on in new iterations. Transcendental selves went out, but 'self-fashioning' came in,[2] followed by the search for subjectivity, for the point when early modern people began to situate themselves in the world around them in discernibly modern ways.[3]

As we seek to close the distance between our postmodern selves and our early modern predecessors, it would seem that any and all written records would be useful, but that some records would be more useful than others. And it would seem that marginalia, the responses that early readers left in their books, would be among the most useful of all, for they bear witness to a consciousness in the process of constituting itself, first by struggling to understand another person's ideas, then by reacting to them. Yet from Burckhardt to Greenblatt, marginalia have played a surprisingly small role in shaping our broader understanding of the early modern individual.

There are several reasons for this. One line of argument claims that after the Middle Ages, people gradually stopped writing in their books. Paul Saenger

---

[1] Jacob Burckhardt, The Civilization of the Renaissance in Italy, 2 vols. (New York; rpt. of New York, 1929 edn.), 1,143–74.
[2] Stephen Greenblatt, Renaissance Self-Fashioning: From More to Shakespeare (Chicago, 1980), esp. 1–9.
[3] Paul Smith, Discerning the Subject (Minneapolis, 1988).

and Michael Heinlen, for example, note that the medieval reader added punctuation and marginalia to clarify the meaning of a manuscript, but that printing presented a clear, unambiguous text that is spoiled by handwritten additions.[4] Mary A. and Richard H. Rouse state clearly what Saenger and Heinlen imply: "... the printed book is not itself an object in which one writes long glosses."[5] Anyone who has looked at a lot of early printed books, however, knows that this is simply not true, a perception which William H. Sherman has recently quantified. His soundings indicate that 60–70% of all incunables are annotated, and that the percentage of books containing annotations was still above 50% in the 1590s. The numbers dip in the early seventeenth century, then go up again in the 1640s and 1650s, while for some genres like religious polemics and practical guides to law, medicine, and estate management, the proportion remains above 50% for the entire STC period.[6]

The problem here is not that marginalia don't exist, but that they were valued more in the seventeenth century than in the twentieth. John Winthrop, for example, wrote a note in 1640 in his copy of Paracelsus which indicated that he had a number of books containing the marginalia of John Dee, "for which they are farre the more pretious"[7] — that is, annotated books were often preferred to unannotated ones because they contained more information. A survey of library sale catalogues suggests that interest in annotated books peaked at the end of the seventeenth and the beginning of the eighteenth centuries. Beginning around 1720 the catalogues stop advertising marked copies, reflecting the beginning of a drive toward 'pure' exemplars that would peak in the nineteenth century, when pages with notes were often washed and bleached, then cropped in rebinding to leave the printed text only.[8]

---

[4] Paul Saenger and Michael Heinlen, "Incunable Description and Its Implication for the Analysis of Fifteenth–Century Reading Habits," in Sandra Hindman (ed.), Printing the Written Word: The Social History of Books, circa 1450–1520 (Ithaca and London, 1991), 253–54. This essay, along with those by Stoddard, Rosenthal (introduction), Chatelain, and Coron in notes 8, 11, and 16 below, can be found in Italian translation in Edoardo Barbieri (ed.), Nel mondo delle postille (Milan, 2002).
[5] Mary A. Rouse and Richard H. Rouse, Authentic Witnesses: Approaches to Medieval Texts and Manuscripts (Notre Dame, 1991), 465.
[6] William H. Sherman, "What Did Renaissance Readers Write in Their Books?" in Jennifer Anderson and Elizabeth Sauer (eds.), Books and Readers in Early Modern England: Material Studies (Philadelphia, 2002), 124.
[7] Qtd. in William H. Sherman, John Dee: The Politics of Reading and Writing in Renaissance England (Amherst, 1995), 79.
[8] Monique Hulvey, "Not So Marginal: Manuscript Annotations in the Folger Incunabula," Papers of the Bibliographical Society of America 92 (1998), 161; Antoine Coron, "Les exemplaires annotés: des bibliothèques érudites aux cabinets d'amateurs," in Revue de la Bibliothèque nationale de France (Le livre annoté) 2 (June 1999), 57–66; and William H.

Collectors, however, are not the only people to have lost the taste for marginalia. Anthony Grafton, alone and with Lisa Jardine, has responded appreciatively to the marginalia of brilliant scholars like Guillaume Budé and Gabriel Harvey, yet he also notes that, for example, the records of classroom activity that fill the margins of early modern textbooks present "the proliferation of discrete items of literary information, almost entirely without cohesive moral and intellectual comment."[9] And the most stimulating recent study of readers writing in their books echoes this disappointment: "discursive and original readers' notes ... are rare before 1700 and increasingly common (in relation to other forms of annotation) thereafter."[10]

I am not going to argue that every schoolboy note construing a difficult Latin sentence is interesting or valuable in and of itself, nor am I prepared to claim that marginalia like those of Coleridge, who introduced the term into English and brought the genre to new literary heights, are common in the sixteenth century. But I do want to argue that even the most routine marking of a text allows us to hear the voice of the reader, and that this voice is often sufficiently personal to provide a reliable source of insight into the early modern self. In the discussion that follows, I will end up privileging commentaries to the poetry of Virgil because these are the early modern books I know best. But since different kinds of books sometimes elicit different responses in their readers, I shall also use some examples that have been mentioned by others who have discussed them with other goals in mind.

**

The catalogue to the Rosenthal collection of printed books with manuscript annotations, recently acquired by the Beinecke Library, describes and illustrates seven early editions of Virgil's poetry that were specifically laid out for

---

Sherman, "'Rather Soiled by Use': Attitudes towards Readers' Marks," The Book Collector 52 (2003), 471–90.

[9] Anthony Grafton and Lisa Jardine, From Humanism to the Humanities: Education and the Liberal Arts in Fifteenth- and Sixteenth-Century Europe (Cambridge, Mass., 1986), 3.

[10] H. T. Jackson, Marginalia: Readers Writing in Books (New Haven, 2001), 15. See, however, the important review by Nicolas Barker in The Book Collector 52 (2003), 11–30, which comes to a different conclusion, that "the reasons for writing in margins and otherwise annotating books have not altered very much" (30). To be fair, Jackson recognizes that "[s]ome early readers engaged themselves in argument with the books they read, or expressed distaste for or disapproval of them" (51), but her generalization is echoed regularly by others: for example Sherman, John Dee, writes that "[t]he tools that Dee (and his contemporaries) used to digest texts and make them useful lack, for the most part, the personal, creative, and emotional intensity that modern readers have come to look for in engagements with texts" (80–81). See also Saenger and Heinlen, "Incunable Description," 250.

the addition of handwritten commentaries, with ample leading and wide margins to hold notes taken in school.[11] Other books with a more usual layout were adapted to similar use. A survey of the classroom notes written in a group of early editions of Virgil now in the Marciana Library in Venice shows that they fall into two broad groups. Some of these notes reveal evidence of students struggling to learn basic Latin vocabulary and grammar, supplemented by the fundamentals of textual criticism, etymologies of words used in the text, the identification of geographical references, myths, and rhetorical figures, and cross–references to other works conveying similar sentiments. Another group of marginal annotations focuses on the moral content of the poetry, either by marking off lines with an aphoristic quality (*improbe amor, quid non mortalia pectora cogis?* "voracious love, to what do you not drive the hearts of men?" Aen. 4.412) or by making notes like the one in the margin of Book 4 that Virgil *incontinentiam ostendit Didonis* ("shows the incontinence of Dido").

On one level, these notes can be seen as impersonal records of institutional activity, but on another level, they have much more to offer. Occasionally one can put names to the annotation, as in a 1578 Virgil edition now in the Biblioteca Comunale, Treviso, whose student owner provided details of his study of the *Georgics:* "Lo incominciaremo alli 19 di Aprile 1610 dichiarato da D. Camillo Setti à me Novello Rosen in Ferrara" ("We shall begin on 19 April 1610, [with the text] explained by Master Camillo Setti to me, Novello Rosen[o], in Ferrara").[12] But even when we can't recover the names of the students and teachers, we can see the educational process at work. The focus on the language is not that of a professional linguist, interested in comparing and analyzing language structures, but of a student seeking to acquire facility in the language through which the deepest level of self–expression was believed to occur. And the focus on the moral content of the poetry is not that of the philosopher, interested in isolating and analyzing logical structures, but of a student seeking to refine his sense of right and wrong, a key element in constructing a self that can interact successfully in the world around it. In both cases, Virgil's text is being studied not for its antiquarian value, but for its insights into how one can learn to speak and act in the world outside the classroom. Annotation, in other words, leads to self–definition.

---

[11] Bernard M. Rosenthal, The Rosenthal Collection of Printed Books with Marginal Annotations (New Haven, 1997), 365–78, nrs. 153–59; see also Roger Stoddard, Marks in Books (Cambridge, Mass., 1985), 30, nr. 47, in which a similar volume is described; and Vincenzo Fera, Giacomo Ferraù, and Silvia Rizzo (eds.), Talking to the Text: Marginalia from Papyri to Print (Messina, 2002), for examples of the research this kind of collection can support.

[12] Craig Kallendorf, Virgil and the Myth of Venice: Books and Readers in the Italian Renaissance (Oxford, 1999), 31–34, 47–49, 57–61.

This becomes clearer when we consider how the annotations in early modern books were designed to be used. Anyone who has looked at any quantity of early printed books has run across volumes like the 1491 Venetian edition now in the Morgan Virgil Collection at Princeton with passages underlined and short 'indexing notes' like *comparatio* ("simile") and *superbia* ("pride") in the margins.[13] Initially these passages were transferred to commonplace books, where headings like the ones marked in the margins were followed by extracts on this subject taken from whatever the reader had been studying.[14] In and of itself, this was a highly personal activity, with the reader selecting the extracts, organizing them as he or she saw fit, and expanding at will on the text.[15] Indeed, during this period an entire genre, the *ars excerpendi*, developed in order to show readers how to make extracts properly.[16] As an example of how this process worked, Anthony Grafton has traced several passages from the annotations in Guillaume Budé's copy of Homer through a group of his notebooks that survive in a private library in Geneva, showing how an initial contact with the text leads to reflection on its meaning. At *Iliad* 1.402–3 in his Homer text, for example, Budé notes that the hundred–handed Briareus was a sea *daimon* who deprived his father Poseidon of his rights. In the Geneva notebooks, Budé expands on the note to suggest that "hundred–handed" can be applied to anyone outstanding in power or strength, including a king or even the Pope, with his power to bind and loose.[17]

---

[13] Shelf mark: VRG 2945 1491q. I am currently preparing a catalogue of this collection.
[14] Battista Guarino, De ordine docendi et studendi, in Craig Kallendorf (ed.), Humanist Educational Treatises (Cambridge, Mass., 2002), sects. 8, 30–31; see also P. Beal, "Notions in Garrison: The Seventeenth–Century Commonplace Book," in W. Speed Hill (ed.), New Ways of Looking at Old Texts: Papers of the Renaissance English Text Society, 1985–1991 (Binghamton, NY, 1993), 131–47; Ann Moss, Printed Commonplace–Books and the Structuring of Renaissance Thought (Oxford, 1996); and Earle Havens, Commonplace Books: A History of Manuscripts and Printed Books from Antiquity to the Twentieth Century (New Haven and Hanover, 2001).
[15] Kevin Sharpe, Reading Revolutions: The Politics of Reading in Early Modern England (New Haven, 2000), 278, notes that preparing commonplace books is an ambiguous practice, in that while the wisdom contained in them derives from a storehouse common to an entire culture, the selection and arrangement of the entries reflects the judgment of the compiler. Jackson, for example, notes that the personality of the English collector William Beckford, his mocking, irreverent spirit that was quick to note and comment on the ridiculous, emerges clearly in the marking, copying out, and light editing of extracts from his books (Marginalia, 38–41).
[16] Jean–Marc Chatelain, "Humanisme et culture de la note," Revue de la Bibliothèque nationale de France (Le livre annoté) 2 (June 1999), 27–30.
[17] Anthony Grafton, Commerce with the Classics: Ancient Books and Renaissance Readers (Ann Arbor, 1997), 170–71.

The notebooks, however, were not an end in themselves, but the means to an end: the production of original compositions in which the reader in turn becomes a writer. If we look at the published notes to the 1656 translation of the first book of Lucretius's *De rerum natura* by John Evelyn, the great English diarist, we can often trace an observation in the notes through Evelyn's commonplace books, which survive in three massive volumes, to a book in his library, where the passage was underlined and marked for retrieval in the margins in the usual way.[18] A similar example is furnished by the 1502 Aldine copy of Statius, now in the Princeton University Library, which contains marginal notes by the Spanish poet Francisco de Quevedo. Quevedo's commonplace books do not survive, but his *silvas* written in imitation of Statius do. In the Princeton volume, for example, Quevedo has underlined *Cum iam fessa dies* (*Silvae* 2.2.48) and written next to it an indexing note, *de occidua die* ("concerning the defunct day"). He then repeated the image in two of his *silvas*: no. 14, l. 5, *difunto día*, and l. 66, *muriendo el día*, and no. 5, ll. 19–20, *morir el día / con luz enferma*. Not only individual words, but longer passages, even themes for entire poems, are reworked in the margins of Quevedo's Statius, showing how underlinings and indexing notes can become the first steps toward the creation of new lyric poems, generally considered the most subjective of genres.[19]

* * *

As William H. Sherman has observed "... by no means all of the notes left behind by readers engage directly with the text they accompany, and more have to do with the life of the reader than the life of the text."[20] Occasionally this is true to the extent that we cannot even figure out why a particular note appears in a particular text. The last leaf of a copy of Terence's comedies now at the University of Alberta contains a veterinary recipe in English, headed "A drinke for beastes,"[21] while the Huntington copy of Boccaccio's 'Amorous Fiammetta' has only one manuscript note, where an early owner has written on the verso of the title page a recipe for leek and herb sauce.[22] And then there's the note in the copy of John Alexander's 'Jesuitico–Quakerism Examined' at the Clark Library that begins "delyvered to Tim. 8 little glasses 5 big

---

[18] Michael Hunter, "The British Library and the Library of John Evelyn," in John Evelyn in the British Library (London, 1995), 84–85.
[19] Hilaire Kallendorf and Craig Kallendorf, "Conversations with the Dead: Quevedo and Statius, Annotation and Imitation," Journal of the Warburg and Courtauld Institutes 53 (2000), 131–68.
[20] Sherman, "What Did Renaissance Readers Write," 130.
[21] John Considine, Adversaria: Sixteenth–Century Books and the Traces of Their Readers (Edmonton, 1998), 38–39, nr. 42.
[22] Sherman, "What Did Renaissance Readers Write," 130.

glasses a decanter and a water bottle ...”[23] These notes, as Sherman observes, "represent the most specific and revealing intrusions of a readerly presence into the margins of an authorial text,"[24] but it is hard to say much about this presence.

More commonly, however, something in the text triggers a personal reaction in the reader that provides insight into both the reader's life and the way he or she makes sense of experience through reading. In a copy of the 1502 Valerius Maximus now at the University of Texas, for example, a seventeenth-century reader has added the most memorable event in his life, the destruction and refashioning of a bell tower in his local church, to the memorable deeds and sayings recorded from antiquity.[25] The Folger Library copy of Plutarch's *Lives* (Venice, 1478) contains annotations by one Calixtus Forcrandus detailing events in his life in Bourg–en–Bresse, near Lyons, between 1504 and 1515.[26] Similarly the Beinecke copy of Michael Beuther's *Ephemeris historica*, which provides a day–by–day listing of events of historical significance from the time of Christ to its publication in 1556, was annotated in two Augustinian convents in Paris and Bourges, where each annotator added "plusieurs choses notables arrivees de son temps", ranging from the death of Luther and a visit by King Henry III to the convent to the expulsion of a student from the convent school and the gift of a pair of slippers to the annotator.[27] And the Folger copy of Solinus's *Polyhistor*, which describes the fauna of the Roman Empire, has a marginal note next to the description of the giraffe that describes how the Soldan of Egypt made a gift of this animal first to King Ferrante of Naples in 1480, then to Lorenzo de' Medici in 1487.[28]

Notes like these can also tell us a good deal about the hopes and fears — the most private emotions — of early readers. Next to Psalm 56, verses 5–6 and 8–9 of Thomas More's prayer book, for example, we see *demones* written twice in the margin, even though demons are not mentioned in the text, leading J. B. Trapp to conclude that "[t]his is the profoundly personal and moving record of More's search for protection from those 'demones', the word occurring again and again in the margins, who were tempting his immortal soul to

---

[23] I owe this reference to Hilaire Kallendorf.
[24] Sherman, John Dee, 83.
[25] The book is described in Craig W. Kallendorf and Maria X. Wells, Aldine Press Books at the Harry Ransom Humanities Research Center, The University of Texas at Austin: A Descriptive Catalogue (Austin, 1998), 93, nr. 56a.
[26] Hulvey, "Not So Marginal," 172–73.
[27] Rosenthal, The Rosenthal Collection, 71–73, nr. 18.
[28] Hulvey, "Not So Marginal," 173–74.

ruin."[29] A 1532–33 Virgil now in Vicenza contains a poem on the back flyleaf, entitled *Invitus in quodam carcere Patavii* ("Reluctant, in a certain Paduan prison"):

> *Non carcer, non vincla viros, non aspera terrent*
> *Tormenta, adversus synceritatis opus.*
> *Ferte, viri, superanda omnis Fortuna ferendo est:*
> *Stat dicus hic, mollit ardua longa dies.*

Neither prison, nor chains, nor harsh tortures terrify men against the exercise of integrity. Endure, men, every fortune is to be overcome by enduring: a dyke stands here, a long day lightens adversity.

Then we find an explicit link between what was thought in prison and what was read in Virgil:

> *Quae conformia sunt dicto Maronis, qui solitus erat dicere, nullam asperam acro [sic] esse fortunam, quam prudenter patiendo vir fortis non vincat, et in V° Aeneidos inseruit.*

These things are in conformity to the opinion of Virgil, who was accustomed to say that for the man of spirit there is no fortune so harsh that a brave man cannot overcome it by enduring wisely, which he put into the fifth book of the *Aeneid*.

A copy of the 1479 edition of Virgil, also now in Vicenza, tells a similarly depressing story, for in the *Priapea*, a series of obscene poems attributed to Virgil in the Renaissance, we find a one–word marginal note, *pedicare* ("to sodomize"), and a weeping face.[30] For the record, though, early annotators also had a sense of humor. The Beinecke copy of Joannes Ludovicus Vivaldus's *De contritionis veritate*, a commentary to the Ten Commandments and the Seven Deadly Sins that focuses on salvation through contrition, has an index, in which we find the word *inebrietas* ("drunkenness"). Next to this entry, an early commen-

---

[29] J. B. Trapp, Erasmus, Colet and Moore: The Early Tudor Humanists and Their Books, The Panizzi Lectures, 1990 (London, 1991), 43–45. See also Adrian Johns, The Nature of the Book: Print and Knowledge in the Making (Chicago, 1998), 409–12, for an account of how John Roberts (b. 1627) also struggled to deal with the demons aroused by his reading. This account is part of a fascinating chapter entitled "The Physiology of Reading," which explains how early modern readers believed that reading helped shape their personalities.
[30] Kallendorf, Virgil and the Myth of Venice, 34–35, 90. A note similar to that of the Paduan prisoner in a slightly earlier copy of Flavius Josephus whose annotator was imprisoned in Saint–Vincent in 1487 is recorded in Chatelain, "Humanisme e culture de la note," 27.

tator has written *dialogi de Ebrietate* ("dialogues on drunkenness"), followed by some three dozen epithets for drink and drunkards.[31]

It is clear, then, that sixteenth–century readers can use their books to make sense of their experiences in ways that resemble very closely those of their twenty–first century counterparts, but we must be careful not to conclude that early modern people are exactly like us. Early readers, for example, habitually read Virgil's poetry through the filter of Christianity. A copy of the 1537 edition now in the Biblioteca Antoniana, Padua, adds a precise reference, *David, Psalm 119*, to an association made by one of the printed commentaries between *Eclogue* 1 and the Christian God. When Servius provides an interpretation of *Aeneid* 4.331 that is consistent with Christian thought, the annotator writes, *vid. bene*, but when Servius glosses *Aeneid* 2.501–2 as meaning that religion is of no benefit, he responds indignantly that as Augustine shows in *De civitate Dei* 1.2, the Trojan gods did not benefit Priam because they were false gods. A note in the Marciana copy of the 1543–44 heirs of Lucas Antonius Junta edition in turn puts a Christian spin on one of Virgil's most famous lines:

Augustinus De civitate Dei, superbis Deus resistit, humilibus autem dat gratiam. Hoc vero quod Dei est, superbae quoque animae spiritus inflatos affectat, amatque sibi in laudibus dici, Parcere subiectis, et debellar[e] superbos.

Augustine says in the 'City of God' [preface], 'God resists the proud, but gives grace to the humble' [Jas. 4:6]. But that which is of God tries to gain control over the swollen pride of the overbearing spirit and loves it to be said in its praise that it 'spares the subjected and tames the proud.'[32]

When the printed commentaries or the minor poems attributed to Virgil ran afoul of the Church, the editions that contained them were to be expurgated, as the annotation at the beginning of the *Priapea* in a Princeton incunable with a clerical provenance indicates: *Hic liber prohibitus est in Concilio Trident. quia est spurcissimus* ("This book has been prohibited in the Council of Trent, since it is most filthy").[33]

Even when they were most unlike us, however, early readers were still revealing a good deal about themselves, for personal judgment came into play even in the effort to deal with the Index. In an expurgated Virgil now in the university library in Padua, for example, Vives's name is cancelled on the title page along with his commentary to *Eclogues* 1–5 and a section of Ascensius's commentary to *Eclogue* 4; in another expurgated text in the same library, the com-

---

[31] Rosenthal, Rosenthal Collection, 378–80, nr. 160.
[32] Kallendorf, Virgil and the Myth of Venice, 91–92.
[33] Shelf mark: VRG 2945 1484q, sig. G1r.

mentary of Ascensius in general is the target. Both authors were good Catholics whose works had been used by most readers of the day to reconcile Virgil and their Christian faith.[34] While the censors who marked passages in these books were unusually zealous, however, others veered wildly in the other direction. Castiglione's 'The Courtier', for example, was placed on the international index in 1590, removed, then put back on in 1623, where it stayed until 1966. Officially copies published before 1590 were supposed to be presented for expurgation, but this was often not done. Two copies now at the University of Texas are nevertheless striking in that they remain unexpurgated even though the first, a copy of the 1528 Aldine edition, was in the library of the Jesuit community in Carpi and the second, a copy of the 1545 Aldine edition, was in the library of Filippo d'Anastasio (b. 1656), the archbishop of Sorrento.[35] Thus the lack of marginalia can also tell us something about the lives of early readers — or to say it a little differently, if we are willing to call expurgation a commentary of sorts, the absence of a commentary may serve as a commentary, too.

The personalities of early annotators probably come through most clearly when they disagree with the text they were reading. Steven Zwicker has recently argued that before 1640 reading tended toward studying a text and mining it for examples of wisdom and stylistic facility, but that after that date many marginalia show a passionate contest between reader and writer, a contest devoted to correcting errors or expressing disagreement with the printed text.[36] Marginalia in early editions of John Dryden, for example, often reveal resistance, with one copy of 'Absalom and Achitophel' eliciting a note in which the poet is condemned as "an Atheist Exceeding Lucretius."[37] Such polemical notes, however, are found in earlier books as well. The reader of the Beinecke copy of the 1512 Giunta Lucretius engages in a running battle with an opponent he names *Inpius*, with this comment being typical: *Nescio quid hic somniat Inpius cum sensus poetae facillimus sit athomos sibi obvias dissilire* ... ("I don't

---

[34] Kallendorf, Virgil and the Myth of Venice, 138–39.
[35] Peter Burke, The Fortunes of the Courtier: The European Reception of Castiglione's Cortegiano (University Park, 1995), 100–6; and Kallendorf and Wells, Aldine Press, 231, nr. 229a, and 272–73, nr. 297. London, British Library C.28.a.4 offers an example of an early edition of Castiglione that was properly expurgated, in this case by one Rosati, Revisor to the Florentine Inquisition (Burke, The Fortunes of the Courtier, 103).
[36] Steven Zwicker, "Reading the Margins: Politics and the Habits of Appropriation," in Keven Sharpe and Steven N. Zwicker (eds.), Refiguring Revolutions: Aesthetics and Politics from the English Revolution to the Romantic Revolution (Berkeley and Los Angeles, 1998), 101–15.
[37] Anna Battigelli, "John Dryden's Angry Readers," in Anderson and Sauer (eds.), Books and Readers, 274.

know why this Inpius nods off, since the poet's meaning is obvious, that atoms burst apart in front of us").[38] These earlier anonymous readers were often not afraid to start a fight with the most famous experts of the day, as shown by the annotator who wrote next to Propertius's verse *Argus ut ignotis cornibus inachidos* in the Beinecke copy of the 1502 Aldine edition this note: *uti notis Sc[aliger], sed male meo iudicio* ("*uti notis* [is the reading of] Scaliger, but in my judgment [it's] badly [emended]").[39] Budé's copy of Cristoforo Landino's *Disputationes Camaldulenses*, a literary–philosophical dialogue that concludes with a detailed commentary on Virgil's *Aeneid*, turns into an extended conversation between two great scholars, with the annotator often challenging the conclusions found in the printed text. Landino, for example, explains that Mary works with her mind, which is immortal and incorruptible and therefore is the "best part" of a person; Martha, on the other hand, works with her senses, which she shares with the animals. Budé notes that *graece non optimam sed bonam legitur, quare tu falso argumentaris* ("in Greek the reading is not 'best' but 'good', for which reason your argument is false").[40]

As we might expect, polemical annotations are common in religious contexts, but again, they are found in pre–1640 books much more often than Zwicker's generalization might suggest. In the copy of Thomas Elyot's 'The Boke named the Governour' (London, 1546) at the University of Alberta, for example, a description of a Catholic mass is crossed out by a Protestant reader, who writes in the margin that "it is nowe for the abhomyna[ble] naughtiness o[f] it, sworne cleane awey god send it n[ever] to returne."[41] Again, however, notes from a religious perspective often reveal an unexpected capacity for nuance. In a 1611 folio containing an early Puritan commentary on 'The Faerie Queene', "a manuscript text in angry dialogue with the printed poem," as Stephen Orgel put it, we see a reader who starts by bringing a basic classical education to his reading of the text, for when Red Crosse Knight draws blood from a tree in Book 1, Canto 2, the reader notes the parallel to Virgil's Polydorus. Poetic conventions, however, are quickly taken as signs of heresy, as when the invocation to the Muses in the proem elicits "Heere hee invocates one of the Muses, as the heathen folk did, and so is an idolater." Anything that smacks of Catholicism is especially irritating, as when a reference to St. George stimulates "A popish saint devised by idle Monks." Yet a critical mind of some acuteness emerges in these marginalia. When Red Crosse Knight kills Sansfoy, for example, the annotater recognizes and appreciates the allegory

---

[38] Rosenthal, The Rosenthal Collection, 200–3, nr. 78.
[39] Ibid., 84–86, nr. 25.
[40] Grafton, Commerce with the Classics, 167–68.
[41] Considine, Adversaria, 32, nr. 34.

but worries about what will happen if some readers don't understand what is going on: "you will say here is a mysticall meaning. I think so, but all know not that, and therefore it is not safe to teach murther under such pretenses." Especially insightful is the note in Book 1, Canto 4, which criticizes Una for not praying: "Heere is no thank[s] to god for her de[li]verance. Is it shame for a po[et] to pray? Not so for heathen Virgi[ls] & Homers have m[ade] prayers to their g[ods]." This note shows a recognition that the ancients had their religion, too, which offers both a threat to and support for Christianity.[42] In this conversation between reader and writer, we hear clearly an annotator who is pious and principled, yet fairly sophisticated as a critic and capable of seeing various shades of gray. In this case, a personality of some complexity emerges in opposition to the text being annotated.

* * *

If annotators like Spenser's Puritan reader can reveal a personality of some interest in the margins of the books they read, it would stand to reason that with an adequate body of surviving marginalia, a great individual could really come alive in the pages of his or her books. Henry Howard, later Earl of Northampton, for example, annotated a copy of Castiglione's 'Courtier' that begins with underlining and marginal summary, but the choice of passages reveals his interests and tells us a good deal about him. He shows a preoccupation with honor that is typical of the Renaissance aristocrat and expresses a keen interest in the visual arts. He clearly saw Castiglione's text as a moralizing work, but he shows special interest in the discussions of grace.[43] If indeed, as Stephen Greenblatt argued in his now–classic study, the Renaissance aristocrat engaged in conscious self–fashioning, there would be no better text than Castiglione's to use as a source for defining the self and presenting it to the world. This is exactly what Howard does in the margins of this text.

Scholars, too, can reveal their personalities in their annotations. For an example, let us return briefly to Guillaume Budé. Like most humanists, he read with pen in hand, and when he found a passage that appealed to him, he launched into vigorous underlining and summary. When he read how Pliny tortured Christians to ascertain their true beliefs, he wrote, "o wretched art thou, Pliny, utterly lost and damned" in the margin next to the offending passage. And Budé even managed to turn his copy of Homer into an extension of himself, although his marginalia showed him struggling to master its difficulties. As a middle–aged man contemplating marriage to a much younger

---

[42] Stephen Orgel, "Margins of Truth," in Andrew Murphy (ed.), The Renaissance Text: Theory, Editing, Textuality (Manchester and New York, 2000), 99–107.
[43] Burke, The Fortunes of the Courtier, 79–80.

woman, next to the passage in Homer which describes how a young woman was cursed by loving old men, he wrote, "mark these verses." In other words, as Anthony Grafton has concluded, Budé's marginalia ended up "transforming the printed text from a standardized product into something unique. His notes recorded an individual's response, laid out in a visually appealing and memorable way, to a particularly important book."[44]

Perhaps the most striking example of this phenomenon is Gabriel Harvey, the English scholar whose voluminous marginalia have been much studied for several generations.[45] Harvey's annotations include the standard underlinings, marked–off passages, and indexing notes, but they extend from there to present a vivid picture of Harvey's inner life, of his own analysis of his intersection with the world around him that is candid and dynamic. Some of the notes record his role in the public life of his day, like the one found at the end of the first three books of the first decade of Livy, which states that he discussed these books at length with Sir Philip Sidney before Sidney's mission as the queen's representative to Emperor Rudolph II in 1576–77. As a scholar and tutor, he reveals his tastes, as in the note in Lodovico Domenichi's 'Facetie, motti, et burle', in which he concludes that Virgil refined Ennius, but Du Bartas refined and improved upon Virgil. Many passages in the printed texts, however, elicit self–analysis from Harvey. Sextus Julius Frontinus's 'The strategemes ... of warre', translated by Richard Morysine, tells of the capture of a formidable Spanish town by Marcus Cato. Next to this passage Harvey wrote, *At nihil tale feci. Ad polyhistorem ista aliquid; sed quid ad Gabrielem Harveium? Nihil Loci Communes, sive propria Industria?* ("But nothing of the sort have I accomplished. [I have progressed] to some extent towards a man of learning but what [have I accomplished] towards the man Gabriel Harvey? Without industry of one's own there are no topics for discussion".) In the margins of John Florio, 'Florio his first fruites: a perfect induction to the Italian and English tongues', Harvey wrote under the pseudonym Axiophilus of his frustrations at not being able to learn Italian as quickly as the other courtiers, encouraging himself with *Repete, repete; ut fervidus lanista* ("Try again, try again, like an enthusiastic gladiator trainer"). Axiophilus is one of a series of pseudonyms that appear in the margins of Harvey's books, allowing him to codify the ideals to which he aspires and exhorting him to try harder in his youth, then helping him to heal the wounds of his later failures, such that we almost feel as if reading Harvey's marginalia allows us to eavesdrop on a series

---

[44] Anthony Grafton, "Is the History of Reading a Marginal Enterprise? Guillaume Budé and His Books," Papers of the Bibliographical Society of America 91 (1997), 139–57.

[45] G. C. Moore Smith, Gabriel Harvey's Marginalia (Stratford–upon–Avon, 1913); and H. S. Wilson, "Gabriel Harvey's Method of Annotating His Books," Harvard Library Bulletin 2 (1948), 344–61.

ing Harvey's marginalia allows us to eavesdrop on a series of therapy sessions.[46] At any rate, as Virginia F. Stern concludes, these notes allow us "to search out ... the inner man: what Harvey thought, his changes of mood, devices he used to cope with the cruelties and injustices he encountered, his views of himself and others, his self-admonitions and precepts, his methods of scholarship, and above all his unceasing efforts toward self-improvement. Glimpses of this sort are obtainable by investigating his personal notes to himself."[47] There is no question that Harvey's notes are more personal, and more interesting, than most of what we find in the margins of early modern books. This, however, says more about the limited emotional and intellectual life of the average person than it does about marginalia as a genre, which have proved perfectly capable of expressing as much subtlety and depth as their author possesses.

* * *

Marginalia like Harvey's reflect a clear effort at self-fashioning, one that begins with defining himself as subject for himself but extends through the regular lending of his books to matters of self-presentation as well. As the notes in his books and those of others show, this process can go on at several levels. The most rudimentary level is the simple act of signing one's name in a book. This is not the neutral activity it might first appear to be, but is rather an act of aggression, a way of claiming what was written by someone else as one's own and defining one's self in relation to it — 'I am what I am as an extension of this book, or in opposition to it, in some way or other.'[48] Those owners who actually read their books — then as now, a book owned is not necessarily a book read — often signalled their progress with notes such as *Nota quod 1606 die 14 Augusti legens hunc locum* ("Note that this place was being read on 14 August 1606," in the Marciana copy of the 1514 Aldine Virgil), allowing us to track their interaction with the texts they were reading.[49]

Other marginalia extend and clarify this initial act of appropriation. The Houghton Library copy of the 'Articles ... According to the computation of

---

[46] Virginia F. Stern, Gabriel Harvey: A Study of His Life, Marginalia, and Library (Oxford, 1979), 135–90; the translations are Stern's. One presumes that Harvey masked some of his thoughts and feelings behind pseudonyms in order to retain some control over how he was presenting himself through his marginalia, for as Eugene R. Kintgen notes, the number of books from Harvey's library inscribed *Gabrielis Harveij, et amicorum* ("[this book belongs to] Garbriel Harvey and his friends") shows that their owner intended to lend his books around freely (Reading Tudor England [Pittsburgh, 1996], 63–64).
[47] Ibid., 137.
[48] Jackson, Marginalia, 90.
[49] Kallendorf, Virgil and the Myth of Venice, 59.

the Church of England' (London, 1612), for example, contains a signed statement on the final blank page confirming that one John Davenport read from this copy before witnesses, thus subscribing to the act of uniformity required of British clergy during this period.[50] Davenport defined himself professionally through this note, as does Christian Beyer, MD, who filled the margins of his copy of Nicolaus Piso's *De cognoscendis et curandis ... morbis libri tres,* now at the Beinecke, with references to other medical texts, case histories drawn from his experience, prescriptions, clinical observations, and descriptions of symptoms drawn from his actual practice. And one of the notes he left in this book stresses the highly personal character of his annotation:

Ad inventorem huius libri[,] *Hic liber Christiani Beyeri Medici supellectili librariae adscribitur. Quem si fors per occasionem invenisti restitutionis memor sis mi lector nam meo non tuo usui inservire potest, ob annotata quae vix legere poteris; amice igitur et obrepe rogo ut librum hunc mihi restitui cures, ni fur aut iniquus possessor alienae rei audire velis.*[51]

To whoever should find this book: it belongs to the working library of Christian Beyer, M.D. If by any chance you should find it, dear reader, please remember to return it to me: because of the manuscript notes that are practically illegible, it is useful only to me, not to you. So, dear friend, I urge you to see to it that it is returned to me, unless you want to be known as a thief and the wicked owner of stolen goods.

A particularly interesting example of this phenomenon is found in the annotations to Giovanni Andrea dell'Anguillara's translation of Book 1 of the *Aeneid,* published in Padua in 1564 by Gratioso Perchacino. Thirty-eight of the forty-six surviving copies that I have been able to see myself or obtain reliable information about have 'Giovanni Andrea dell'Anguillara dona di propria mano' ("Giovanni Andrea dell'Anguillara makes a gift [of this book] from his own hand") written in the handwriting of the author on the back of the title page; fifteen of these thirty-eight also contain the name of the recipient, also in Anguillara's hand. This book is a trial run, as it were, a sample of the kind of translation Anguillara could write. There were eleven more books of Virgil's poetry to do, but in order to finish his work, Anguillara needed a patron, someone who believed in his project and could provide the financial backing needed to support the translator while he worked and finance the publication of his book when it was finished. Anguillara's marginalia show that he planned to hand out his translation of Book 1 to those who might be able to help him. The translation was never finished, which suggests that Anguillara never

---

[50] Stoddard, Marks in Books, 23, nr. 35.
[51] Rosenthal, The Rosenthal Collection, 274–76, nr. 114.

found the patron he needed, making the marginalia in his book a particularly interesting record of an unsuccessful attempt to define one's self professionally.[52]

Annotators could define themselves genealogically as well in the margins of their books. In the margins of his copy of the Welsh laws of Hywel Dda, John Dee drew a line from the first word of the text (Hywel) to the margin, where this name is the third one in a marginal genealogy beginning with *Rodericus Magnus Rex totius Cambriae* in 843 and ending with Dee himself, his wife Jane, and their eight children.[53] A similar process of self–definition takes place in the margins of a 1610 edition of the 'Mirror for Magistrates', in which Lady Anne Clifford writes "some part of this I red over my selfe and the rest of [it] Wm. Watkinson read to me the 30:31st of March 1670 in Brough Castle." Then a few pages later she places herself in relation to her family by writing next to a passage in praise of 'Renowned Clifford' "this was my ffather George erle of Cumberland"; then beside a passage on Sir William Russell, "hee y^t was my Mothers younger Brother."[54]

In these examples, the process of self–definition is triggered by the name of a family member, but an explicit trigger is not necessary for a book to be used in similar ways. A copy of the Venice, 1551 Virgil now in Verona contains this note:

> *Memoria quando morse la venerabile signora gridonia filio primo del signor conte Gaihes* [?] *conte de Sartero qual fu molier del venerabile signor conte aurelio Becaria conte de la pieve morse alle 16 die novembre a hore 10 de note del ano 1579.*[55]

> A memorial of the death of the venerable Signora Gridonia, first child of Gaihes, count of Sartero, who was the wife of the venerable Count

---

[52] Craig Kallendorf, "In Search of a Patron: Anguillara's Vernacular Virgil and the Print Culture of Renaissance Italy," Papers of the Bibliographical Society of America 91 (1997), 294–325.

[53] Sherman, John Dee, 87 and fig. 6, 108.

[54] Stephen Orgel, "Margins of Truth," in Murphy (ed.), The Renaissance Text, 95–99. For an interesting extension of the points being developed in this essay, see M. E. Lamb, "The Agency of the Split Subject: Lady Anne Clifford and the Uses of Reading," English Literary Renaissance 22 (1992), 347–68. Obviously Kevin Sharpe is (uncharacteristically) mistaken when he writes that "Lady Clifford, however, did not annotate her books and she does not comment on the books she read" (Reading Revolutions, 298).

[55] Kallendorf, Virgil and the Myth of Venice, 162. Books were also used in a similar way to record births: see, for example, the 1528 Galen in which the Spanish physician Francisco Ximenez of Cordoba recorded the birth of his daughter, "Jueves en dos de diciembre ... de 1540 años nascio mi hija Augustinica" (Rosenthal, The Rosenthal Collection, 144–46, nr. 53).

Aurelio Becaria, count of the parish; she died on 16 November, at 10 at night in the year 1579.

This book was being used like a family Bible, to record the death of an important person by (presumably) a family member. Petrarch's famous Virgil in the Ambrosian Library was used in the same way, for it records in his handwriting the dates when he first met his Laura and when she died.[56] A 1507 Virgil now at Princeton in turn bears the note *Anno 1568. Die 19 Junij Hunc Vergilium filio suo Joanni Rinckio perlegendum et ediscendum transmittit Antonius Rinckius* ("on the 19th of June, 1568, Antonius Rinckius passed on this copy of Virgil to his son Joannes to be read through and learned by heart").[57] This book, in other words, serves as a tangible record of how one father sought to shape the character of his son in relation to a beloved and valuable book.

* * *

As these examples have shown, early readers often defined themselves in the margins of their books. When they marked passages of stylistic value in their Latin texts, they were solidifying their control of the preferred language for self expression in their day; and when they marked passages of moral value, they were refining their sense of right and wrong in preparation for action. In both cases, the marked passages went into notebooks that expressed their values and priorities, as preparation for original compositions of their own. In conversation with their books, the voices of early readers emerge, revealing both the patterns of their logic and the emotions and values that made them unique. Sometimes a truly great personality emerges in the margins of early books, but in any event, early readers defined themselves both professionally and genealogically through the marks they left in their books.

For scholars who prefer more traditional methods, this information is valuable enough to merit the often considerable effort it takes to find and use it. Until someone invents a time machine that works, we will never be able to go back into the past and interrogate those who have lived before us. All we can do is to use the written records they have left behind. There are many sources for important battles and who held what office when, but there are not many sources that really help us see individual people as people. Few things are as personal as reading, so the notes readers have left in their books offer a rare opportunity to see the reflections of someone else's soul.

---

[56] This volume, of course, is a manuscript rather than a printed book. It is described in Marco Bunocore (ed.), Vedere i classici: l'illustrazione libraria dei testi antichi dall'età romana al tardo medioevo (Rome, 1996), 257–59, nr. 46, which contains references to older bibliography.

[57] Shelf mark: VRG 2945 1507, on front pastedown.

For those scholars who prefer some of the latest methods, marginalia are of even greater potential importance. The American 'new historicists' and the British cultural materialists, for example, often feel uncomfortable with the idea that a person possesses a transcendental essence. As Jean Howard puts it, "[o]ne of the most striking developments of contemporary thought is the widespread attack on the notion that man possesses a transhistorical core of being. Rather, everything from maternal 'instinct' to conceptions of the self are now seen to be the products of specific discourses and social practices."[58] If there is no soul, but only a series of interventions in which the individual defines himself or herself in reaction to events, ideas, and other people, then it becomes crucial to recover each and every one of these interventions, because (as Ralph Hanna III puts it) when an annotator is annotating, "he is in fact creating himself as reader."[59] In other words, early modern subjects create themselves in the margins of their books, and we postmodern scholars would be well advised to search for them there.

And in the end — perhaps surprisingly — this is important. Contemporary reader–response theory has taught us that the meaning of a classical text like Virgil's poetry rests not in the timeless intention of the author, but in a negotiation between text and reader that is very much timebound, linked inextricably to the values and ideas that the reader brings to the text and enters into his or her marginal comments.[60] This being the case, our critical and interpretive skills are therefore improved significantly if we take the time and trouble to recover as much as we can of the ideas and values of the annotator who has written a commentary into the margins of a printed book.

Craig Kallendorf   Texas A&M University

---

[58] Jean Howard, "The New Historicism in Renaissance Studies," in Arthur F. Kinney and Dan S. Collins (eds.), Renaissance Historicism: Selections from English Literary Renaissance (Amherst, Mass., 1987), 10.
[59] Ralph Hanna III, "Annotation as Social Practice," in Stephen A. Barney (ed.), Annotation and Its Texts (New York, 1991), 181.
[60] The now-classic articulations of this position may be found in Wolfgang Iser, The Act of Reading: A Theory of Aesthetic Response (Baltimore, 1978); and Hans Robert Jauss, Toward an Aesthetic of Reception, trans. Timothy Bahti (Minneapolis, 1982).

Index of manuscripts

Assisi
> Biblioteca e Centro Documentazione Francescana (Sacro Convento), *303* 10

Augsburg
> Staats- und Stadtbibliothek, *2° Cod. 305* 10

Bern
> Burgerbibliothek, *ms. 411* 7, 10

Bologna
> Biblioteca Universitaria, *ms. 124* 80n56
> Biblioteca Universitaria, *ms. 1438* 87n3

London
> British Library, *King's 32* 52

Modena
> Biblioteca Estense, *Est. lat. 306 (α.W.4.13)* 32n9
> Biblioteca Estense, *Ms. Campori App. 324 (γ.S.5.25)* 87n2

Munich
> Bayerische Staatsbibliothek, *Clm 7612* 10, 32n9
> Bayerische Staatsbibliothek, *Clm 19480* 19n20
> Universitätsbibliothek, *2° Cod. 548* 32n9

Naples
> Biblioteca Nazionale, *IV C 3* 32n9

Padua
> Biblioteca del Seminario, *142* 10

Rome
> Biblioteca Corsiniana, *Cors. 1836 (43 F 11)* 10

Vatican City, Biblioteca Apostolica Vaticana
> *Vat. lat. 1801* 30n5
> *Vat. lat. 2184* 17n19
> *Vat. lat. 6737* 50n6
> *Vat. lat. 6835* 52
> *Vat. lat. 6848* 51, 51n10
> *Chigi F.VIII 193* 66n5
> *Ottob. lat. 179* 17n19

Ottob. lat. 1389 17n19
Ottob. lat. 3291 10
Pal. lat. 1279 71
Urb. lat. 301 52
Urb. lat. 1180 59

Venice
   Biblioteca Nazionale Marciana, *lat. XIV 179 (4488)* 32n9

Yale
   ms. 358 10

Index of persons and works

Abano, Pietro de, *Conciliator* 75n34
Actaeon 92
Aesop 10
Alberti, Leon Battista, *De re aedificatoria* 4.1 83
Aldus Manutius, ed. of *Catullus, Tibullus, and Propertius (1502)* 107–108n63
Alexander, John 116
Amor, *s.* Cupid
Anastasio, Filippo d' 120
Anguillara, Giovanni Andrea dell' 125
Anonymus, *Sallust commentary (Bern ms. 411)*, *accessus* 12; — *De coniuratione Catilinae* 1.1 15, *1.1–4* 16, *1.2* 17, *5.1–6* 18, *5.9–6.2* 19, *9.1–5* 20, *13.3* 21, *14.1–3* 22, *17.1* 22, *31.4* 23, *32.2* 25, *33.1* 24, *35.1* 24, *35.2* 24, *51* 25, *51.1* 26, *52.1–2* 26, *61.1–9* 27; — *s. later version attr. to Ognibene da Lonigo*
Appius Claudius 31
Apuleius, 88–109; — *Apologia 22.9* 90n11; — *De diphtongis (attrib.)* 59, *f. 113v–114r* 59; — *Metamorphoses (Golden Ass) 2.4.10* 92n16, *2.5.1* 92n17, *5.1.3* 101, *9.4.3* 90n11; — *De mundo 20* 96; — *Florida 9.9* 90n11, *16* 109n69; — *s.* Beroaldo
Arabic authors (Mauretani) 70
Aristoteles 65, 72, 72n19; — (attrib.) 50; — *De plantis (attrib.)* 66, 68, 81; — *Metaphysics* 68
Arnulf of Orleans, *commentary on Lucan* 11
Articles ... According to the computation of the Church of England *(1612)* 124–125
Ascensius, *s.* Bade
Atedius Melior 96
Athenaeus, *Deipnosophistae 9.49* 80n54
Augustine, *De civitate Dei, 1 praef.* 119, *1.2* 119
Avicenna, *Canon 2.159* 70
Avienus 10
Axiophilus (pseudonym of John Harvey) 123

Bade, Josse (Jodocus Badius Ascensius), 34, 40–41, 43, 45, 119–120; — *Familiaris explanatio* 39; — *Cat. 1.1* 15, *3.1* 40, *61.3* 40
Bakócz, Tamás 107n61
Ballistreri, G. 9
Balsamo, Jean 45n47
Barbaro, Ermolao, the Younger, 65–84; — *Castigationes Plinianae* 68, *praefatio (ed. Pozzi, vol. I p. 3)* 74, *monitum (I 4)* 81, *Ca. primae 1.7 (I 17)* 81, *1.54 (I 33)* 84, *4.74 (I 214)* 81, *5.202 (II 433)* 80, *7.15 (II 540)* 79, *8.23 (II 583)* 80, *9,10 (II 604)* 74n30, *10.2.2 (II 629)* 80, *11.32.5 (II 667)* 83, *14,31 (II 739)* 70n16, *18.18 (II 795)* 70n16, *26.1 (III 923)* 66n6, *26,13 (III 926)* 74n30, *29.29 (III 988)* 66n6, *Ca. secundae praefatio (III 1213)* 79, *Ca. in Melam, praef. (III 1307)* 69n14, *Ca. glossemata, praefatio (III 1353)* 82, *O 14 (III 1417)* 76, *S 75 (III 1452)* 83, *T 6 (III 1464)* 80; — *De coelibatu, praef. 3* 80n53, *3.5.79–80* 74n31;

— *Dioscorides* 67–84, print of *1517* 68, *Corollarium in Dioscoridem, 1* 71n17, *4* 70n16, *5* 69, *9* 72n19, *12* 70n16, *28* 81, *83* 84, *98* 70n16, *124* 72n19, *134* 68n11, *173* 72n19, *195* 72n19, *206* 72n19, *221* 81n64, *240* 72, *256* 72n19, *303* 72n19, *312* 72n19, *314* 72n19, *322* 72n19, *385* 72n19, *410* 81n64, *414* 72n19, *425* 72n19, *461* 71n17, *469* 72n19, *472* 72n19, *543* 71n17, 72n19, *562* 72n19, *567* 72n19, *616* 72n19, *625* 72n19, *628* 72n19, *695* 72n19, *740* 72n19, *904* 72n19, *922* 73; — *Epistolae, 2* (ed. Branca, vol. I p. 5) 80, *12 (I 17)* 74, *17 (I 26)* 84, *18 (I 26)* 81, *19 (I 29)* 81, *27 (I 42)* 75n34, *31 (I 47)* 75, *56 (I 74)* 73n26, *108 (II 29)* 74n28, *115 (II 33)* 80, 81, *123 (II 39)* 80, *125 (II 41)* 74, *132 (II 50)* 72n21, *135.36* 74, ep. non datate *5 (II 89)* 74, ep. n. d. *7 (II 91)* 84, ep. n. d. *8 (II 92)* 74, ep. n. d. *10 (II 93)* 75n34

Barbaro, Francesco 65; — *De re uxoria* 68, 80; — *Epistolae, 278* 75n34, *293* 75n34, *344* 75n34

Barker, Nicolas 113n10

Basilius 50

Bauhinus, Caspar, *Pinax theatri botanici* 71

Baxendall, Michael 93n18, 94, 94n21

Bayle, Pierre 32

Beckford, William 115n15

Bembo, Pietro, *De Aetna* 83

Benedetto d'Ettore 107n62

Benedictus Presbyter 35

Bentivoglio, Antongaleazzo 93–96, 93n19

Beroaldo, Filippo, the Elder, 87–109, *courses, on Apuleius* 88, 108, *on Cicero* 108, *on Pliny the Younger* 103n52, *on Statius' Thebaid* 87n4; — *Annotationes centum, praef.* 8 83, *62.1* 82n69; — *Commentarii in Asinum Aureum, dedication (sig. a2r)* 109n70, 109n71, 109n72, *(sig. a4v)* 102n51, 107–108n63, *praefatio (2v)* 91, *1.1.1 (5r)* 89, *2.4.3–10 (33v–35r)* 92–97, *2.4.7 (34v)* 93, 94, 95, 96, *4.28.1 (95r)* 97, *4.28.1 (95v)* 98, *5.1.3 (100v)* 101, 102, *5.1.3 (100v–101r)* 97, 103n52, *5.1.3 (101r–v)* 103, *5.6.9 (103v)* 100, *5.10.6 (105v)* 100n40, *5.23.3 (111r)* 100, *6.23.3 (132r)* 100n40, *6.23.4 (132r–v)* 100n41, *6.24.4 (134r)* 100n41, 105, *6.24.4 (134r–v, 135r)* 105, *6.24.4 (134r–135r)* 97, *6.24.4 (135r)* 105, 106, *6.5.4 (120r)* 100n39, *6.9.2 (122v)* 100n39, *6.9.4 (122v)* 100n39, *6.9.6 (123r)* 100n41, *8.22.2 (180r)* 91n13, *8.29.2 (188r)* 90, *9.5.1 (193v)* 92, *9.24.2 (207r)* 90, *10.23.3 (239r)* 92n14, *11.25.1–6 (275v)* 91; — *Oratio habita in narratione Lucii Apuleii, sig. m8v* 108n67, *sig. n1r* 108n67; — *Oratio proverbiorum (Bologna, 1499), sig. a3r* 99n37, *c4v–c7r* 108n65, *c6r* 109n70, *c6v* 108n66, *c7r* 108n66; — poem, *"Quod veriores ...", vv. 7–14* 109n70

Bessarion 50

Beuther, Michael 117

Beyer, Christian 125

Bible, Psalm 56.5–6 + 8–9 117, *119*

119
Black, Robert 44n43
Boccaccio, Giovanni 49, 116
Boethius 80
Bonisoli, *s.* Ognibene da Lonigo
Brugnoli, Benedetto 37, 38n27
Bruni, Leonardo, *De studiis et litteris* 57
Budé, Guillaume 59n23, 113, 115, 121, 122
Burckhardt, Jakob 111

Caesar, C. Julius Caesar 12, 25, 77
Calderini, Domizio 49; — *Commentarii in Martialem* 79; — *Commentarii in Statium, Silv.* 2.7.16 82n69, *epilogus* 80
Calfurnio, Giovanni 8, 34
Camillus (*model for Lorenzo Valla*) 37, 61
Carrara, Michele Alberto da 72n21
Castellanus, Vincentius 34
Castiglione, Baldassare 111, 120, 120n35, 122
Catiline 12, 23
Cato, Marcus 21, 26; 123
Catulus, Q. Lutatius 12
Cellini, Benvenuto 111
Censorinus, *De die natali 17, 10–11* 78
Charlet, Jean–Louis 60
Cicero, M. Tullius 8, 10, 12, 23, 31, 41, 58, 59, 77, 80; — *Ars vetus = De inventione* 31; — *Brutus 164* 77; — *De natura deorum 1.10* 84n75; — (attrib.) *In Sallustium* 11
Clemens, *Stromateis* 78
Clifford, Anne 126
Coleridge, Samuel Taylor 113
Columella 72, 72n19

Cortesi, Mariarosa 29, 29n2
Crassus, M. Licinius 22
Crucius Bononiensis, Jacobus 34
Cupid and Psyche 97–106

Davenport, John 125
De Gregori (press) 37
Decembrio, Angelo, *Politia litteraria 1,1,1* 78, *1,2,4* 78
Dee, John 112, 126
Diana (goddess) 92
Diana, Francesco 36
Dioscorides, 65–76, (*variant readings*) 72n19; — *s.* Barbaro; Ruel
Domenichi, Lodovico 123
Donato, Gerolamo 74
Dryden, John 120
Du Bartas, Guillaume de Salluste 123

Egnazio, Battista 76n36
Elyot, Thomas 121
Ennius 123
Epictetus 50
Este, *s.* Leonello d'Este 58
Estienne, Robert, *Thesaurus Latinae linguae* 51
Evelyn, John 116

Federigo da Montefeltro, *s.* Montefeltro
Felice di Santa Sofia, *s.* Santa Sofia
Feltre, Vittorino da, *s.* Vittorino da Feltre
Fera, Vincenzo 61
Ferrante, King of Naples 117
Ficino, Marsilio 79; — *Commentarium in Convivium Platonis 6,1* 81; — *Epistolae, 6 (ed. Hartkamp)* 83
Fileno dalla Tuata 87n3
Flavius Josephus 118n30

Florio, John 123
Forcrandus, Calixtus 117
Francia, Francesco 93
Frontinus, Sextus Julius 123
Fulgentius 97–100; — *Mythologiae 3.6* 98

Galeatius de Santa Sofia, *s*. Santa Sofia
Garin, Eugenio 99n37
Gaza, Theodore 66, 80
Gellius, Aulus 83
St. George 121
Gian Pietro da Lucca 36
Giustiniani, Bernardo, *De origine urbis Venetiarum* 37
Glareanus (Loriti), Heinrich, 34, 45; — *In Sallustium Annotationes* 39, 41, dedication 41, 42, *in Catil. 24.2* 43; — *In Titum Livium Annotationes* 43
Glossae, *Corpus Glossariorum Latinorum V. 578.3* 20n21
Gombrich, E. H. 93n18, 94, 94n21
Grafton, Anthony 44n43, 113, 115, 123
Greenblatt, Stephen 111, 122
Gregori, *s*. De Gregori
Guarini, Battista 34, 40, 58n21
Guarino Veronese 9, 10, 58

Hankins, James 44, 57, 44n45
Hanna III, Ralph 128
Harvey, Gabriel 113; 123–124; — *s*. Axiophilus
Heinlen, Michael 112
Henry III 117
Herodotus 37; — *s*. Valla, Lorenzo
Homer 115, 122–123; — *Iliad 1.402-3* 115
Horace 10; — *Ars poetica 16* 19

Howard, Henry 122
Howard, Jean 128
Hywel Dda 126

Isidore 22
Isocrates 58

Jackson, H. T. 115n15
Jardine, Lisa 44n43, 113
Juvenal 8, 9; — *s*. Merula

Kallendorf, Craig 45, 44n45, 58n20, 59n23
Kintgen, Eugene R. 124n46
Krautter, Konrad 88

Landino, Cristoforo 121
Latro, (attrib.) *Declamatio in Catilinam* 11
Leonardi, Gerolamo 75n34
Leonello d'Este 58
Leoniceno, Nicolò, *De Plinii in medicina erroribus* 66n6, 75n34
Leto, Pomponio 29, 32, 34, 35, 38, 49, 50, 51, 52, 53
Libanius 50
Livy 31, 41; *1.3.1* 74n30, *8.7* 20, *9.17.1* 104n55
Lowry, Martin 35n20
Lucan 8, 11, 21
Lucca, Gian Pietro da, *s*. Gian Pietro da Lucca
Lucretius 116, 120
Luther, Martin 117

Macrobius 97; — *Commentarii in Somnium Scipionis 1.2.7–11* 98n31, *1.2.11* 98n33
Maffei, Agostino 32
Mancinelli, Antonio, *Lima in Vallam* 37, 41

INDEX OF PERSONS AND WORKS 135

Manlius 12
Manlius Torquatus, *s.* Torquatus, T. Manlius
Marcius Rex, *s.* Rex
Marlianus, Bartholomaeus 34
Marsi, Paolo 67n9, 79
Marti, Berthe 11
Martial 49; — *6.1.3* 75n32, *14.191* 47
Martianus Capella 10, 81, 97
Mary (Virgin Mary) 91
Mattioli, Pier Andrea 76
Medici, Lorenzo de' 117
Mela, Pomponius 10
Melanchthon, Philipp 39
Meliavacca, Baldassare 80n55
Merula, Giorgio 41; — *Martial* 73; — *Juvenal, dedication* 79n52
Mino de' Rossi 97
Monfasani, John 8
Montefeltro, Federigo da 52, 53, 56, 61, 64, 79n52
More, Thomas 117
Moreto (or Moretto), Antonio 32, 34, 35, 37
Morysine, Richard 123
Most, Glenn W. 8

Nicholas V, pope, 30

Ognibene Bonisoli da Lonigo (Omnibonus Leonicenus) 7–28; — *commentary to Sallust (attrib.)* 39, 34, *accessus* + *Catil. 1.1* 14, *in Catil. 1.1* 15, *3.1.* 24, *5.1–5* 18, *5.9–6.2* 20, *9.1–5* 21, *11.4* 21, *13.3* 22, *14.3* 22, *17.1* 22, *18.2–3* 23, *31.4* 23, *35.2* 24, *37.11* 25, *37.11–38.1* 25, *35.1* 24, *35.2* 25, *51* 26, *51.1* 26, *61.1–9* 27; — *s.* Anonymus

Orgel, Stephen 121
Ovid 10; — *Metamorphoses, 1.84–86* 17, *14.610* 74n30

Pade, Marianne 37n26, 43, 43n41
Panormita, Antonio 49
Paracelsus 112
Pazzi 57
Pensis, Cristoforo de 35
Perchacino, Gratioso 125
Percival, Keith 44n44
Perotti, Niccolò 39n29, 49–64, *Martial autograph* 51, ed. *Martial 1473* 53; — *Cornu copiae, praefatio 2* 53, 54, *praef. 3* 54, 58, *praef. 6* 55, 63, *praef. 7* 55, *27.3* 69n13, *31.18* 84, *41.33* 83, *44.9* 82, *44.9–10* 78, *75.1* 53n14, *99.14* 56n17, *127* 56n18, *epilogus* 60–61, *1–2* 57, *epil. 2* 62; — *Rudimenta grammatices* 50; — *De componendis epistolis* 50, 60
Perotti, Pirro 52, 53, 54, 60
Persius 8, 9, 10
Petrarch 127; — *Contra medicum quendam 3.10* 75n34
Phidias 96
Pico della Mirandola, Giovanni, — *Adversus astrologiam divinatricem 1 p.24* 79, *1 p. 48* 81, *8.5 p. 452* 79; — *Conclusiones DCCCC, concl. sec. op. propr. 2.43* 82; — *Epistolae 21.70* 81, *22* 79; — *Oratio de dignitate hominis 30* 81, *35* 81
Pins, Jean de, *Philippi Beroaldi vita* 107n61
Pinzi, Filippo 31, 33, 34, 35, 37, 38n27
Piropilo, Antonio 75n34
Pio, Giambattista 99, 100
Piso, Nicolaus 125

Plato, *Laws 888–9 tr. Ficino* 95
Plautus 72; — *Mercator 490* 74n28,
 — *Pseudolus 1167* 74n28
Pliny the Younger 122; — *Epistulae 2.17* 102–103, *5.6* 102–103
Pliny the Elder, 41, 68, 70, 72, 83;
 — *Naturalis historia 1.14* 81, *34.61* 95, *36.19* 96n27
Plutarch 31, 50, 68, 117
Poliziano, 73; — *Miscellanea prima, praef. 13* 78, *praef. 63* 81, *praef. 91* 73, *1.13* 75n32, *1.59* 75n32, *4.3* 73, *7.12* 81, *9.11* 78, *54.2* 78, *58.27* 78, *58.35* 78, *58.49* 79, *90.4* 75
Polybius 50
Pontano, Giovanni 39n29
Porphyrio 82
Priapea 118, 119
Priscian 82
Propertius, *1.3.20* 121
Psyche, *s.* Cupid

Quevedo, Francisco de 59n23, 116; — *silvas, 14.5 + 14.66* 116, *5.19–20* 116
Quintilian 58, 81; — *Institutio oratoria 10.1.101* 30, 42, 47, *11.1.27* 84n75

Ramminger, Johann 53n16
Reggio, Giovanni da 32
Regio, Raffaele 34, 35, 41; — ed. *Quintilian, Institutio oratoria* 41
Rex, Q. Marcius 12
Rhetorica ad Herennium 3.22 94
Riddle, J. 76n36
Rinckius, Antonius 127
Rinckius, Joannes 127
Rischach, Johannes Wernherus von 41

Rivius, Johannes 34, 39
Robathan, Dorothy M. 9
Roberts, John 118n29
Rosati (revisor to the Florentine Inquisition) 120n35
Rosen, Novello 114
Rossi, Mino de' 101–104
Rouse, Mary A. and Richard H. 112
Rudolph II, Emperor 123
Ruel, Jean 76, 76n36
Russell, William 126

Sabellico, Marcantonio, — *De latinae linguae reparatione dialogus* 37, 73, 84; — *Epistolae* 78
Saenger, Paul 111
Sallust 7–28, 29–46; — *De coniuratione Catilinae 1.1* 15, *1–18* 12–23, *3.1* 30, *5.1–5* 18, *5.9–6.2* 19, *9.1–5* 20, *20.12* 31, *21.2* 31, *31* 23, *31–37* 12, 23–24, *33* 24, *34* 24, *35* 24, *51* 12, *51–52* 25–26, *52.30–31* 21, *61.1–9* 27, *61.7* 40; — *De bello Iugurthino* 13; — comparison with Thucydides, *s.* Quintilian, *Inst. 10.1.101*
Sanford, Eva M. 9, 16
Santa Sofia, Felice di 71
Santa Sofia, Galeazzo di, *Onomasticon de simplicibus* 71
Scaliger, Joseph 121
Serapion iunor, *Liber aggregatus de simplicibus* 66
Servius 31; *Commentarius in Aeneida 2.501–2* 119, *4.331* 119
Servius Danielis (= Servius auctus), *Commentarius in Aeneida 1.273* 20n21
Setti, Camillo 114
Sforza, Francesco 111

INDEX OF PERSONS AND WORKS

Sharpe, Kevin 115n15, 126n54
Sherman, William H. 112, 113n10, 116–117
Sidney, Sir Philip 123
Sidonius Apollinaris, *Epistulae*, *2.10.5* 106n60
Silvaticus, Matthaeus, *Opus pandectarum medicinae* 67n8
Simon Januensis, *Synonyma medicinae* 67n8, 71n18
Sofia, *s.* Santa Sofia
Soldi, Giovanni Crisostomo 33, 39
Solinus 117
Spenser, Edmund 121; — *Faerie Queene, 1 canto 2* 121, *1 canto 4* 122
Statius, P. Papinius 50, 52, 116; — *Silvae 2 praef.* 96n26, *2.2.48* 116
Stern, Virginia F. 124
Stok, Fabio 56, 60
Suetonius 83
Sylvius, Franciscus 34

Terence 10, 11, 116
Themistius 65, 68
Theophrast 66, 68, 70
Thucydides 30, 30n7; — *s.* Valla, Lorenzo; — comparison with Sallust, *s.* Quintilian, *Inst.* 10.1.101
Tomasi, Pietro 75n34
Torquatus, T. Manlius 21
Tortelli, Giovanni 50; — *De orthographia, praefatio* 73n24, 78, *De syllabis desinentibus in M* 82
Trapp, J. B. 117
Tuata, Fileno dalla 87n3

Ulery, Robert W. 29
Urbino, Duke of, *s.* Montefeltro

Valerius Maximus 8, 10, 31, 117; — *8.15 ext.1* 84n75
Valla, Giorgio 75n34
Valla, Lorenzo 50, 60; — *Antidotum in Pogium II* 36n24; — *De falso credita et ementita Constantini Donatione* 30; — *Elegantiae* 41, *proemium primum* 22–23 and 29ff. 29, *praefatio 2–31* 61n29, *praefatio 30* 62n30, *praefatio 32* 62n31, *1.14* 40, *2.15* 83, *3.82* 40, *4.21* 78, 82, *6 praef.* 73n24; — *Gesta Ferdinandi regis Aragonum* 41, 44, *proemium* 30, *3.10.8* 83; — Herodotus 41; — *emendations of Livy* 31n8, 41, *21–26* 43; — *In latinam novi testamenti interpretationem* 41; — *In Benedictum Morandum et Bartolomaeum Facium* 41; — *Opuscula quaedam nuper in lucem edita* 35; — *Oratio in principio studii* 30; — commentary on *Quintilian's Institutio oratoria* 34; — *Reconcinnatio totius Dialecticae* 41; — commentary on Sallust (attrib.) 11, 12, 29–46, *Catil. 1.1* (= *proemium or vita Sallustii*) 29, 31, (edition) 47–48, *2.5* 31, *3.1* 40, *17.4* 36, *21.2* 31; — Thucydides 30n7, 43, dedication 30; — *De voluptate ac vero bono* 41; — *s.* Camillus; Mancinelli
Varadi, Pietro 87n2
Vecce, Carlo 41n36
Vernia, Nicoletto 74
Vinsauf, Geoffroy of 10
Virgil 10, 11, 72, 113, 114, 126; — *Aen. 1.600–601* 31, *5.710* 118, *6.853* 119, *8.313* 19; — *Eclogue 1* 119; — *s.* Servius
Virgilio, Marcello 67
Vitruvius *9.8.5* 74n30

Vittorino da Feltre 8, 9
Vivaldus, Joannes Ludovicus 118
Vives, Juan Luis 119

Wartenberg, Johannes von 102
Winthrop, John 112

Ximenez, Francisco 126n55

Zanchus, Bartholomaeus 34
Zwicker, Steven 120

Table of Contents

Marianne PADE, Preface	5
Robert ULERY, Sallust's *Bellum Catilinae* in the Edition of Venice, 1500: the Medieval Commentary and the Renaissance Reader	7
Patricia J. OSMOND, The Valla Commentary on Sallust's *Bellum Catilinae*: Questions of Authenticity and Reception	29
Marianne PADE, Niccolò Perotti's *Cornu Copiae*: Commentary on Martial and Encyclopedia	49
Johann RAMMINGER, A Commentary? Ermolao Barbaro's Supplement to Dioscorides	65
Julia Haig GAISSER, Filippo Beroaldo on Apuleius: Bringing Antiquity to Life	87
Craig KALLENDORF, Marginalia And The Rise Of Early Modern Subjectivity	111
Index of manuscripts	129
Index of persons and works	131